Years of Decision

Critical Episodes
in American Politics
Robert A. Divine, Editor

Years of Decision: American Politics in the 1890s

R. HAL WILLIAMS
Southern Methodist University

JOHN WILEY & SONS
New York
Santa Barbara
Chichester
Brisbane
Toronto

Cover designed and executed by Mark E. Safran
Production supervised by Joseph P. Cannizzaro

Library of Congress Cataloging in Publication Data:

Williams, R Hal.
Years of decision.

(Critical episodes in American politics)
Includes index.
1. United States—Politics and government—1889-
1893. 2. United States—Politics and government—1893-
1897. 3. United States—Politics and government—
1897-1901. 4. Political parties—United States—
History. I. Title. II. Series.

E701.W54   320.9'73'08   78-6407
ISBN 0-471-94877-2
ISBN 0-471-94878-0 pbk.

Printed in the United States of America

10 9 8 7 6 5 4 3 2 1

FOR LINDA, LISE, AND SCOTT

Foreword

The resurgence of political history is one of the most intriguing developments in recent American historical scholarship. In the years immediately following World War II, scholars tended to dismiss the study of past politics as mundane and old-fashioned as they focused on cultural, psychological, ethnic, and intellectual approaches to the American experience. But the enduring importance of political events, brought home to scholars as well as journalists by the tumultuous events of the 1960s and the devastating Watergate scandal, led historians to examine the political past anew. Many borrowed ideas and techniques from social scientists to probe into such new areas as voting behavior, party fluctuations, and the role of ethnocultural factors in politics. Others relied on more traditional studies of campaign rhetoric and the impact of charismatic leaders on the political process. The result was a new flowering of political history.

Critical Episodes in American Politics is a series of interpretive volumes designed to bring the new scholarship to bear on eight major episodes ranging from the origins of the first party system in the 1790s through the trauma of Vietnam and Watergate. Each author examines the political process at a critical time in the American past to demonstrate the way the democratic system functioned under great stress. Employing different techniques and approaches, the authors seek to explain the distinctive events in their respective periods to give the reader an insight into both the strengths and weaknesses of the American political tradition.

In this volume, Professor Williams traces the transformation of the American party system during the crisis of the 1890s. Focusing on the nationalistic program of the Republicans, he shows how the GOP championed such measures as the protective tariff and a stable currency to forge a national consensus that would endure for the next three decades. In his analysis, both the Democrats and the Populists failed because they did not anticipate the needs of an emerging industrial-urban society. The result was a political upheaval that changed the evenly balanced and essentially localized party structure of the Gilded Age into a national political system in which the Republicans, the party of energy and change, were dominant. Professor Williams's provocative thesis and incisive characterizations provide a new and challenging view of a watershed decade in American political history.

Robert A. Divine

Preface

This book attempts to tell the story of American politics during the 1890s, a fascinating, exciting, and turbulent period in American history. It focuses on national events and figures, tracing the decade's party battles and the development of a national party system. Conflicting parties and philosophies fought it out in this decade, with the Republicans—the party of central government, national authority, and activism—soundly defeating the Democrats—the party of states rights, decentralization, and limited government. A third party, the People's party, flourished briefly and added to the decade's vitality. Out of the party battles, patterns emerged that governed the nation until the 1920s and 1930s. In that sense, and others, the 1890s became a critical decade, marking the passage between an older era and a new.

The story begins in 1888 rather than 1890, for the presidential election that year turned out to be the first in a series of important elections that distinguished the decade. It ends in 1901 in Buffalo, New York, with the assassination of President William McKinley, himself a symbol of the transition between eras. McKinley, in many ways a modern president, was also the last veteran of the Civil War to sit in the White House.

In the dozen years between 1888 and 1901, something recognizable as modern America took shape. People who lived through the years knew somehow they were important. Cities, factories, science, and technology were changing the country. When the decade began, Benjamin Harrison occupied the White House and Nellie Bly, a New York reporter, raced around the world in a record 72 days, 6 hours, and 11 minutes. When it ended, Wilbur and Orville Wright were nearing the birth of powered flight at Kitty Hawk, North Carolina. The decade brought major challenges: growth, political struggles, depression, war, social and economic turmoil, a sense of world power, imperial responsibilities. Each found an outlet in politics, for politics was the period's fascination, its mass entertainment and participatory sport. Millions of Americans read party newspapers, hung on the words of party leaders, and in elections turned out in enormous numbers. In the presidential elections from 1888 through 1900, well over 70 percent of the eligible electorate voted, a figure that arouses envy today.

The book seeks to be analytical and interpretive. It does not take sides. The Republicans won, the Democrats lost, and the Populists died: but in the fashion of American politics, another day and another chance would always come. Our politics also tend to be cyclical in nature, so the effects of this critical decade lasted for years to come, until FDR, the Democrats, and the New Deal constructed from another depression a political coalition that resembled in outlook and dimension the McKinley coalition of the late 1890s. Until then, however, the Republicans ruled, and the patterns of the 1890s persisted.

I am indebted to the staffs at the various libraries mentioned in the notes. Friends at the Yale University Library, Southern Methodist University Library, and the Manuscript Division of the Library of Congress were particularly helpful. John G. Hall of the Fondren Library, SMU, acquired needed materials, and Linda E. Sellers and Carl F. Prestfeldt answered many questions. A sabbatical leave from SMU enabled me to complete the book.

Michael E. McGerr sharpened my understanding of the tariff (and other issues) in the 1890s. Jeremy duQ. Adams, a model for colleagues, eased the burdens. Bonnie P. Wheeler and David J. Weber gave much. Mick and Janet McGill added things of great importance. Lydia Clay helpfully checked final details. Lewis L. Gould shared time, knowledge, and encouragement, and improved the manuscript from beginning to end. Robert A. Divine, a delightful editor, read chapters swiftly and critically. Marylee A. Skwirz contributed in many ways. Linda, Lise, and Scott know how much they helped.

Dallas, Texas   R. Hal Williams

Contents

Years of Decision

ONE

☆

The Party
Setting, 1888

Elections were social events in late nineteenth century America. They brought people together, in ways since forgotten. City dwellers joined local party organizations, donned uniforms to march in parades, distributed literature to the wavering, and heeded closely the orders of favorite ward captains. In rural areas the pattern was similar, with appropriate variations. Picnics and rallies, often with a prominent speaker imported for the occasion, lured large crowds, and some members of the crowd traveled a day or more to get there. Ministers included political injunctions in church services, and local postmasters, usually party appointees, passed out campaign pamphlets with the mail. Election-eve brought thousands into the streets to discuss that morning's betting, evaluate late rumors, and await slowly arriving returns. Most onlookers had voted, for elections seemed to have meaning in terms of issues and personalities. A substantially larger proportion of the population voted in Gilded Age elections than at any earlier period, or during the subsequent Progressive era.[1]

The presidential election of 1888 was no exception. By midnight of election day the crowds gathered outside newspaper offices could see

1

that the Republican party, with Benjamin Harrison as its nominee, was on the way to the biggest election victory for either party in almost two decades. Grateful politicians, who had had to wait several days for the results in 1880 and 1884, and several months in 1876, analyzed the returns and went to bed. The Republicans had registered sizable gains in crucial New York State, carried all but two northern states, and showed strength in West Virginia and the border South. Although definite figures would have to wait, Republicans might also control the two houses of Congress, the first party to command both legislative and executive branches since 1875. Former President Rutherford B. Hayes, who knew something about waiting for election results, was delighted with the outcome and the conduct of the campaign. "The best and decentest election I ever knew," he wrote in his diary.[2]

The incumbent president, Grover Cleveland, had followed the returns through the telegraph room near the White House library. Placidity and a certain detachment marked his actions on election day, as they had throughout the campaign. Exactly 11 months before, on December 6, 1887, Cleveland had stirred the country with an annual message to Congress devoted to tariff reform. The tariff drew on deepseated feelings and touched sensitive economic interests, and Cleveland recognized the need for a campaign of education to sway voters. But resisting appeals from Democratic leaders, he declined to take an active hand and remained quietly in Washington or at his summer home.[3] On election day he told friends of his hope for Democratic success but expressed willingness to retire from office. "You know how I feel in the matter and how great will be the *personal* compensations of defeat," he wrote one friend. "I am very sure that any desire I may have for success rests upon the conviction that the triumph of my party at this time means the good and the prosperity of the country."[4]

Cleveland's outward detachment concealed strong ambitions and a lively sense of his own importance. As the defeat's dimensions became clear, he angrily rejected suggestions that his tariff message had been a mistake. "Damn it, it was right," he exclaimed to supporters; and declared to a reporter: "It is better to be defeated battling for an honest principle than to win by a cowardly subterfuge."[5] Friends were bitter, blaming defeat on Republican corruption and Democratic treachery in New York State. "One week more of instruction would have given us the day." Preferring approval to criticism, Cleveland unintentionally fostered a sycophancy among followers, which came out at moments like these. "But you will conquer," a follower assured him. "Your message last December came to us as a gleam in the midst of darkness, bringing faith and hope after years of error, outlining the policy upon which shall rest the basis of our freedom and national wealth and prosperity. Its truths were not alone for this day and generation, but for all time, and all parts of the world."[6]

Perhaps. But for this particular day another man had conquered. After voting early at a nearby livery stable, Benjamin Harrison spent November 6 relaxing at home in Indianapolis. Harrison was weary, for unlike Cleveland he had conducted an energetic campaign, traveling seldom but speaking almost daily to groups visiting his home. In 16 weeks he made over 80 speeches to nearly 300,000 people. "I am quite tired of hearing my own voice," he wrote his running mate, Levi P. Morton of New York, in late October, "and if there was a party pledged to the prohibition of public speaking I would join it."[7]

Knowledge of his effectiveness made the weariness worthwhile. In short, eloquent speeches Harrison had deftly deflected the Democratic tariff thrust, explained and defended the protective system, and pledged federal action to solve a variety of problems. He expressed dismay over disfranchisement of black voters in the South, promised to advance civil service reform, suggested policies to meet the growing issue of the trusts, and urged liberal treatment for aging veterans of the Civil War. Above all there was the tariff and the Democratic attack on it. "It is not a contest between [tariff] schedules, but between wide-apart principles. . . ," Harrison announced in his letter of acceptance, published in September. "The assault upon our protective system is open and defiant." "The Democratic party has challenged our protected industries to a fight of extermination," he told a cheering audience a month later. "The wage-earners of our country have accepted the challenge. The issue of the contest will settle for many years our tariff policy."[8]

The victory in hand, hundreds of townspeople celebrated around the Harrison home, and messages of congratulations and support came in from Republican leaders. "Your election opens a patriotic epoch in the history of the country," James G. Blaine, the most popular Republican of them all, wired Harrison. The president-elect knew it was possible. With Republicans in charge of the White House and Congress, party measures that had been stalled for years could now be enacted. The responsibility was sobering, and Harrison, cool and austere, felt it. As he turned to constructing his cabinet and inaugural, he voiced apprehension about the challenges ahead. To Republicans who talked only of party opportunities, Harrison spoke thoughtfully of "grave responsibilities and shadowy troubles."[9]

☆☆☆

Responsibilities came in legions. There were party leaders to satisfy, policies to define, expectations to fulfill. Republican newspapers were predicting that an effective administration and Congress would ensure Republican rule into the next century. "Are the Republicans In to Stay?" George F. Hoar, the respected senator from Massachusetts, asked in the *North American Review.* The answer: barring accidents, the party could rule for several decades, perhaps even have "a permanent tenure of power."[10]

It would not be easy. The coming decade of the 1890s would present challenges enough to test any political party, or society. Change and movement were everywhere, in many cases reflecting century-long developments. Industrial expansion, urban growth, spreading agricultural and labor unrest, economic depression, problems of race and religion—all demanded adjustments and solutions. The approach of the twentieth century bred self-consciousness, and observers sensed the importance of this final decade, a fact confirmed in retrospect. "Politically," one of the shrewdest among them wrote, "1889 might be called the end of the houp-la. The partisan clamor of the years following the Civil War was to be subdued by the new problems of the 'nineties. We lost zest after that for expressing and explaining everything with silver-tongued oratory and brass bands. Torchlights went out."[11]

More than torchlights were going out. The 1890s would mark the passing of the Civil War generation, that unusual group of people who rose to early prominence and power in the turbulent 1850s. In both North and South they had ruled longer than most generations, and with the consciousness, as Oliver Wendell Holmes, Jr., put it, that the war experience had set them apart. "In our youth our hearts were touched with fire." Five of the six presidents elected between 1865 and 1900 had served in the war, as had many social, economic, and religious leaders. In 1890 there were well over a million veterans of the Union Army still alive, and Confederate veterans numbered in the hundreds of thousands. For this generation the influence of the Civil War and its related issues was incalculable.[12]

But time was now catching up. Benjamin Harrison, who had marched through Georgia and risen to command the 70th Indiana, was 56 in 1889 as he sketched out his administration. James G. Blaine was 59, and in fewer than four years would be dead. Senator John Sherman of Ohio, who had first entered Congress in 1855, was 66. Many Democratic leaders had also grown old, and like their Republican counterparts had somehow to adjust to new problems and people, while giving continued meaning to the experiences of their youth. Suggestions that they relegate war issues entirely to the past baffled them. These issues—of nation, and section, and race, and economic policy—had been present since the beginnings of the republic. Surely they still merited discussion.

Tensions between old and new marked both political parties, but particularly the Republicans. With increasing impatience they had worked during the 1880s to retain old loyalties and build new constituencies to break the stalemate that followed Reconstruction. For nearly a dozen years before 1889 the two parties had been so evenly balanced that neither dared take chances. In 1880 the Republicans had won the presidential race by only 7000 votes out of more than nine million cast; in 1884 they had trailed Grover Cleveland by only 63,000 votes out of ten million. Congressional races were equally close. Less than two percentage points separated the total Republican and Democratic vote for congressmen in all but one election between 1878 and 1888. Such margins affected the party system, making politicians extremely cautious and giving no one the majority needed to govern.[13]

The Democrats found this situation rather congenial. Like all politicians they enjoyed winning elections, but usually for their symbolic value and to keep activist-minded Republicans from power. Democrats believed in states rights, decentralization, and limited government—a trilogy as suited to stalemate as to victory. "No man," one of their leaders had once written, "has the right or duty to impose his own convictions upon others."[14] The remark measured Democratic policy, since government in almost any form meant imposing convictions on others. In the late 1880s Cleveland, William E. Russell, the young governor of Massachusetts, William L. Wilson, an upcoming congressman from West Virginia, and other Democrats kept the tradition alive. Wilson in particular liked to quote Albert Gallatin's early dictum: "We are never doing as well as when we are doing nothing."[15]

As a consequence most Democratic policies took on a distinctly negative cast. In the language of party platforms, Democrats "viewed with alarm" rather than "pointed with pride." They sought to slash

5

federal activity, cut expenditures, repeal laws, and end governmental interference in the affairs of private citizens. Even their latest issue, tariff reform, which had a positive and constructive sound, reflected the party's traditional demand for the separation of government and business. Although a few Democrats worried about the effects of negativism, wondering whether the party might become incapable of governing, most preferred to follow the popular Cleveland whose term in the White House had lifted Democratic spirits and defined the party's vision. While president, Cleveland had vetoed over two-thirds of the measures presented to him, more than all his predecessors combined.[16]

Whenever doubts arose, Cleveland and the Democrats had only to point to the obvious appeal of their policies. Unlike the Republicans, whose strength dwindled south of the Potomac, they won adherents throughout the country. Southerners embraced Democratic *laissez faire,* not simply for reasons of tradition. Energetic governments might intervene to protect minority voters in southern elections.[17] Elsewhere, people weary of Reconstruction commitments, resentful of taxation, and suspicious of centralization gravitated toward Democratic ranks. In an era when religious affiliation helped mold political views, Roman Catholics, German Lutherans, and other nonmoralistic groups welcomed Democratic opposition to prohibition, sabbatarian legislation, and similar attempts to use government to control individual standards of behavior. From immigrants to entrepreneurs there were many in the late nineteenth century who approved the Democratic "master-wisdom of governing little and leaving as much as possible to localities and to individuals."[18]

Democratic negativism irritated Republicans, who enjoyed governing. A party that had started by telling slaveholders to keep slavery out of the territories was seldom afraid to display its convictions to others. Since then, according to party histories, Republicans had won the Civil War, emancipated the slaves, reunited the nation, guided Reconstruction, and passed the legislation that had brought the country to its present peak of industrial and agricultural growth. The Democrats had opposed it all.[19] "The Republican party has walked upon high paths," Benjamin Harrison declared in an 1888 campaign speech. "It has set before it ever the maintenance of the Union, the honor of its flag, and the prosperity of our people." "Progress is of the essence of Republicanism," said Thomas B. Reed of Maine. "To have met great emergencies as they arose has been our history. To meet emergencies as they shall arise must be our daily walk and duty, or we cease to be."[20]

Republicans took immense pride in their party's record. Large differences in outlook and issues set them apart from their Democratic opponents. While Democrats stressed the local and negative, Republicans pursued a national vision, in which local interests merged into nationwide patterns and government became an instrument to promote moral and material growth. Reed captured some of the distinction with his biting wit. "The Republican party does things, the Democratic party criticizes; the Republican party achieves, the Democratic party finds fault." It was a partisan judgment, which outside observers confirmed. Beatrice Webb, the British socialist, noted that Republicans "represented a faith in centralized power, in the capacity of the few who are in authority at the centre of the state or the municipality to regulate the many and manage the affairs."[21]

Party differences contained one of the era's interesting ironies. The Republicans built on power but found it difficult to acquire. The Democrats, who distrusted power, often had it thrust upon them by an approving electorate. Republican programs appealed to millions of voters, yet seldom the hoped-for majority. The party's share of the presidential vote declined through the 1880s, and Republicans controlled the House of Representatives, the popularly elected branch, for only two years between 1874 and 1888. Such figures preoccupied Republican strategists, who during the 1880s saw the need to devise policies to boost party fortunes. Somehow Republicans must increase their strength in the critical East and Midwest, and reach further into the developing Far West. Then there was the South—for Republicans there was always the South.

Once the proud focus of Republican plans, the South had come to symbolize the party's good intentions and frustrated hopes. During the early years of Reconstruction it had seemed to offer an unusual combination of the moral and political. Republicans would protect southern Unionists and pass measures to help black freedmen, which in turn would foster strong Republican organizations. The strategy had not worked. Southern white resistance, northern white racism, misguided policies, and other difficulties had soon thwarted it, and northern voters had since tired of the problem's complexities. "It is clear," suggested a Republican newspaper in January 1888, "that there is no longer a majority in the North to respond to the nobler issues on which the Republican party has so long stood." Republicans could continue to support the nobler issues, but must adjust to altered opinion in the North, and the realities of power in the South.[22]

The realities were not always pleasant. Democrats ruled the South, and used fear of Negro domination, Confederate war loyalties, and a mixture of fraud and intimidation to keep voters in line. They acquiesced in limited Republican campaigns, but met efforts to build opposition with bitter resistance, sometimes violence. Although national Republican candidates ran fairly well in the region, Republicanism itself was in danger of withering under the harsh sun of Democratic supremacy. Over the years party members had become a tattered lot: some worked for patronage, others for money, and some simply believed enough in Republican principles to brave ostracism and intimidation. Few hoped for victory. By 1888 white Democrats governed every southern state. With unusual candor a Mississippi Democrat explained how: "it is no secret that there has not been a full vote and a fair count in Mississippi since 1875, that we have been preserving the ascendancy of white people by revolutionary methods. In other words, we have been stuffing ballot boxes, committing perjury, and here and there in the state carrying the elections by fraud and violence."[23]

For years Republicans had sought answers, without success. They received no help from northern Democrats, who had little taste for southern elections but liked the political security the South provided. It was pleasant in presidential campaigns to be able to count on 153 electoral votes from the South, when it took only 201 to elect. Nor did help come from Mugwumps, Independent Republicans, and other intellectual leaders who had once professed great interest in the southern question. Now they practiced a fine discrimination between similar activities on either side of the Mason-Dixon line, praising Democrats who adhered to wartime loyalties, accusing Republicans of raking up old memories and "waving the bloody shirt." The distinction was absurd; it also missed the fact that Republican charges usually reflected present grievances, not stale memories. "Our complaint," as Benjamin Harrison told a Chicago audience in early 1888, "is against what was done [in the South] in 1884, not against what was done during the war. Our complaint is against what will be done this year, not what was done between 1861 and 1865."[24]

Worthy motives were fine, but still the problem remained: to break the stalemate and assemble a coalition that would enable a party to govern. As 1888 approached, few in either party guessed it would signal the long-awaited break and, in a sense, usher in the newer concerns and alignments of the 1890s. Voters, it was true, seemed reasonably content with Cleveland's Democratic administration. They expected little in the relatively placid 1880s, and Cleveland had given them that, with a firmness they admired and a blend of mild policies they liked.[25] Republicans drew on traditional strengths, but were tired and listless, on the defensive against the administration. Prospects in the upcoming presidential election seemed even, with chances in favor of the Democrats. When at last the break came, nearly everyone was surprised at its source. It came from Grover Cleveland himself.

☆☆☆

In the early summer of 1887 James G. Blaine took his family off to Europe, to tour, visit old friends, get away from newspaper speculation about his presidential plans, and perhaps even find a cure for recurring headaches and the gout. It was also something to do. Blaine had been away from official life since 1881, and retirement, at first an enjoyable opportunity to write his memoirs, had begun to bore him. The memoirs were finished, and seemed premature for a man at the height of his abilities. Only 57 years old, Blaine was still energetic and ambitious, a commanding party leader, the most popular figure of his time.

Of medium height, handsome, with a pale face and captivating black eyes, he blended formidable talents. His charm was legendary. "Had he been a woman," remarked a colleague's wife, "people would have rushed off to send expensive flowers." Born in western Pennsylvania, he entered college at age 13, taught for a few years in Kentucky and Pennsylvania, and in 1854 moved to Maine to edit a newspaper. Soon he became Maine's leading Republican, in an era when that state greatly influenced national affairs. From 1863 to 1876 Blaine served in the House of Representatives, including a period as Speaker of the House from 1869 to 1875. His quick wit, sharp tongue, and extraordinary memory made him a feared debater. "On the whole," said his friend James A. Garfield, "he is the completest gladiator in debate I know of."[26]

Followers—they were legion—called him "The Magnetic Man" and "The Plumed Knight," and touted him for the presidency. Opponents were less generous, pointing to his partisanship, occasional indecisiveness, and questionable dealings with some railroad bonds while Speaker. Elected to the Senate in 1876, Blaine led the Republican "Half-Breeds," a forward-looking faction in the party, against Roscoe Conkling and the "Stalwarts." The Half-Breeds were diverse in outlook, but they generally embraced economic nationalism, tariff protection, and the developing urban-industrial society. The Stalwarts looked backward, reluctant to play down older issues like the South and Reconstruction. In 1881 Blaine became Garfield's secretary of state, a position he had desired, but resigned soon after his friend's tragic assassination.

In 1884 he ran for the presidency himself, and though losing narrowly to Cleveland, slowed the recent decline in Republican fortunes. Disgusted with the dirtiness of the campaign, he lost interest in the White House but not in the GOP. He wrote his memoirs, pressed new issues, and worked to build Republican majorities. Surely there were ways to end the party stalemate. Traveling through Europe during 1887, Blaine worried about Republican chances the following year. Letters from party leaders, also concerned about the prospects, added to his doubts. Then, one December day in Paris, he shook open his newspaper and read about Cleveland's tariff message.

It was the break Blaine had been waiting for. Immediately he called in a reporter from the New York *Tribune* to give the Republican party's answer. Cleveland's proposed tariff reduction would unsettle business, lower wages, damage markets for farm products, and open the country to ruinous competition from British manufacturers. If the Democrats were worried about the surplus revenue the tariff currently was bringing in, they should spend it on education, public works, coastal defense, and other worthwhile projects, not use it as an excuse to undermine the nation's economy. Cleveland's message had one virtue, Blaine concluded: it set the issue clearly and voters could respond, as he had no doubt they would. "The Democratic Party in power is a standing menace to the prosperity of the country."[27]

The tariff was not a one-sided issue; protection and reform offered political benefits to both parties. But it was a complex one, and needed explaining to voters, who in this politics-minded period were eager to listen. The Republicans explained, the Democrats waffled. Ironically, Cleveland soon became alarmed over possible losses from his reform stand, and attempted to back down in the Democrats' 1888 platform.[28] The Republicans nominated Harrison, a midwestern friend of Blaine's and a thoughtful proponent of the tariff, and trumpeted protection's virtues. Couched in straightforward economic terms, the tariff made sense to a nation in the process of rapid industrialization. It appealed to local interests, which it merged into a national system. Finally, it had a patriotic dimension in a patriotic era, setting up barriers against Great Britain, the country's traditional opponent, and "the terrible competition beyond the sea."[29]

Properly handled, the tariff appealed to voters in city, factory, and farm. By closing out competition from low-wage areas abroad, it boosted the demand for American-made products, kept factories at full production, and raised wages for American workers. Prosperous workers in turn bought finished goods from urban tradespeople and merchants. They also bought food and agricultural staples from farmers who then no longer had to depend on the unstable world market. Everyone, Republican orators explained, benefited from the tariff: the industrial East, the diversified Midwest, the burgeoning Far West, the industrializing South. "It is a policy broad enough to embrace within the scope of its beneficent influence all our population."[30]

In Republican hands the tariff had both social and economic dimensions. It built healthy societies as well as economies. Effectively administered, it brought occupations, classes, and sections together, interweaving them all under the wholesome influence of common interest and prosperity. You have "the perfect results of protection in bringing the consumer and the producer close together," a Republican speaker once told an Indiana audience. "The farmer needs the home market which the manufacturing towns afford, and the manufacturing towns must have the supplies furnished from the farms. Each is required by the other, and both working together make a prosperous community of people."[31]

Republicans focused their tariff strategy on the East and Midwest, the critical heart of the party's territory, and cast longing glances at the South, which in 1888 beckoned once again. Blaine had run well in several southern states in 1884, and now there was talk of "a revolution in sentiment" following Cleveland's tariff message.[32] The Democrats were reportedly in trouble in the iron regions of Tennessee, Alabama, and West Virginia, among sugar growers in Louisiana, and in the scattered industrial areas of Virginia, Florida, Georgia, and North Carolina. Republican leaders knew enough to discount the most optimistic reports, but still the prospects were intriguing. Harrison needed only to emphasize the tariff and play down the "bloody shirt," some southern Republicans advised, and he might carry five southern states. "Meet Cleveland on his own ground and beat him there is my advice," wrote a Tennessee industrialist. "Let us wage the battle for the protection of American Industry and win the fight."[33]

Tempting, the advice appealed to many influential Republicans. Blaine for one liked the relative novelty of the tariff issue. It could attract young voters uninterested in Civil War issues and win over protectionist Democrats unhappy with Cleveland's message. It might break the party stalemate. Blaine returned home from Europe in August 1888, to a hero's welcome. Fireboats played in New York harbor, and crowds chanted "Blaine, Blaine, James G. Blaine" and "No, no, no free trade." Europe, Blaine told them, was watching the presidential campaign. "It is the opportunity of England. It is the wished-for and longed-for occasion upon which the cheaper fabric of the Old World expects to invade the New and lower the standard of American labor to the European level."[34]

A night's rest at home in Augusta, Maine, and the active Blaine was on the stump again, with an energy that contrasted with Democratic lassitude. On occasion he gently waved the "bloody shirt," to keep the Democrats off balance, but most often he lectured to large and enthusiastic audiences on the intricacies of the tariff. By mid-October, dozens of speeches later, he reached Indianapolis where he joined Harrison, who was already a bit weary from his front-porch campaign. The two men made an effective team: Harrison, quiet, thoughtful, in command, eloquent and forceful when speaking to small groups; Blaine, quick, impulsive, charming, incredibly popular, able to attract publicity and crowds to the Republican standard. Blaine exploited the Republican party's tariff opening. Harrison touched on all issues, including the tariff and the party's long commitment to civil rights in the South.[35]

Proud of the party's moral tradition, intensely conscious of his own Civil War service, Harrison rejected advice to stress the tariff to the exclusion of other issues. He would give the tariff due emphasis, but would not relinquish the civil rights issue. "I feel very strongly upon the question of a free ballot," he told Whitelaw Reid, editor of the influential New York *Tribune,* who had written for instructions. "It is one of the few essential things. I have never failed in any campaign to speak upon it and to insist that the settlement of that question preceded all others in natural order. There would be no tariff question now, if the labor vote of the south had not been suppressed."

The problem, Harrison noted, was far broader than the South or the momentary interests of the Republican party. Election fraud— whether accomplished through bribery, intimidation, or ostensibly legal means—was a disease that should concern voters everywhere. It tainted by example, infecting other areas of the country and damaging confidence in the political process. The problem was "a national, not a sectional one, for these vile southern methods are spreading their contagion, like the yellow fever, into our northern States." An issue of such magnitude could not be ignored, Harrison instructed. Republicans must discuss it, though in moderate terms and always in the context of present circumstances, not as part of a so-called "bloody shirt" or Civil War association. "I would not be willing myself to purchase the Presidency by a compact of silence upon this question."[36]

Presidencies could easly be won or lost on such decisions, as Harrison might have reflected as he walked home from the livery stable that morning of November 6, 1888. By one o'clock the next morning a pleased Harrison had retired to bed, now virtually the president-elect, happy with a victory won on his own terms. The tariff issue, traditional Republican voting blocs, and Democratic mistakes had proved effective in the Northeast, Midwest, and Far West, where the Republicans lost only two states and carried New York State by more than 14,000 votes. In the important Midwest Harrison ran 120,000 votes ahead of Cleveland, while his party won five of six congressional delegations. It was a heartening victory, not diminished by Cleveland's small lead in the popular vote, based largely on increased Democratic pluralities in the deep South.[37]

Eager to assess the tariff's impact, analysts watched the returns from urban-industrial areas and the border South. In the former the outcome was mixed, with Republican gains in Cincinnati, Milwaukee, and other industrial centers offset by losses in New York City, Boston, Chicago, Detroit, and San Francisco, some of them normally Democratic. Both parties claimed success among urban workingmen, and recognized that local issues and organizations always played an important role in city elections. In the border states the returns on the whole favored the Republicans, who at first believed they had managed even to carry West Virginia. "It is the beginning of the break in the Solid South," boasted Blaine, who had helped devise the strategy to engineer the break. Later returns altered the results but not the encouraging patterns. The Republicans came within 500 votes of carrying West Virginia, 1600 votes of carrying Virginia. They also cut into Democratic margins in Maryland, Kentucky, North Carolina, and Delaware.[38]

The election over, the Republicans celebrated. The victory was narrow and included some disappointments, yet was the most decisive in nearly 20 years. Proper work on the tariff held out hope of further gains. The party seemed strong across the North, and portions of the South appeared within reach, a conclusion that would influence

Republican strategy in the upcoming Fifty-first Congress. That Congress, for the first time in years, would have a Republican majority in both houses. The margin was thin, but it existed, and with chances for expansion. Once in power the Republicans planned to admit to statehood the two Dakotas and Washington, which could add six new Republican senators. The prospect delighted Republican leaders, who saw long-term opportunities. As Blaine told Harrison, "It gives you (with a Republican House) the amplest power for a useful, strong and impressive Administration."[39]

☆☆☆

Harrison, who had a minister's conscience and a lawyer's regard for the precise and particular, was preoccupied with responsibilities. The scion of a politically prominent family, he was born near Cincinnati, Ohio, in 1833, the grandson of William Henry Harrison, the country's ninth president. Graduating from Miami University in 1852, he practiced law in Indianapolis, joined the new Republican party, and fought bravely in the Civil War. Returning home, he resumed his law practice and earned a reputation for probity, candor, and ability. Cool and reserved, Harrison won respect more easily than affection. He relished truth and cared little for flattery. Pushed for public office, he lost a close race for the Indiana governorship in 1876, but came back to win a Senate seat five years later. A national-minded Republican, he spoke for tariff protection, civil rights, sound currency, civil service reform, and generous benefits for Union veterans.

The weeks after his presidential victory strained his patience. Letters and delegations, all bearing advice, pleas, and demands, poured into Indianapolis. "I am worked to the verge of despair in receiving callers and trying by the aid of two stenographers and typewriters to deal with my mail," Harrison wrote a cousin only two weeks after the election. "One person could not open and read the letters that come to me. I have been compelled to put them up in bales." The mail measured a country's interest and expectations. Citizens and Republican party leaders wrote to suggest personnel and policies for the new government. Party workers begged for patronage, the customary reward for victory. It was all very tiring, and very necessary. Late nineteenth century Americans demanded access to their president, who surrounded himself with little pomp and panoply.[40]

Delegations came from veterans' groups to congratulate their fellow member and request liberal pensions. Businessmen and congressional leaders sought information on the new administration's tariff policy. Southern whites stopped in, to ask generous treatment for their region and a minimum of black appointments to office. Delegations of Negroes called, to urge the appointment of a strong attorney general and vigorous enforcement of the Fifteenth Amendment, guaranteeing suffrage regardless of race or color.[41] The whole southern question continued to fester, as scattered violence broke out in the South in the aftermath of the election. Trying to head off investigations of election irregularities, nightriders badly wounded a representative of the GOP national committee in Tennessee, and killed the brother of a prominent Arkansas Republican. Black spokesmen showed a renewed militancy, insisting that Harrison and the party help the millions of people currently disfranchised in the South. "We have had emancipation for twenty-five years," one remarked. "It is about time we have recognition."[42]

In the intervals between callers Harrison worked on his cabinet, which emerged a reasonably strong one, with Blaine as secretary of state. He also considered and finally rejected advice to call an extra session of Congress to deal immediately with the difficult tariff question. At last it was time to leave for Washington and the inauguration. Harrison and his family traveled in a private car over the Pennsylvania Railroad, but still there were calls for speeches from the rear platform and talks with Republican politicians. Governor Joseph B. Foraker, a Harrison rival, boarded the train near the Ohio border and rode part way to the inauguration. The two men dined, then retreated to the end of the car to talk politics. Harrison's wife followed, with their daughter's infant son. "You hold him, Ben," she said, and left. As the baby crawled over his lap, Harrison discussed with Foraker the tariff, the possible extra session, Indian policy, and other matters.[43]

Inauguration day, Monday, March 4, 1889, might have been an omen. It poured most of the day, with rain slanting into faces and drenching clothes. "Such a day as yesterday!" Mrs. Blaine wrote her son the day after. "My prevailing impression is one of vast ranges of umbrellas, black bubbles." Storekeepers along Pennsylvania Avenue, recognizing a good thing, packed people into windows at $6 a head. Onlookers joked about the "Harrison hoodoo" and the "Harrison luck," in unkind reference to Harrison's grandfather, William Henry Harrison who died from pneumonia supposedly caught on his own rainy inauguration day in 1841.[44] At the Capitol the Cleveland administration went through the rituals of its final hours. To reporters' amusement Cleveland signed into law the last three bills presented to him, in counterpoint to his record of 278 vetoes, 157 more than all previous presidents combined.[4 5]

Standing in the rain on the Capitol portico, Harrison read his inaugural address, while on the plaza below a sea of umbrellas surged here and there as people tried to catch his words through the downpour. As expected, the address urged friendly relations with foreign governments, praised the benefits of the tariff, asked Congress to adjust the revenue system to reduce the surplus money in the Treasury, promised to enforce civil service reform, cautioned against trusts, and pledged an economical administration. Southerners listened attentively for hints of the administration's southern policy. Harrison was firm. He promised even-handed treatment for all sections, but vowed strong action if needed to safeguard voting rights. "The freedom of the ballot is a condition of our national life, and no power vested in Congress or in the Executive to secure or perpetuate it should remain unused upon occasion."[4 6]

This year 1889, the centennial of the United States Constitution, held special significance, Harrison concluded. As the nation entered on its second century under the Constitution, it could take pride in past achievements and faith in continued progress. Thirty-eight states had grown out of the original thirteen. Thanks to economic growth, Americans were better fed, clothed, and housed than any people before them. In the recent war they had settled permanently the shape of their government. "No other people have a government more worthy of their respect and love or a land so magnificent in extent, so pleasant to look upon, and so full of generous suggestion to enterprise and labor. . . . We must not forget that we take these gifts upon the condition that justice and mercy shall hold the reins of power and that the upward avenues of hope shall be free to all the people."[4 7]

The upward avenues of hope: the graceful phrase caught the spirit of a confident, expansive society. As Harrison left the Capitol to review the inaugural parade, the Clevelands prepared to move to New York, where the former president would practice law, snipe at the Republican administration, and prepare for 1892. Outwardly Cleveland seemed happy to be free of duties, and would soon write his closest friend: "You cannot imagine the relief which has come to me with the termination of my official term." His wife, the pert Frances Folsom Cleveland, was more open, instructing an old White House servant to take care of the furniture and ornaments. "I want to find everything just as it is now, when we come back. . . . We are coming back just four years from today." For now the Harrisons were settling in, excited over the prospects, the new president having comfortably survived his rainy inauguration day. He had worn a complete outfit of chamois leather underneath his outer suit, his wife later said. "No inauguration pneumonia for him!" The incident, if true, said a good deal about Harrison's foresight, and caution.[48]

In the coming years he would need both qualities, in plentiful measure. He would preside over the onset of the 1890s, an exciting and challenging time, which in retrospect would clearly occupy a critical place in our history. As a decade the 1890s today seem both modern and remote, a blend of Civil War and twentieth century, a time of genuine transition between centuries and periods. When Harrison took office in 1889 industrialism, large-scale enterprise, and specialized, mechanized agriculture already signaled the way of the future, yet older economic patterns still existed. Cities grew and captured the imagination, but the great majority of Americans still lived on farms and in villages. They pursued old faiths, particularly religious ones, with all the efficiency of modern technology.[49]

The nation believed in moral and material progress, and could justify the belief. Slavery had been eradicated, and a similar fate seemed in store for the liquor traffic and other evils. Economic expansion, based on enormous resources and energy, offered benefits to all. With thrift, hard work, and talent, people bettered themselves, rising through social classes, acquiring more of the world's goods, traveling those upward avenues of hope. As a newspaper put it as late as 1892: "the rich are growing richer, some of them, and the poor are growing richer, all of them." Henry George, Hamlin Garland, and others raised protests, warning against increasing concentrations of wealth and power, but for a time they seemed out of place. Progress was afoot in the country. An onlooker only 50 years old at Harrison's inaugural had witnessed the advent for practical purposes of steel, oil, electricity, the electric light, telephones, telegraphs, the phonograph, iron-clad warships, the use of steam in ocean travel, the vast railroad network integrating the country, and a good deal more. The automobile and the airplane were only a few years away.[50]

By 1901 attitudes would be different. The 1890s worked great changes, on and under the surface, in outlook and structure, in ways that would shape twentieth century life. By decade's end the country had added seven new states, the first such admissions since the Civil War, and had admitted almost four million immigrants to strain class lines and swell burgeoning cities. It had overtaken Europe in some measurements of industrial production, survived a massive economic depression, experienced the celebrated presidential election of 1896, crushed Spain in a brief and popular war, and extended American influence deep into the Caribbean and Pacific. Major shifts in voting alignments and other fundamental patterns made the 1890s a vital decade, linking the nineteenth and twentieth centuries in more than chronology. Somehow they became known as the "gay nineties," but the term was misplaced. At the time they were more often called the grim or shattering nineties.

Gay and shattering: an unusual juxtaposition, but not inappropriate. The 1890s both shattered and built, worried and enjoyed. Benjamin Harrison little suspected what lay ahead in March 1889. "I do not mistrust the future," he said in his inaugural address. "Dangers have been in frequent ambush along our path, but we have uncovered and vanquished them all."[51] The years ahead would try this spirit, as older values gave way to new, and dissident groups swept the South and West like shadows across the landscape. Populism would rise and fall, and in the process question the country's direction, disrupt political alignments, and lend its decline to the drama of the McKinley-Bryan contest in 1896. Labor would adopt a new militancy, immigrants would demand tolerance and recognition, the issues of tariff, silver, civil rights, and political reform would require treatment. Through it all ran challenges that tested political parties and party leaders, who responded in meaningful ways. Out of the exciting and difficult conditions of the 1890s they created patterns that carried the nation into the twentieth century.

TWO

☆

The Republicans Govern, 1889-1891

It was a good thing, Mark Twain liked to say, that Congress had not been present when God said "Let there be light," for otherwise the world would still be in darkness. Twain enjoyed poking fun at his era, and Congress was an easy target. Its record during Reconstruction had alienated many people, and since then scandals and other problems had further damaged its reputation. More than ever before, the business community siphoned off talented youth, who preferred a chance at a railroad presidency to a low-paying career in Congress. The era's narrow margins between political parties did not help. With neither party able to exercise effective control, Congress passed little legislation and took on a helpless, inept air. Antiquated rules, more suited to antebellum needs than to the late nineteenth century, also blocked legislation and mystified the public, who lost track of the complex maneuvering. As Jonathan P. Dolliver, a newly elected representative, told his family in 1889: "I believe I shall enjoy the work of the House, though I confess it is a little in the nature of a bear garden to the uninitiated observer."[1]

With these problems in mind, Republican party leaders conferred frequently as the date approached for the opening of the Fifty-first

Congress in December 1889. For years they had derided Democratic inaction and had promised much in the way of tariff, currency, pension, and other legislation. Now, as the country watched expectantly, they were in a twofold difficulty: a very thin majority in Congress and congressional rules that further eroded such majorities. With the addition of new states the Republicans could count on a plurality of about ten in the Senate, sufficient for action. In the House of Representatives matters were different. The new House would have 330 members, with a quorum placed at 166. The Republicans had 169 members, quickly reduced to 168 when one died soon after Congress opened. The Democrats had 161. The critical figure involved the quorum, for the Republicans could have only two or three of their number absent at any time for illness or other reasons, a virtually impossible task. Yet without a quorum the party could not govern.[2]

No aid would come from the Democrats or the current rules of the House. Since the days of Thomas Jefferson the Democrats in the House had perfected dilatory tactics to impede legislation, a party strategy that had assumed fresh urgency during the slavery, secession, and Reconstruction crises. Traditional American respect for the rights of legislative minorities lent support to the strategy, until by 1889 the rules governing the House stressed minority over majority, inaction over action, the right to block legislation over the right to pass it. Besides procedural roll calls and other time-tested methods of delay, the Democrats particularly liked the "disappearing quorum," which permitted House members to participate in debate, then refuse to answer to the roll call to determine whether a quorum was present. In the previous Congress, the Fiftieth, they had carried this tactic to such an extreme that the House had accomplished virtually nothing. They had been pleased with the result. During 1889 Democratic leaders served notice that similar tactics would prevail in the Fifty-first Congress, even if it destroyed the session.[3]

The threat troubled Republicans, who recognized that it cut to the heart of the democratic process. A system that elected and then emasculated a majority was headed for difficulty. In a September 1889 article in the *North American Review,* Henry Cabot Lodge, a young congressman from Massachusetts, showed the drift of Republican thinking. The House must adopt new rules to fit itself for the business of governing. "If a majority cannot be trusted to rule in this country," Lodge wrote, "then we should try something else; but while we live under the majority system a majority ought to have, and must have, a chance to act." In the months before the House convened, Lodge and other Republicans discussed possible rules changes, but reached no firm conclusions. As early as April 1889, the Philadelphia *Press* threw out the suggestion that a desperate party might follow the example of David B. Hill, the Democratic governor of New York, who had solved the "disappearing quorum" in the state senate. He simply counted as present all members who were in the hall, whether or not they had answered to the roll call. "But there is no danger of a Republican adopting such partisan tactics to carry through any measure," the *Press* added.[4]

A great deal would depend on the firmness and ingenuity of the new Speaker of the House, to be chosen by the Republican caucus when Congress opened in December. Fortunately, the Republicans had just the person. Fifty years old in 1889, Thomas Brackett Reed had put a lifetime's experience into a belief that legislative bodies must function. Born in Portland, Maine, he graduated with honors from Bowdoin in 1860, taught school and practiced law, and entered Congress in 1877. There, he soon won fame for partisan loyalties, parliamentary skill, and acidulous wit. Few people crossed him, and those who did were never forgiven. As his friend Lodge later said of him, "when he hated or disliked he could not bridle his tongue & the bitter things he said, charged with wit & humor, flew everywhere."[5]

Reed fascinated his fellow politicians, who feared and respected him. Dressed in his customary dark suit, with baggy trousers, he towered over most of them, at 6 feet 3 inches and nearly 300 pounds. He seldom mentioned his weight. "No gentleman ever weighed over two hundred pounds," he once remarked to an inquirer. Newspaper reporters savored descriptions. "He has the frame of a Japanese wrestler, and his head might serve for that of a Chinese giant." Reed's head was nearly bald, his face broad and fat, with a red mustache straggling across his upper lip. At moments of tension he affected a bland and cheerful smile, which infuriated opponents and reminded others of a cherub. During his years in Washington he lived very simply in a pair of small, sparsely furnished rooms near the attic of a rooming house. Books and a picture of Abraham Lincoln were the rooms' main features.[6]

Widely read, Reed had an excellent mind which he sharpened throughout his life. Deciding in middle age to learn French, he nightly kept his diary in that language. His wit awed and intimidated. "He can say more bright things in the space of ten minutes than any other man in congress can get off in the course of an hour," noted a reporter. During his first six months in Congress, Reed said, he felt like a fly in a bowl of molasses: "there was plenty of sweetness, but no light." He coined the definition of a statesman as a dead politician. Addressing a crowd liberally sprinkled with Democrats, Reed suggested that a photograph of everyone in the Democratic party would show them doing some "mean, low-lived, and contemptible thing." He listened calmly to the resulting catcalls and jeers, and remarked: "There, I told you so." Democrats were his favorite target, including the Democratic orator who grandly stated that he had rather be right than president. Said Reed: "The gentleman need not be disturbed, he never will be either." Sardonic and cynical, Reed had few illusions. As he put it, "One, with God, is always a majority, but many a martyr has been burned at the stake while the votes were being counted."[7]

The wit nearly always had purpose. Reed liked to govern, and to discomfit those who opposed or lagged behind. "Did it ever occur to you," he asked one audience, "that the road in front of the chariot of Progress is never macadamized? It is only the fellows lagging behind that are on the beaten track, and it is those men who make the outcries; other men are too busy trying to find a passage in front." Reed wanted to keep the Republican party and himself in front. He had presidential ambitions and resented the pervasive shadow of his fellow Maine Republican, James G. Blaine. In December 1889, thanks to his election as Speaker, he was about to emerge from that shadow and become one of the most famous men in the country. Reed had signaled his intentions in a magazine article published the previous March. "The danger in a free country," he had written, "is not that power will be exercised too freely, but that it will be exercised too sparingly." The statement might have served as the keynote for Reed, the Republican party, and the Fifty-first Congress.[8]

Congress opened on December 2, 1889, and a week later Speaker Reed announced the membership of the major House committees. "It means business," said a shocked Democrat. In the previous Congress his party had delayed action for six weeks before even announcing committees.[9] The committee chairmen reflected the Republicans' activist mood, with Reed himself at the head of Rules and William McKinley, a talented veteran of Ohio politics and an expert on the tariff, at the head of Ways and Means. McKinley immediately began to gather data for a new tariff bill, while the House as a whole turned to its first order of business, disputed elections cases. As feared, the Republicans had difficulty mustering a quorum, and their opponents, seizing the advantage, soon brought the House to a standstill. The method was simple, honed during recent Democratic Congresses: offer dilatory motions, then refuse to vote on the roll call—the "disappearing quorum." For weeks the House accomplished nothing.[10]

Democrats grew smug, Republicans angry and impatient. Tensions mounted, as it became clear that Reed and other Republican leaders had had all they could stand. The crisis came on Wednesday, January 29, 1890, shortly after the noon opening hour. Lines of people crowded into the House galleries, alert to rumors that the Republican leadership had reached its decision. On the day's first important vote, a motion to take up an election case, the Republicans fell two votes short of a quorum, 161 to 2, with 163 members not voting. During the vote, anxious Democrats had moved about the chamber, whispering together and watching Reed who was busy making notations on a separate list. The vote completed, a Democrat shouted the usual "No quorum." The moment had come, and Reed in a clear calm voice made congressional history. "The Chair," he said, "directs the Clerk to record the following names of members present and refusing to vote."[11]

A moment's disbelief, then pandemonium. The Republicans cheered, Democrats rushed into the aisles. Through it all Reed calmly intoned names: Bland, Blount, Breckinridge of Arkansas, Breckinridge of Kentucky. Normally mild-mannered, the latter Breckinridge interrupted, furious. "I deny the power of the Speaker and denounce it as revolutionary." The Democratic side erupted in yells and cries of czar! czar! The names continued: Lawler, Lee, McAdoo, McCreary. "I deny your right, Mr. Speaker, to count me as present," shouted McCreary. Reed's face took on that cherubic smile. "The Chair is making a statement of the fact that the gentleman from Kentucky is present. Does he deny it?" Amid laughter and applause from the Republicans, Reed finished his list and then explained his decision. He pointed to precedents in the British Parliament and some state legislatures, including David B. Hill's New York. Besides, he concluded, the House simply needed to adopt procedures that would enable it to act. "The Chair thereupon rules that there is a quorum present within the meaning of the Constitution."[12]

The tumult continued the following day, and for days after. The galleries remained crowded, as President Harrison's family and others came to watch the drama. Newspapers analyzed the events closely, aware of the importance of the issues at stake. Reed evolved a standard patter after votes. He would announce the actual totals, then add: "which, in addition to the gentlemen present and declining to vote, constitute a quorum." For several days outraged Democrats surged through the House aisles, shouting and gesturing at the Speaker, denouncing him as a tyrant and czar. They caucused nightly, to vent feelings and discuss strategy. On January 31, after listening to an emotional letter from Samuel J. Randall, an old leader dying of cancer, they settled on their strategy. They would use parliamentary motions and delaying tactics to halt all action in the House until the Republicans acknowledged the error of their ways.[13]

Reed was too much for them. That same day he cooly deflected their strategy, crossing in the process another significant legislative line. When House members resort to ordinary parliamentary motions to halt business, he announced to the House, "it is the right of the majority to refuse to have those motions entertained, and to cause the public business to proceed." The ruling set off a nationwide debate over the nature and aims of constitutional government. It dazed even some Republicans, although in a broad sense it reflected a logical extension of the party's activist approach. It represented a large expansion of the Speaker's power. In his earlier ruling, which had won wide support as a sensible one, Reed had simply said that a member present for one purpose (to make parliamentary motions) was also present for another (to make a quorum). Now, he was saying, a Speaker need not recognize motions from the floor if in his judgment they were intended for delay or obstruction.[14]

Some young Democrats, impatient with the negativism that pervaded their party, voiced admiration for the ruling. A harbinger of a fresh strain in the party's thinking, Tom L. Johnson, a reform-minded Ohio congressman and later the progressive mayor of Cleveland, considered it silly to elect representatives whose main task was to obstruct business.[15] Most Democrats were aghast over the ruling, and were certain that voters would not support it. On February 4 they issued an address to the country, which a former Speaker of their own, John G. Carlisle of Kentucky, composed, that accused Reed of destroying the limitations "the Constitution has wisely imposed upon the legislative department. Constitutions are made to restrain majorities and protect minorities." It was a revealing phrase, echoed in much of the nation's Democratic press. Southern journals reacted with particular bitterness, alert to the impact an unrestrained congressional majority might have on their local racial arrangements.[16]

Republicans on the whole were delighted. If Congress and the voters agreed, Reed's actions could mark a new era in legislative accomplishment. Reed had happily freed the House from "the seedy statesmen who have for so many years kept famous on motions to adjourn," boasted Jonathan P. Dolliver. On February 14, 1890, House Republicans formally adopted the Reed rules, together with others designed to regularize procedures, tighten restrictions on filibusters, and expedite business.[17] Three days later the Democrats admitted temporary defeat, amid final warnings that a Republican-run Congress would loot the Treasury. Carlisle announced that they would await a chance to test the new rules' constitutionality and the voters' judgment in November. Jubilant, Reed, McKinley, and other Republican leaders turned their attention to the party's legislative program, confident now that it all could be passed. It could at least be considered and debated, as an exuberant Theodore Roosevelt noted. "I swear by Tom Reed . . . ," he wrote a friend. "No one man can filibuster and beat a bill now. A house may do well or ill; but at least it can do *something* under the new dispensation."[18]

☆☆☆

The first thing to do was to tackle the tariff issue. As much as Republicans hesitated to open up the complicated issue, they knew that something had to be done about the current revenues. Government revenue in the late nineteenth century came from two sources: tariff duties on imports and internal revenue taxes, primarily on tobacco and whiskey. For the fiscal year ending June 30, 1889, the total revenue had amounted to $387,000,000, of which nearly 60 percent came from tariff duties. The problem seemed a pleasant one: during the same period federal expenditures had amounted to only $282,000,000, leaving a handsome surplus in the Treasury of $105,000,000. Treasury officials used some of the surplus to reduce the government debt, but still it was embarrassing to the Republicans. It implied unnecessary taxation and, so long as it went unspent, could dampen economic growth. Democrats like Cleveland exploited it effectively in calls for tariff reductions. Worse, projections for the fiscal years 1890 and 1891 showed a surplus of about $92,000,000 yearly. Something had to be done, and in their first annual reports Harrison and his secretary of the treasury, William Windom, suggested that "a revision of the tariff and customs laws is urgently needed."[19]

Revision was a neutral word—it could mean up or down—and the tariff was an extraordinarily complex question. Tariff duties could not be casually tinkered with, for they affected a multitude of interests and provided the bulk of the government's revenue. Were revenues too large? Then lower the tariff a corresponding amount, came the quick answer. Unfortunately, the tariff was not that simple. Lower duties could encourage greater imports, which in turn could actually increase revenues. In addition, there were complicating problems within the Republican party. Decades old now, the protective system had been in effect long enough to raise questions about its specific benefits. In the Midwest a whole segment of the party, behind Joseph Medill's influential Chicago *Tribune,* urged a restructuring of the tariff to lower duties on necessities, boost them on luxuries, and place some raw materials like lumber and iron ore on the free list. There and in the Plains states, restive farmers openly wondered what the system offered them, a question that intelligent Republican politicians like senators Preston B. Plumb of Kansas and William B. Allison of Iowa quickly picked up.[20]

In the Northeast, still a stronghold of protectionist sentiment, changing economic patterns fostered new doubts. Needing to cut costs to meet competition, some manufacturers toyed with the benefits of undutied raw materials such as hides and wool for the shoe and clothing industries. At the moment, in Midwest and Northeast, they were only doubts, but with mistakes they could swell easily into discontent and Republican defeats. One danger lay in the tendency of avid protectionists to miss the point that voters in 1888 had voted for the protective system and against Cleveland's attack on it. They had not voted for higher tariffs. Republican protectionists, including Whitelaw Reid's New York *Tribune,* often a voice for Blaine, wanted to raise tariffs in order to reduce revenues. This was a perfectly logical though politically dangerous approach. Blaine himself was moving in a different direction, building visions of what could be done in foreign policy with a few tariff manipulations. Always the Republican strategist, Blaine also fretted about the party's tariff timing. He knew his history well, and historically it had been a serious mistake to pass a tariff bill just before an election, as the Republicans were about to do.[21]

McKinley's Ways and Means Committee, in charge of preparing the bill, pushed it along as fast as possible. While Reed and the Democrats fought for control of the House, the committee met almost daily, listening to testimony from hundreds of witnesses, juggling rates to meet this need or that. On April 16, after nearly four months of deliberation, McKinley presented the bill to the House. It raised some duties, lowered others, and added 37 articles to the free list. To New England's dismay, it boosted duties slightly in the wool schedule, but offered free hides in return. It retained existing duties on iron ore and pig iron, and reduced those on steel rails. Prohibitive rates on tinplate, used in the canning business, represented an attempt to construct an entirely new domestic industry, drawing on tin ores in South Dakota's Black Hills.

Other experimental features marked the bill. In a significant departure designed to soothe Midwestern and Great Plains unrest, it raised duties on a range of farm products, including eggs, potatoes, barley, oats, and hops. Another sweetener appealed to the West: sugar would go on the free list, lowering the price to consumers, with a bounty of two cents a pound to domestic sugar producers. The bill's sponsors estimated it would reduce revenue by about $71,000,000, some of it from adjustments in the tobacco tax. Although rates were generally higher than before, Republicans on the committee sought to label it the "farmer's tariff," with benefits for all, consumers and industrialists, farmers and laborers, West and Northeast. As McKinley told the House in introducing it: "This bill is an American bill. It is made for the American people and American interests."[22]

Many of the people seemed less sure. Joseph Medill, among others, welcomed the bill's several concessions, but still questioned its provisions and intent. The lumber, linen, wool, and tinplate duties were too high, dictated by "the sharkish plutocrats of the East, who are greedy for larger profits." Medill's *Tribune,* the St. Paul *Pioneer Press,* and other leading western Republican papers scoffed at the "farmer's bill." "The farmer is to be benefited not by cheapening what he buys but by an attempt to advance the price of what he sells," a "wrong-headed" approach. More unfortunate, current farm problems stemmed from overproduction, and in promising higher prices for farm products, the bill could stimulate production. With his many followers around the country, Blaine learned early of the incipient consumer revolt. A proposal in committee to take hides from the free list, thus adding to the price of shoes, brought a quick letter from Blaine to McKinley. "Pray stop it before it sees light," he urged. "Such movements as this for protection will protect the Republican party into a speedy retirement."[23]

Harrison and Blaine followed the bill closely through the House. Both men wanted some lower rates, for foreign as well as domestic uses. They also wanted one higher rate, on sugar, to use as a bargaining point for trade concessions from sugar-producing countries in Central and South America. In letters and conversations between the two, the idea of reciprocity took firm shape, in which trade agreements would gradually and reciprocally lower duties on noncompeting products. The idea had commercial and political advantages, appealing to consumers through reduced prices, farmers and manufacturers through a larger market for surplus foodstuffs and industrial products. Each country would profit because agreements would cover primarily goods not produced in the country. As Blaine declared in a public letter: "We ought to have in exchange for free sugar from certain countries a free market for breadstuffs and provisions, besides various fabrics from all parts of our country. In short, we ought to secure in return for free sugar a market for $60,000,000 or $70,000,000 worth of our own products."[24]

Blaine explained the concept to the Ways and Means Committee on February 10, but convinced only Chairman McKinley. The other committee members needed more time, especially in the face of popular pressure for immediate nontaxed sugar. Harrison and Blaine would give them time, and meanwhile keep up a steady flow of publicity to persuade the Senate to adopt the reciprocity idea when the tariff bill reached there. Western Republicans were happy with the idea, but strong protectionists were doubtful, afraid that reductions in some duties might undercut the whole protective system.[25] Free sugar remained in the bill, which came to a vote in the House on May 21, 1890. Reduction-minded Republicans threatened defections until the end, but the veteran McKinley knew that tariff bills seldom pleased everyone, particularly in their initial stages. With aid from Reed's rules, the bill sped through by a party vote, 164 to 142, and moved on to the Senate. The unaccustomed air of activity alarmed Democrats, who renewed their protests against the new rules. For the moment it was not the tariff bill that worried them most. The Republicans seemed ready to act on a measure to protect black voters.[26]

The race question was as complex as the tariff issue, and far more difficult to solve. By 1890 the nation was in the midst of a sentimental effusion that glorified the Old South and pointed hopefully toward a New. In December 1889, Henry Grady, the young, attractive editor of the Atlanta *Constitution,* came north to woo Boston audiences with appeals to leave the South alone to solve its own race problem. The applause that followed Grady's tour, given added point when he returned home and died unexpectedly, persuaded many that his appeal would be answered. Senator John T. Morgan of Alabama, a man of long political experience, was sure the South could exploit northern indifference and economic interest to head off action on the Negro question. "Protectionists want markets," he wrote, "and the silver men want free coinage, and these and other craving people want the help of the South against their own people, and they prefer to leave the negro to work out his own salvation, rather than lose money. Money, my dear friend, is the real power in American politics at this day. I am glad to have its shelter, just now, when it is the most efficient barrier to a new descent upon the South."[27]

Morgan was in for a surprise. Money was a power, then as now, but so were political and moral considerations. The latter especially moved Henry Cabot Lodge, the patrician friend of Roosevelt and Reed, who introduced in the House on March 15, 1890, H.R. 8242, a bill "to regulate elections of Representatives in Congress." Son of a wealthy and prominent Boston family, Lodge seemed out of place in the blustery House, yet came naturally to his role as sponsor of the federal elections bill, one of the most important bills in American racial history. From his family he had acquired an early dislike for slavery, a respect for human rights, and a close acquaintance with Charles Sumner, Massachusetts' great abolitionist senator, who was a frequent visitor to the Lodge home. Though only a teenager at the time, Lodge had been deeply affected by the Civil War, and as a historian would later resent the fake glorification of the Old South. "No good is ever done by falsifying the past," he wrote in 1913. "There was a right and a wrong in the Civil War. . . . The North was right and the right won."[28]

This sense of place and rectitude would serve Lodge well in his famous fight with Woodrow Wilson over the League of Nations. In 1890 it turned him toward a concern for the race problem and a conviction that the Republican party, at last in control of the government, must do something about it. He found willing collaborators in senators George F. Hoar of Massachusetts and John C. Spooner of Wisconsin, who like him had been upset at events in the South during the fall elections of 1889. Violence, fraud, and Republican defeats had marked the elections, discrediting for many Republicans the gradualist theory that time and the tariff would bring new elements to the leadership of southern society. Virginia, the special focus of Republican hopes, had been a particular blow. There, the Democrats had learned from 1888's close margin and engineered a sizable victory that changed the minds of many Republican leaders. Legislation, not time, was needed, as the New York *Tribune,* once a vigorous supporter of the gradualist theory, declared. "A National measure for guarding the purity of the registration and the suffrage has become a necessity." President Harrison agreed, and with his active encouragement Lodge, Hoar, and Spooner set about drafting such a measure.[29]

In some fashion, the three men knew, the measure would have to solve the South's own version of the "disappearing quorum." In charge of their own congressional elections, southern states counted virtually all voting-age citizens to determine their representation in Congress, then disfranchised huge numbers of them. In some states the congressional vote had shrunk by half in less than a decade, while representation remained the same. As a result, one vote in a Georgia or South Carolina congressional election had as much weight as five votes in Oregon, Nebraska, and Minnesota, four votes in New Hampshire or Kansas, and three votes in California or Wisconsin. The seven states of Alabama, Arkansas, Florida, Georgia, Louisiana, Mississippi, and South Carolina had 45 members in the present House, elected by a total of 864,025 votes (an average of 19,200 per member). In contrast, the seven states of California, Kansas, Minnesota, Nebraska, New Hampshire, Oregon, and Wisconsin had only 33 members, elected by a total of 1,557,629 votes (an average of 47,200 per member). The imbalance was pronounced, and could be solved either by reducing southern congressional representation to its appropriate level or by opening up the ballot to all qualified voters.[30]

Committed to a free and open ballot, Lodge and his colleagues naturally chose the second method. As it finally evolved, H.R. 8242 sought to facilitate suffrage and bring congressional elections under federal control. It authorized the federal circuit courts, on petition from 100 or more voters in a congressional district or a city of sufficient size, to place the law in effect in that district or city. The circuit courts would then appoint bipartisan boards to supervise voter registration, oversee election procedures, and canvass the returns. In cases of bribery or fraud, the courts could also appoint investigators, and in the event of a disputed election they, not state officials as before, would certify the winner to the House. Restrained in language and intent, the bill seemed nonpartisan enough. It applied equally to all districts and sections, relied on legal sanctions rather than outright force, and seemed likely to affect northern urban elections as much as anything else. In many of its provisions it resembled the Voting Rights Act of 1965.[31]

It promptly set off a storm of denunciation rarely equaled in congressional history. Outraged Democrats, rightly convinced that the measure had been devised primarily with them in mind, labeled it the "force bill" and conjured up visions of federal troops stationed at every polling place. In 1890 the entire United States Army had fewer than 28,000 men, and the bill prescribed courts and bipartisan boards rather than troops, but no mind. The "force bill" label stuck, and in a nation wary of repeating Reconstruction experiences became an effective opposition weapon. For years Democratic leaders and newspapers had polished alarmist rhetoric, seemingly for this moment. The bill, they charged, would end American civilization as it had been known—a great deal for one measure to accomplish. It would corrupt the ballot, bring federal judges and courts into politics, demoralize the southern labor force, stifle industrial development in the South, centralize power in federal hands, destroy individual freedoms, and bankrupt the Treasury to pay for enforcement.

"It is a dark blow at the freedom of the ballot," announced Cleveland, who neglected to mention the millions of people his fellow Democrats disfranchised in the South. Carlisle predicted economic depression and massive social disorder should the bill pass. "It is the most outrageous and iniquitous measure ever brought before Congress for passage," said Charles F. Crisp of Georgia, who would later replace Reed as Speaker of the House. Arthur P. Gorman of Maryland, a leading Democratic senator, called it "radical and vicious." The Florida *Times-Union* said: "The gleam of federal bayonets will again be seen in the South." The Mobile *Daily Register* claimed it "would deluge the South in blood."[32] For weeks the denunciations continued, with spiraling predictions. Amazed, Republicans began to lose their tempers. "Good gracious. . . ," exclaimed one, answering a complaint the law might cost ten million dollars a year to enforce. "It cost us six billions of dollars to give the ballot to the negroes of the South. I should think ten millions a year was cheap . . . to make sure that they had a fair chance to use the ballot, now that they've got it!"[33]

Democrats in the House tried to filibuster and delay, but the Republicans' new rules cut them off. With Reed's aid, Lodge marshaled his forces, and shortly after nine o'clock in the evening on July 2, the federal elections bill cleared the House, 155 to 149. The swirl

of controversy had not ended, only shifted to the Senate. Some southern newspapers plotted a boycott of northern products, while others
spoke the old language of nullification. "The negro can go or stay, as
he chooses," said the Charleston *News and Courier,* "but he will never
be permitted to rule over the Southern white man." For black leaders,
who had crowded into the House galleries to watch, the vote was a
significant occasion, though many were apprehensive over a possible
backlash in both North and South. They had no illusions about the
extent of racism in either section, and for that reason considered it all
the more striking that the House Republicans should pass the elections
bill at their first opportunity. It seemed to confirm an earlier prediction
which a leading advocate of black rights made: "For the Negro in the
United States, the year 1890 is destined to be the most important that
elapsed since the black man first touched . . . the ballot."[34]

☆☆☆

Republicans were pleased, and could even accept for a time the
stifling heat of a Washington summer. Two major pieces of legislation
seemed done: both devised carefully over several months, debated and
passed through the House in a matter of weeks. Congress had not seen
action like this in a generation, at least since the early days of Reconstruction. There was more to come. In June 1890, a third important
piece of legislation, the Dependent Pensions Act, moved quickly
through both houses and was signed into law. It granted liberal pensions
to Civil War veterans and their dependents, fulfilling a Republican campaign pledge. A month later Harrison signed two other major laws,
these dealing with trusts and silver. Democrats were dazed. "From its
organization down," complained one, "this Congress has been a raging
sea of ravenous legislation. . . . The friends of the people have only a
moment to cry out before they are swept overboard to make their
moans to the winds and the waves. It is not the voice of the people.
It is an instrument of tyranny."[35]

Ohio's aging Republican senator John Sherman introduced the
antitrust measure, and though it underwent sweeping changes in committee, it still emerged under his name. A measure of great importance,
it grew out of a spreading concern with the problem of business consolidation, which the Standard Oil trust and others touched off in the
1880s. Politicians responded quickly to the problem, Democrats naturally working on the state level, Republicans more often focusing on

national remedies. Business consolidation aroused conflicting emotions. Americans relished industrial growth, as evidence of national progress and superiority over Europe. They enjoyed the benefits of vigness, yet distrusted its impact on local enterprise and individual opportunity. The tension between the two views circumscribed the legislative response. Sherman and others somehow had to define an effective middle way, to spur growth and hold open opportunity, to discriminate between good and bad trusts, to harness bigness without harming it.[36]

The Sherman Antitrust Act, passed in June 1890 with only one dissenting vote, tried to do just that. Like most experimental measures, its terms were often vague and left precise interpretations to later experience and the courts. It declared illegal "every contract, combination in the form of trust or otherwise, or conspiracy, in restraint of trade or commerce among the several States, or with foreign nations." Penalties for violation were stiff, including fines and imprisonment, dissolution of guilty trusts, and the award of triple damages to successful plaintiffs. In a quiet ceremony Harrison signed the bill on July 2, 1890, the same day the controversial federal elections bill passed the House. In long-term effects, the Sherman Act was the Fifty-first Congress' most important measure. It made the United States virtually the only industrial nation to regulate business combinations. During the coming decade the law suffered from damaging court decisions and the distractions of depression and the Spanish-American War, but it took on fresh power after the turn of the century. As the nation's initial attempt to deal with the problem of trusts and industrial growth, the Sherman Act shaped all subsequent antitrust policy.[37]

Silver was a far more difficult matter. In 1890 it had not yet acquired all the sectional, economic, and emotional dimensions it would soon possess, but was vital enough to its supporters. As one of the two precious metals, it had once played a substantial role in world currencies, then had slipped into relative disuse in mid-nineteenth century. With the discovery of the great bonanza mines in Nevada, American silver production quadrupled between 1870 and 1890, at times glutting the world market and helping to persuade many European nations to demonetize silver in favor of the scarcer metal, gold. In 1873, during a momentary lull in the silver agitation, the United States also dropped silver coinage except for minor coins, but readopted it five years later under renewed pressure from silverites and others. The 1878 Bland-Allison Act remonetized silver, though with strict limitations. It required the government to purchase and coin between

$2,000,000 and $4,000,000 worth of silver monthly. Treasury officials usually purchased the minimum amount, but during the next twelve years the act added nearly $400,000,000 to the currency.[38]

For many silver adherents this was not enough. The price of silver fell steadily after 1878, and successive presidents continued to regard gold as the heart of the financial system. Resentful, silver adherents wanted either a silver-based currency or at the least a true bimetallic system that would rely equally on both metals. They marshaled numerous arguments. Unlike paper money, silver was found in nature and thus accorded with natural law. More plentiful than gold, it could reverse the recent deflationary trend reflecting the failure of world gold production to keep pace with increases in population and business transactions. Once placed on an equal footing with gold, it would safely inflate the currency, raise wages and crop prices, and reduce debts. Like the tariff, silver also had an attractive patriotic dimension, enabling the United States, one of the world's largest silver producers, to declare its financial independence of Europe. As a leading silverite put it: "Standing among the nations of the World as a giant among pygmies, why should we ask the aid or advice of baby England, baby Germany, or lilliputian France, in establishing for ourselves a bimetallic system?"[39]

By 1890 silver had wide appeal. Silver miners and mine owners had obvious reasons to favor it, as did the businessmen, railroads, farmers, and merchants who served them. But silver sentiment spread far beyond a few mining regions, and drew on emotional and sectional considerations as much as economic ones. It spread particularly through the South and West, where adherents touted it as a cure for depressed conditions and a chance to throw off the hated financial yoke of the gold-oriented Northeast. In 1890, however, sectional lines were not yet drawn with the clarity and bitterness they would soon attain. Northeasterners, it was true, were harder to persuade of silver's benefits, for they were closer to a financial world tied to European nations that relied on gold. But many of them, including even some business and financial groups, were willing to compromise with the silver interests. A gesture on the issue would aid sectional reconciliation, and if limited in scope would not necessarily harm a healthy economy. Above all, a satisfactory compromise might resolve the troublesome issue once and for all, ending its unsettling effect on monetary values and business growth.[40]

Silver worried Republican party leaders, who knew it held the key to the Fifty-first Congress. The tariff and elections bills, safely through the House, faced serious dangers in the Senate. There, Reed's rules did not apply, and a dozen or more silver Republican senators, led by Plumb of Kansas, William M. Stewart of Nevada, and Henry M. Teller of Colorado, demanded action on silver before other legislation passed. Teller's colleague from Colorado, Edward O. Wolcott, made the priorities clear. Silver, he told the Senate, "is of vast importance; of far greater importance than a new election law . . . or a tariff law."[41] The silver senators worked for a free coinage measure, which would direct the government to coin all silver presented at the mints, but recognized that Reed, a supporter of gold, would kill such a measure in the House. Harrison tried to steer a cautious middle course, hoping to keep the party together and devise an acceptable compromise. "What he wanted," the president told Teller in January 1890, "was a Republican law and one he could approve. With a fair silver measure, a good dependent pension bill and a revision of the tariff, he thought the Republicans would be in pretty good shape."[42]

Easier said than done, as Harrison soon learned. To his embarrassment silver Republicans in both houses promptly turned down his own mild compromise proposal. The silverites tied up the Senate, pointedly postponing consideration of the tariff bill, while they worked on a silver bill. On June 17, 1890, they stunned Harrison and moderate Republican leaders by pushing through a free coinage bill, 42 to 25. Fifteen Republican senators, nearly all from the West, joined the Democrats to pass the bill.[43] Hurriedly, Reed, McKinley, and others beat back a similar measure in the House, then put together a House-Senate conference committee to devise a solution. Temperatures hovering in the 90s frayed tempers, already stretched thin by swirling rumors that some silver Republicans had promised to sabotage the elections bill in return for southern Democratic votes for free silver.[44]

In the committee the Republican factions fought briefly and moved to a middle ground. The wily John Sherman took the lead, exerting all his talents at conciliation. The resulting Sherman Silver Purchase Act represented a major compromise between contending forces in the tradition of American politics. It directed the Treasury to purchase 4,500,000 ounces of silver a month, and to issue legal tender Treasury notes in payment for it. Opponents of silver had headed off free coinage and had gained some minor restrictions on silver's use. The silverites had won important concessions. The prescribed monthly purchases would absorb most of the country's silver production. The Treasury notes were redeemable "in gold or silver coin," a gesture toward a true bimetallic system. And the law declared it "the established policy of the United States to maintain the two metals on a parity with each other," another gesture toward bimetallism.[45]

The compromise sped through Congress, measuring everyone's weariness with the issue. It passed the Senate on July 10, the House two days later. Plumb spoke the feelings of the silver leaders. "I shall vote for [it], regretting that it is not better, immensely glad that it is not worse. . . . It is a fair compromise." Relieved to have the issue out of the way, Harrison invited Republicans to a White House celebration. The measure, he wrote his wife the next day, "was very gratifying to all our people. . . . It is not just what I wanted, but it is not so far away but that I shall be glad to end a controversy by signing it." Other observers wondered whether the Sherman Act had actually ended the controversy, though few guessed the extent to which the silver issue would dominate the coming decade. For the moment Harrison and the Republicans had more pressing concerns. It was already mid-July. The fall elections were rapidly approaching, and Congress still had to deal with the complex tariff and elections bills.[46]

☆☆☆

A cautious man, Benjamin Harrison did not set out to transform the presidency, but he added important new dimensions to it. In particular he rejected the older view that the Constitution—aside from the veto power—did not permit presidential meddling in the legislative process. A former lawmaker himself, Harrison knew the potential value of presidential advice and pressure, a well-timed message to Congress, a trial balloon leaked to the press, a quiet conference with key congressional leaders. He evolved many techniques, but came especially to favor informal dinners in the White House, where he brought together McKinley, Reed, Sherman, and others to discuss developments on Capitol Hill. In this manner he had shaped the silver law just passed, and kept in close touch with the elections and tariff bills. It was all accomplished in milder ways than later presidents would develop, yet it set precedents. William McKinley, one of the most frequent visitors to the White House, would use similar techniques during his own administration, which in fundamental ways would inaugurate the modern presidency.[47]

In late July, the silver bill signed into law, Harrison thought it safe to escape to the cooling sea winds of Cape May, New Jersey. Telephone and telegraph kept him informed of events at the Capitol. So did Secretary of State Blaine who arrived to discuss strategy on the tariff and reciprocity.[48] Strategy was needed, for in Washington the Senate had bogged down again, this time at the mercy of Democrats determined to kill the "force bill." Fatigue, as it often did, had begun to influence the lawmakers. They had been in continuous session since December 1889, nearly eight months before. Filibuster and delay, easy tactics under current Senate rules, worked to the advantage of the Democrats. Republican leaders divided over methods to deal with the problem. Cloture, though wistfully discussed, was out of the question, with too little precedent for it. Harrison hoped Republicans would stand firm behind both the tariff and elections bills, then take the result to the people in November. Others, much more pragmatic, argued that the two measures had to be separated if either was to be passed.[49]

Matthew S. Quay, a senator from Pennsylvania and the influential head of the Republican national committee, led the pragmatic. Enemies charged that Quay often confused pragmatism with economic self-interest, in this case land speculations in the South that would suffer if the "force bill" revived sectional antagonism. Quay professed a more political motive. With scarcely twelve weeks remaining before the elections, he said, both bills could not get through Congress. Republicans must choose between them—an easy choice for the high-tariff Pennsylvanian. Consulting only Gorman, the Democratic floor leader, Quay made his move on August 12, 1890, in the midst of desultory Senate debate over the tariff. He proposed a bargain to Democrats to end their logjam. The Republicans would agree to postpone the elections bill until the second session, which would meet in December. In return, the Democrats would stop their obstruction and allow the tariff bill to reach a vote in August or September.[50]

Taken completely by surprise, Hoar and Spooner, the Senate sponsors of the elections bill, were furious. They lobbied bitterly against the bargain and circulated anti-Quay editorials from Republican newspapers. Harrison caught an early train back to Washington to help, but found the forces against him insurmountable.[51] Too many Republicans shared Quay's priorities. They were anxious to pass the tariff and adjourn to mend electoral fences at home. Beaten, Hoar fought a skillful rear guard action, refusing to give way until he had the signatures of 41 of the 42 Republican senators to an agreement pledging to give the elections bill absolute priority at the second session. The Democrats were jubilant, certain they had killed the detested bill. Harrison, Hoar, and other Republicans showed outward confidence. The Quay bargain, they argued, insured the bill's passage in December. Privately, some of them expressed doubt, aware that Democratic hysteria had taken its toll. Any Republican reverses in the elections would give wavering senators an excuse to back out. Unfortunately for the history of American race relations, December would confirm their doubts.[52]

In one thing, of course, Quay had been absolutely right. Without possibility of cloture, the Republicans could not have passed both bills before the elections. As it was, they still took six weeks to pass the McKinley tariff over a suddenly quiescent Democratic minority. The Senate had added nearly 500 amendments to the House bill, many of which brought fresh protests from concerned Republicans. Wool duties moved slightly higher, glass schedules were raised, and some sugars vanished from the free list. As always happened in tariff bills, an item such as binding twine became a central issue. New England cordage interests, who produced it, wanted a high duty to guard against European competition, while western farmers, who used it, wanted a low duty to encourage importation. In this case the farmers won, but not without lengthy debate. Through the summer the Chicago *Tribune* and its allies continued to argue for wholesale reductions, warning of a rising revolt among western merchants, consumers, and farmers. The mail brought dire predictions to Republican congressmen. Should the present bill become law, Dolliver of Iowa was told, "both Iowa and the nation will go Democratic by astonishing majorities."[53]

Since Iowa had not gone Democratic for nearly forty years, such predictions naturally troubled Republican leaders. Harrison and Blaine thought they had the answer, if only they could convince Congress. Reciprocity would dull the discontent, give hope of tariff adjustments, and open foreign markets to American products. As secretary of state, Blaine had already explored the possibilities with Latin American governments, and had found, he thought, a market of 40,000,000 people for American foodstuffs, machinery, and raw materials.[54] Encouraged, Harrison threw administration influence behind the concept. In June 1890, Blaine testified dramatically before the Senate Appropriations Committee. Without reciprocity the McKinley bill had little to offer, he said. "If I were in the Senate I would rather have my right arm torn out of its socket than vote for this bill." The Republican senators were doubtful. Was not reciprocity simply another name for tariff reduction? Blaine grew agitated. The Democrats were already predicting higher prices if the McKinley tariff passed. Reciprocity promised lower prices on noncompeting products. Rather than undercutting the tariff system, it would save it. "Pass this bill" without reciprocity, Blaine told the Republicans in parting, "and in 1892 there will not be a man in all the party so beggared as to accept your nomination for the presidency."[55]

The same day Harrison kept up the pressure with a special message to Congress touting reciprocity's benefits. American wheat and flour would flow south, in exchange for sugar, coffee, molasses, and tea. A friendly senator introduced a Blaine-drafted reciprocity amendment to the McKinley bill, and Blaine himself followed with a drumfire of speeches and public letters. "The charge against the protective policy which has injured it most," he wrote on July 11, "is that its benefits go wholly to the manufacturer and the capitalist, and not at all to the farmer." The present bill helped disprove the charge, but not enough: "there is not a section or a line in the entire bill that will open a market for another bushel of wheat or another barrel of pork." Democrats relished the phrase, which they would exploit to full effect in the upcoming elections, but the Republicans understood Blaine's meaning. Tariffs had never been used to open foreign markets, only to protect domestic ones. Now there were new opportunities, for both protection and expansion. "Shall we seize the opportunity," Blaine asked, "or shall we throw it away?"[56]

As it turned out, the Republican lawmakers had little choice. Their constituents were demanding action, persuaded by the Harrison-Blaine campaign. "Blaine's plan has run like a prairie fire all over my district," noted one congressman.[57] The breakthrough came two weeks after the Quay bargain. Sugar had remained the problem until the end: Blaine was insisting on a sugar duty to use as a bargaining tool with other nations, while congressmen hesitated to remove household sugar from the free list. With characteristic directness Harrison found the solution. Instead of imposing a sugar duty that could later be reduced if reciprocity succeeded, why not start with no duty and authorize later increases if reciprocity failed? It was simple and effective, and quickly adopted. Sugar stayed on the free list, and a bounty of two cents a pound compensated domestic producers. After July 1, 1891, the president could raise rates on sugar, molasses, coffee, tea, and hides from countries refusing to sign satisfactory reciprocity agreements.[58]

A House-Senate conference committee ironed out the other details. On September 26 McKinley reported the final bill to the House. In essential outlines it closely resembled the bill that had passed the House five months before. Three features set it apart from previous tariffs: reciprocity, significant protection for agricultural products, and the use of duties to promote whole new industries. The tinplate industry alone, sponsors predicted, would soon employ 50,000 workers. The bill would also cut government revenue by about $86,000,000 a year, solving the problem of the surplus.[59] On September 27 it easily cleared the House, 151 to 81. Relieved Republicans laid plans for a quick adjournment, and crowded the Senate aisles to cheer the bill on. Resistance there was more stubborn. Plumb and two other western Republicans voted against the bill, but it passed, 33 to 27. The long process was over. In Chicago, the *Tribune* praised the outcome, though there were hints of continuing dissent. Pro-tariff newspapers were exuberant. "For years to come, perhaps for a generation," boasted the New York *Tribune,* "the policy of this Nation has been fixed by the action of Congress."[60]

The first session of the Fifty-first Congress came to an end on Wednesday evening, October 1. Symbolizing the administration's ties to the session, Harrison and his cabinet rode to the Capitol to witness its final moments. Harrison went to the presidential room behind the Senate chamber, where he signed last-minute bills. The tariff bill reached him at three o'clock in the afternoon, and McKinley, Blaine, and others gathered to watch the signing. "Does your hand tremble?" asked Blaine, with a smile. "Not a bit," replied Harrison. "I shall be able to put on a good signature." Harrison's secretary held out the blotter, but Blaine caught his arm. "Don't blot that signature. Let it stand out bold and clear." It did. At 3:22 the ceremony was finished, and people began to drift away. Harrison and Blaine lingered, discussing the session and listening to the nearby sounds of adjournment. Adjournment came at six o'clock. Harrison left for the White House, and congressmen scattered for home, glad to be released. They had been in session 303 days, missing a record by only 18 days.[61]

It had been a remarkable session, one of the most productive in American history. The contrast with previous sessions, under the Democrats' rules, was pronounced. Together the House and Senate had passed a record number of laws. They had passed tariff, silver, pension, and antitrust laws, all of large importance. They had admitted two new states to the Union (Idaho and Wyoming); established a territorial government for Oklahoma; strengthened the Army and Navy; and required the inspection of meat products intended for export. They had come reasonably close to passing a major civil rights bill, in an era that did not reward displays of concern for the rights of black citizens. As Republican congressmen headed home, they were tired, consciously proud, and somewhat bewildered by all they had done. They had accepted Reed's challenge, and tried to exercise power freely and responsibly. Now all that remained was to explain the new laws to their constituents.[62]

That would not be easy. Parties that did things were vulnerable to attack, as Reed noted waspishly. "Human nature seems incapable of prolonged virtue. It is hard to keep people always up to the Republican program." It would certainly be hard in this particular election. Voters were restive, uncertain about the activism of the Fifty-first Congress. The Democrats labeled it the "Billion Dollar Congress," and charged that the Republicans had spent that much in appropriations, subsidies, and pension grants. It is "a Billion Dollar Country," retorted Reed, answering the charge without really deflecting it. Voters at least had a clear choice, for the Fifty-first Congress had set the issues and outlooks for the coming decade: the tariff, silver, sectionalism, agricultural unrest, industrial growth, economic policy, party leadership and party responsibility.[63]

Given power, the Republicans had governed. It was as simple as that. Did voters approve, or did they prefer the more negative approach of the Democrats? Time and again during the 1890s voters would be asked the question, which ultimately they would decide in favor of the Republicans and the Fifty-first Congress. In November 1890, their answer was strikingly different. For Republicans the result was disaster.

THREE

Democratic Victory, 1890-1893

Grover Cleveland could scarcely believe what the Republicans were doing in Washington. To his mind they were making blunder after blunder, overturning his administration's policies, committing the nation to dangerous new courses. On leaving office he had moved to New York City, and begun living in the comfortable fashion he had long coveted. He purchased a large home at 816 Madison Avenue and joined the prestigious law firm of Bangs, Stetson, Tracy, and MacVeagh, where he usually handled routine matters. Summers were spent fishing at Buzzards Bay on the Massachusetts coast, initially at the cottages of friends, later at Gray Gables, the Clevelands' own cottage bought in 1891. It was all very pleasant and flattering. Ex-presidents received constant attention from the public and press. For a time Cleveland concealed his rising anger with the Harrison administration, for he believed comment on politics unseemly. Besides, he enjoyed private life. "The fact is, Colonel," Cleveland wrote his trusted private secretary, Daniel S. Lamont, in the fall of 1890, "that the inclination is growing on me, daily, to permit things other than politics to claim the greatest share of my attention."[1]

Then patience ran out, and ambition, always large, reasserted itself. Soon Cleveland was recalling more and more his own years in office, the time spent "endeavoring to give our countrymen good government." "I hardly believed . . . such retrogression could be made in so short a time." The Republicans, he was sure, had lost all sense of restraint. Centralizing power under Harrison and Reed, they were giving the president unconstitutional authority to meddle in private affairs, even to juggle tariff rates at will, and allowing the Speaker to destroy liberties in the House of Representatives. It was the kind of abuse Cleveland had predicted, and evidence that voters shared his anger gratified him. Democrats across the country reported encouraging signs. Henry Watterson, an influential Kentucky newspaper editor, stumped the Midwest and Plains states, and found widespread discontent. "I think the Republicans have 'bit off' more than they can 'chaw' . . . ," Watterson concluded. "It is inconceivable that a party so dishonest and reckless can again carry the country."[2]

Cleveland agreed. Reading the news reports from Washington, he watched the Republicans, in his opinion, "getting deeper and deeper into the mire." "Our policy," he instructed Democratic party leaders, "should be to let them flounder." The Democrats did, though not without giving their opponents a frequent push. During the summer and fall of 1890, Democratic orators spread through the nation, assailing the Harrison administration and the Billion Dollar Congress. The reception dazzled them. Every issue they touched gushed profit and applause. Best of all, they could tailor issues to suit localities. Reed's rules and the "force bill" aroused antagonism in both North and South, as evidence of government centralization and party usurpation. Audiences in the economy-minded Northeast savored assaults on Republican extravagance, while their southern counterparts cheered attacks on liberal pensions for Union Army veterans. In the Midwest and Plains states, as everywhere, listeners wanted to hear about the McKinley tariff and its probable effect on prices. The Democrats responded eagerly, and created a "high price scare" that stunned Republicans.[3]

They did it in the simplest way: by actually raising prices. They paid peddlers to sell household goods at inflated prices, with signs that blamed the McKinley law. Dismayed housewives, asked to pay twice the usual amount for tinware and other items, wondered what was to come. Democratic newspapers told them, printing circulars from merchants announcing still higher prices.[4] Legitimate importers and shopkeepers used the new tariff law as an excuse to boost prices across the board, even on products not affected by the law. By election day in November 1890, veteran Republican politicians were reporting a "stampede" on the price issue, among both urban and rural voters. Cleveland and other Democrats were delighted. For years they had tried to convince voters that the tariff was a tax, paid by consumers on every tariff-protected product they bought. "The McKinley bill is with us always," a Detroit audience was told on election eve, "at the table, at the bedside, in the kitchen, in the barn, in the churches and to the cemetery." At last such arguments seemed to be taking hold.[5]

Republicans had perfected answers for decades, but now found the going surprisingly tough. For the first time in history large numbers of people had begun to think of themselves as consumers, and as such they were clearly apprehensive, worried about the tariff's impact on prices in an already-troubled economy. As Blaine had warned, the Republicans had also passed the McKinley law too late, giving themselves barely a month to explain its complexities to the voters. Worse, undutied sugar, one of the law's most popular features, would not take effect for another six months. The outlook was bleak. The September elections showed strong Democratic gains in Republican Vermont and produced expected Democratic wins in Kentucky, Alabama, and Arkansas. Reed won reelection handily in his safe Maine district, but in Ohio William McKinley, the very symbol of the tariff system, was obviously in trouble. The Democrats in the state legislature had gerrymandered his district, awarding him a Democratic constituency that come November could be expected to repudiate the tariff's author.[6]

Farther west, in Iowa, Illinois, and Wisconsin, the Republicans faced troubles of a different sort. There, as on the national level, they had used the power of the state to pursue party ideals. They had governed, again in ways that intruded in private affairs and offended large numbers of voters. In Iowa they fought for prohibition, hoping to end the evils of drink as they had earlier ended the evils of slavery. In Illinois and Wisconsin they passed public school laws, well-intentioned measures that required children to attend school a prescribed number of weeks each year. All three states illustrated broader Republican trends, since at the same time Republicans in Boston and elsewhere were "reforming" public school laws, and Republicans in Ohio, Indiana, and Nebraska were working for temperance. In cities and states across the nation, it seemed, local Republicans were trying, as a prominent Iowa Republican put it, "to make a police sergeant out of the party," and now, in November 1890, they were discovering that thousands of voters did not like the idea.[7]

In particular many voters did not like the way Republican measures reflected certain religious precepts. Religious views, especially the tensions between liturgicals and pietists, strongly shaped political alignments in late nineteenth century America. Members of liturgical religions—Catholics, German Lutherans, Episcopalians, orthodox Calvinists, and others—stressed the institutions and rituals of the church, assigned the church responsibility for individual morality and salvation, and consequently restricted the role of the state in prescribing personal morality. As a rule, they tended to cast their lot with the Democratic party, which also set strict limits on state authority. Members of pietist churches, on the other hand, tended to prefer the Republican party, with its expansive, activist outlook. Pietists—Methodists, Congregationalists, some Presbyterians, and others—played down church ritual and believed in individual salvation, confirmed in a life of pure behavior. The state, they thought, was an appropriate instrument to achieve those ends. It should promote morality and purify society, through prohibition, Sunday-closing laws, and other measures.[8]

In Iowa Republican pietists took control of the state party during the 1880s and pushed prohibition measures through the legislature. "A school house on every hill, and no saloon in the valley," became their slogan. Soon there were also fewer Republicans in Iowa hills and valleys, as angry German Lutherans and Catholics flocked in protest to the Democratic party.[9]   In Illinois Republican pietists in 1889 passed the Edwards law, which served as the model for Wisconsin's subsequent Bennett law. Both laws mandated school attendance, and defined a school in terms of teaching certain subjects "in the English language." Liturgically minded voters, including the region's German immigrants, numbering in the tens of thousands, were aghast. The Republicans were threatening church, family, and language.

Democrats skillfully exploited the opening, pointing out the larger pattern. In both nation and state—whether it was the McKinley tariff, prohibition, the Lodge elections bill, Reed's tyrannical rules, or the Bennett law—the Republicans seemed bent on abusing power and encroaching on individual liberties. The issues were emotional, and extremely effective. Roger Q. Mills, a leading Texas stump orator, brought a Wisconsin audience to its feet. "Who has given to any State," he thundered, "the right to invade the family fireside and deprive the mother who has nursed the child, and upon whose bosom it has lain, of the right of training the child?"[10]

No one, if the region's voters had their way. In the November 1890 elections they swept the Republicans out of office in all three states. Wisconsin Republican leaders, surveying wreckage that included a lost governorship, legislature, Senate seat, and congressional delegation, spoke of "the terrible blizzard" that had struck their party. "The worst feature of the situation," noted the state chairman, "is the almost hopeless task of getting back our German Republicans without whose help it is impossible to carry Wisconsin."[11] The results in Illinois were only slightly less spectacular. Republican candidates fell everywhere, as Democrats took the governorship, a Senate seat, and majorities in the legislature and Congress.

Iowa, which had once seemed so safely Republican that Jonathan P. Dolliver predicted "Iowa will go Democratic when Hell goes Methodist," again went Democratic, as it had the year before. In 1889, thanks largely to the temperance issue, it had elected its first Democratic governor in a third of a century. Now, with the same prohibition-sparked influences at work, it elected Democrats to six of its eleven seats in the House of Representatives. Republicans were stunned, uncertain how to reverse the forces they had set in motion. Jubilant Democrats believed they had suddenly found the key to hegemony in the Midwest. For the moment, at least, they were right, but Republicans were resourceful, and the battle was far from over. It would not really end until the exciting, crucial contest of 1896.[12]

☆☆☆

The elections of 1890 rank among the most important in American political history. They were decisive, and they produced clear patterns that shaped the history of the decade. They also drew people's attention to a burgeoning movement among farmers, a movement soon known far and wide as Populism. It had begun rather quietly, in places distant from normal centers of attention, and for a time it went almost unnoticed in the press. But during the summer of 1890, in the South and West, wagonloads of farm families were converging on camp-grounds and picnic areas, to socialize and discuss mutual grievances. Farmers came by the thousands, tired of deprivation, drought, burdensome mortgages, and low crop prices. They came on horseback and on foot, in caravans that sometimes stretched for miles. At the camp-grounds they picnicked, talked, sang favorite songs, and listened to recruiters from an organization called the National Farmers' Alliance and Industrial Union, which promised unified action to solve agricultural problems. Farmers were joining at the rate of a thousand a week; the Kansas Alliance alone claimed 130,000 members in 1890. It was "that wonderful picnicking, speech-making Alliance summer of 1890," a time of fellowship and spirit long remembered among farmers.[13]

Spirit was plentiful, and spread quickly into politics. Many farm leaders advised against political involvement, fearful of the divisive effect of party loyalties and ambitions. But in late nineteenth century America the temptation was almost irresistible. Politics was the system's focus, an essential point of attack for a group discontent with its lot. "There has been to much Legeslation in favor of Capital and we will work hard to Elect men that will Rrepresent us," as an Alliance leader in Wisconsin put it. Kansas organizers went further than others, and in June 1890, formed the first major People's party. They named a third-party ticket for the November elections. Elsewhere in the Midwest and Plains states, especially in Nebraska, Iowa, and the Dakotas, farm strategists used independent tickets and selective endorsements to bring old-party politicians into line. Alliance chapters closely questioned local Democratic and Republican candidates, then endorsed those who answered satisfactorily on the currency, tariff, trust, and other issues.[14]

Southern farmers were particularly bitter, victims of a regional economy that lagged far behind the rest of the nation. By 1890 many of them had had their fill of its chief characteristics: crop liens, depleted lands, cheap cotton, sharecropping, and living standards comparable to those of European peasants. They "seem like unto ripe fruit," an Alliance organizer noted, "you can garner them by a gentle shake of the bush." In 1890 the southern wing of the Alliance had over a million members; some said nearly three million, though doubtless with exaggeration.[15] It turned to politics early, but recognized the dangers of independent action in the South. People who defied the section's dominant institution, the Democratic party, faced ostracism, sometimes even injury or death. Better to work within the party, using Alliance numbers to take control.

Thomas E. Watson and Leonidas L. Polk, two politically minded southerners, led the strategy. Georgia-born, Watson was a talented orator and organizer, small and active, with a thin face and dark-red hair brushed back from his forehead. In 1890, fed up with the desperate conditions of Georgia farmers, he planned to run for Congress as an "independent" candidate on the Democratic ticket. Polk hailed from North Carolina, where he had served as the first commissioner of agriculture and founded the *Progressive Farmer,* an influential farm journal. Colorful, engaging, and eloquent, he believed in scientific farming and cooperative action to solve farm problems. In 1889, at an Alliance meeting in St. Louis, he was elected president of the National Farmers' Alliance. (POLK)

In the West the movement's leaders faced different situations, but had equal talent. Jeremiah Simpson of Kansas, probably the most able among them, also planned to run for Congress in 1890. Reflective and well-read, a follower of Henry George, Simpson pushed for social and economic change. "We reformers," he said, "are fighting for a mud ball as big as a boulder; what we permanently win will be no larger than a diamond, but it will be a diamond."[16] Mary E. Lease—"Our Queen Mary," her Alliance friends called her—joined Simpson on the Kansas lecture trail. Thirty-seven years old, tall and slender, she had trained herself as a lawyer and become interested in women's suffrage, temperance, and other reform issues. On the lecture platform she sparkled, hurling sentences "as Jove hurled thunderbolts." Mrs. Lease made 160 speeches during that Alliance summer of 1890, calling on farmers to rise against Wall Street and the manufacturing East.[17]

Annie L. Diggs, far brighter than the more famous Mrs. Lease, attracted a sizable following in a movement remarkably open to female leadership. William H. Peffer also worked in Kansas, a rich breeding ground for the Alliance. An able lawyer and editor, with a bushy brown beard that reached his waist, Peffer early cast his lot with Kansas' new People's party. Farther north, in Minnesota, Ignatius Donnelly brushed aside other leaders to take charge of the burgeoning movement on the northern Plains. Donnelly was restless and irascible, a nationally known social critic who wrote several utopian novels, dabbled in reform politics, and "proved" that Shakespeare had not written his own plays. In 1890 he pushed long-cherished reforms and had large political ambitions, which the Alliance movement might satisfy.[18]

Alliance growth, swift and startling, upset political patterns and dismayed politicians in the South and West. As a southern Democrat said: "I don't know how it is in the West, but in my country these blatant demagogues that the Farmers' Alliance send out have raised the very deuce." Republicans knew how it was in the West. Farmers were breaking away from the Republican party, with a determination that resisted the normal blandishments. "I never seen the time before but what I could soothe the boys down and make them feel good," a Dakota Republican wrote in July 1890, "but seemingly this fall they are not to be 'comforted.'"[19]

Voters went to the polls on Tuesday, November 4, 1890, and deserted the Republican party in droves. "It Is Revolution," headlined the St. Louis *Republic.* "On the face of the first returns, it is hard to see what the Republicans have left." The truth was, the Republicans had virtually nothing left. They lost 78 seats in the House, a reversal of political fortunes rarely equaled in the history of congressional elections. No longer could Reed build dreams, and rules, on 166 Republican members. In the next Congress he would have 88. The Democrats would have 235 members. The totals were stunning, as was the extent of the devastation. Republican candidates were overwhelmed even in areas of traditional party strength. They lost badly in New England, the Midwest, and on the Plains. The "force bill" and other issues inflated the usual Democratic majorities in the South. Dazed, President Harrison called it "our election disaster," and hoped it indicated only the midterm reversal customary to American politics.[20]

Privately, of course, Harrison knew better. The elections ruptured party alignments that had existed since the Civil War, thirty years before. Of the tier of Republican states that had once stretched from New England to the Pacific, only California, Colorado, Maine, Vermont, and a few other outposts remained. New England Democrats, accustomed to Republican supremacy, could scarcely credit the returns. William E. Russell, a Cleveland protégé, won the governorship of Massachusetts, and the state chose seven Democratic congressmen. For the first time in decades, the Democrats had a majority of the New England delegation in the House. In Ohio McKinley lost as expected, though he foreshadowed the Republican future with an extraordinary pro-tariff campaign that brought him within 300 votes of victory in his gerrymandered district. But still he lost, and such party luminaries as John C. Spooner and Robert M. La Follette, both from Wisconsin, Joseph G. Cannon of Illinois, chairman of the House Appropriations Committee, and John J. Ingalls of Kansas, a Republican patriarch who had been in the Senate since 1873, joined him in retirement.[21]

Retirements were numerous. The Republicans lost six House seats in Wisconsin, seven in Illinois, four in Iowa, one in Indiana, six in Michigan, nine in Ohio, five in Kansas, three in Nebraska, and four in Missouri. As older faces disappeared, new politicians vaulted into sudden prominence, including a young man from Lincoln, Nebraska, William Jennings Bryan, who was swept into Congress by the Democratic landslide of 1890. Attuned to farm problems, Bryan and others welcomed evidence that the Farmers' Alliance had scored heavily in the elections. Alliance leaders boasted that the movement had influenced or controlled 2,500,000 votes, almost a quarter of the total votes cast for president in 1888. No one could confirm the figure, but it was impressive nonetheless. Polk, the tireless president of the Alliance, claimed 38 avowed Alliance men elected to Congress, with at least a dozen more pledged to Alliance principles. The *National Economist,* the official newspaper of the order, raised the estimate to 44 Alliance members in Congress, and sympathetic senators from six states.[22]

In Kansas the Alliance-related People's party, organized just a few months before, shocked the Republicans. It elected four congressmen, including Jeremiah Simpson, took control of the lower house of the legislature, and deposed Senator Ingalls, "the innocent victim," he said, "of a bloodless revolution—a sort of turnip crusade, as it were." Peffer replaced Ingalls. In nearby Nebraska, farmer-sponsored Independent tickets also did reasonably well. The returns there displayed the effect of agricultural unrest, as Republicans held their own in the towns and villages, but lost heavily to the Democrats and Independents in rural precincts. Nebraska elected a Democratic governor for the first time in its history.[23] Thomas E. Watson won his House race in Georgia. Across the South the Alliance won a swath of victories based on "The Alliance Yardstick," a demand that Democratic party candidates pledge support for Alliance measures in return for the organization's endorsement. When the elections were over, Alliance leaders claimed on that basis a majority in eight southern legislatures, and six Alliance-elected governors, including those in South Carolina, Georgia, Tennessee, and Texas.[24]

Success had come so swiftly, so easily: it was all a little dazzling. Exuberant Alliance songwriters composed a new song:

You can no longer keep us in serfdom,
  For the people have opened their eyes;
In the next Presidential election
  We will give you another surprise.

Republican and Democratic politicians hoped to avoid another surprise. Undecided about strategy, they wavered between wooing farm dissidents and attacking them. Conservatives in both parties fretted about agrarian radicalism, "the irruption of cranks charging like Cossacks, . . . and swarming to possess the land." President Leonidas Polk stirred the cauldron. Expansive in victory, he called in reporters. "We are here to stay," he told them. "This great reform movement will not cease until it has impressed itself indelibly in the nation's history." A few days later he talked with reporters again. Democrats should be delighted with their sweeping victory, Polk said, but victory also brought responsibility. They must now enact Alliance reforms, or "a third party is inevitable," in the South as well as the rest of the country. We "are determined to gain the ends [we] are striving for, and will smash any party that opposes them."[25]

The elections had already shattered one party's confidence. In their aftermath a kind of paralysis crept through the Republican party. Newsmen caught Matthew S. Quay, the Republican national chairman, in early November as he hurried off for a Florida vacation. What would Republicans do now, they wanted to know. Quay smiled, but the reply was serious. "It looks to me as if the best thing to do just now is to saw wood." Like Quay, many Republicans searched for a quiet haven in which to ride out the storm. Others squabbled over blame for the defeat. Republicans everywhere were in disarray. "You cannot get ten of them together without finding wide disagreements as to tariff, election bill, and every other Republican measure or principle," a party worker noted.[26]

Blaine was unhappy, fearful the debacle might undercut his reciprocity negotiations. He immediately set up a special office in his home on Lafayette Park across from the White House, where he conferred daily with Latin American diplomats, pressing for specific agreements, assuring them the administration stood firm despite the setback. Reed was bitter, aware the defeat had tarnished the Fifty-first Congress and ended his hopes for a presidential bid in 1892. "It looks just for the moment as if this was a world made mostly for cowards and laggards and sneaks," he wrote Lodge the day after the elections. Joseph Medill and his allies were irate. Blaming the election "cyclone" on the McKinley tariff, they angrily reminded Harrison of earlier warnings and urged him to call Congress into special session to lower duties. Harrison ignored the advice, but the size of the defeat daunted him. Should present trends continue, he confided to one Republican correspondent, "our future is not cheerful."[2 7]

As Harrison recognized, the year's devastation indicated dramatic shifts in voting patterns, perhaps even the onset of Democratic hegemony. It thrust the Democrats far into the lead for the presidential election of 1892. Somehow, since 1888's lifting victory, Republicans had lost touch with the people, a touch they would have to reestablish if victory were to come again. On one level, they needed to take a close look at that "police sergeant" impulse toward moral and social reform, which apparently alienated more people than it converted. On another, they needed to review the first session of the Fifty-first Congress, its measures and outlook, and the way both had been presented to the people. Public opinion seemed clear, at least for the moment. The Republicans had gone too far, raised tariffs too high, legislated too much. The judgment galled Republican leaders, who believed they had acted constructively in a fashion rarely seen in the past. "The sting of the present defeat," as Lodge said in his diary, "lies in the fact that the Republican party never since the war deserved so well." Lodge and other Republicans would never forget the sting of 1890. It hurt too much for that.[2 8]

☆☆☆

Elections always contain ironies, as Grover Cleveland and Benjamin Harrison both knew. Cleveland, who was not a candidate for any office in 1890, was the year's biggest winner; Harrison, also not running for anything, its biggest loser. Considered a triumph for tariff reform, the elections spurred talk of a third presidential bid for Cleveland, the issue's chief spokesman. Letters poured into 816 Madison Avenue, congratulating him personally for the victory, though he had played little direct role in it. The elections also rekindled Cleveland's appetite for office. They showed, he thought, a "moral awakening" in behalf of decentralization, limited government, and other Democratic doctrines. Pursuing his usual strategy, he maintained an outward disinterest in the nomination, but worked privately with loyal aides to head off competitors and signal his intentions to key Democratic leaders. By early 1892, the groundwork carefully laid, he was ready to move more openly. "I shall be obedient to the call of my country and my party," Cleveland said in May, six weeks before the opening of the Democratic national convention.[2 9]

Distrustful of the press, Cleveland relied on occasional speaking engagements to build on 1890's victory and keep himself before the public eye. An awkward, labored speaker, he overwhelmed audiences rather than stirred them, usually with lessons of moral courage, individualism, fidelity, and patriotism. Ray Stannard Baker, later a biographer of Woodrow Wilson, always remembered the occasion in February 1892 when Cleveland spoke at the University of Michigan Law School as part of his preconvention campaign. The speech, entitled "Sentiment in our National Life," simply urged students to have faith in the value of "a good conscience and a pure heart," yet impressed the youthful Baker. Cleveland was "a great slow-moving hulk of a man, ponderous in what he said, but with something about him, some authority, some inherent power, that impressed me more profoundly than any other speaker I had ever heard up to that time." Afterwards, Baker and others crowded forward to shake Cleveland's hand. "I remember the thick, soft, warm feel of his fingers, like a handful of new-baked breakfast rolls." Years later the impression still lingered, said Baker: "weight, power, greatness."[30]

In November 1890, Cleveland went to McKinley's Ohio to attack the tariff. Two months later, in Philadelphia, he attacked again, calling the McKinley law "an unjust tariff which banishes from many humble homes the comforts of life, in order that in the palaces of wealth luxury may more abound." In Buffalo during May 1891, he denounced the "reckless and wicked" spending of the Billion Dollar Congress; in Boston late that year he accused Republicans of ignoring the needs of consumers and the poor; in New York early in 1892 he pledged to lighten the burdens of taxation. "We have insisted on tariff reform and on abandonment of unjust favoritism. . ," he reminded fellow Democrats. "The least retreat bodes disaster."[31] Gathering momentum, Cleveland steadily eclipsed rival candidates for the nomination. Carlisle, the renowned Kentucky congressman, and Horace Boies, the governor of Iowa, fell easily. David B. Hill, Cleveland's own successor as governor of New York, fought more stubbornly.[32]

Bitter enemies, Cleveland and Hill played to different audiences in the country. Cleveland liked independence, and carefully preserved an air of detachment from politics. Hill loved politics, considered himself a party man, and made famous his personal motto, "I am a Democrat." While Cleveland enjoyed political maneuvering, yet tried to hide it, Hill made no pretense. It was his joy, and had been his vehicle to power. Working his way up, he had patiently climbed rungs that Cleveland had skipped in his own swift rise. In 1882 Hill had resigned as mayor of Elmira, New York, to become Cleveland's lieutenant-governor. He assumed the governorship when Cleveland moved to Washington, then won the office on his own in 1885 and 1888. A hard-working governor, he compiled a decent record that included several important reforms, but never received credit for it in the Cleveland camp. Cleveland detested him, suspicious of his higher ambitions, disdainful of his "shiftiness and cheap expediency." Hill wanted the presidency. In January 1891, he took a useful step, winning election to the Senate, yet decided also to hold on to the governorship for another year, a mistake that cost him dearly.[33]

A month later it was Cleveland's turn to stumble, or so his rival initially hoped. On February 10, 1891, disturbed by a bill then before the House authorizing the free coinage of silver, Cleveland spoke out on the sensitive issue. In a letter distributed to the press he predicted "disaster, if in the present situation we enter upon the dangerous and reckless experiment of free, unlimited and independent silver coinage."[34] Skillfully worded, the letter left ample room for maneuver. It was firm on free coinage, but implied approval of limited silver coinage, raised hopes of an international agreement to promote silver, and avoided calling for repeal of the recently passed Sherman Silver Purchase Act. Cleveland made sure no one missed the point. "Note carefully the wording of the letter and see how much room after all there is for the action of judgment and conviction below the line of free coinage of the silver of the world," he wrote a friend. Hill, who had counted on exploiting Cleveland's anti-silver reputation in the hunt for convention delegates, must have been bewildered. Had the letter come from his pen, it would likely have been treated as further evidence of shifty equivocation. From Cleveland's, it won widespread praise for flexibility and forthright courage.[35]

Cleveland was certain the letter would work to his benefit. It would bind New England Democrats even more firmly to his cause, and prepare the way for an appeal to sound-money Republicans in the 1892 election. It would alienate extreme silverites in the South and West, who were unlikely to support him anyway, but might woo moderate silver men and bimetallists. The strategy worked. Amid the loud outcry following the letter's publication, some silver Democrats angrily abandoned Cleveland, but many others counseled moderation, and praised his courage and candor. Most important, the entire Democratic party, hungry for unity and victory in 1892, moved toward a decision the silver Democrats would soon bitterly regret: to accept Cleveland's plea to subordinate the silver issue to the tariff issue in the 1892 campaign. The Democratic party "is united on the tariff," as the pro-silver San Francisco *Examiner* put it succinctly. "Let the issue on which it is divided wait."[36]

Robbed of issues and support, the luckless Hill never had a chance. Unable to resist the sly maneuver, he used chicanery in February 1892 to capture New York State's delegates, another costly triumph, and then watched helplessly as Democratic state conventions across the country declared for his opponent. A genuine groundswell of popular support for Cleveland, which his managers skillfully tapped, carried state after state, even in areas where the party hierarchy preferred Hill.[37] By June 21, when the national convention opened in Chicago, the former president had the nomination firmly in hand. On the first ballot Hill received 114 votes, Cleveland 617⅓ and the nomination. Cleveland, his wife, Governor Russell of Massachusetts, and other close friends followed the balloting with a special telegraph wire in the gunroom at Gray Gables. As the satisfying totals mounted, Cleveland startled everyone, suddenly remembering: "I forgot to dry my [fishing] lines today." He went outside to hang them up, and was there at 3:20 A.M. when the nomination became his. Dawn came shortly thereafter, a good omen, Mrs. Cleveland calmly thought.[38]

There were favorable signs everywhere. Normally fragmented, Democrats for once were united, and sensed certain victory. A proven vote-getter headed their ticket, and they could appeal to the same elements, national and local, that had created 1890's triumph. They had done well in the recent 1891 elections, though the Republicans, fighting to recover lost ground, had also made some gains. In November 1891, with strategists from both parties nervously watching for a continuation of the 1890 trend, the Democrats had won the governorship of New York, reelected Russell as governor of Massachusetts—the first time that had happened since the formation of the Republican party in the 1850s—and again exploited the prohibition issue to reelect Governor Boies in Iowa.[39] The Chicago convention over, a confident Cleveland met with advisers to lay plans for the election. He disliked the aggressive tariff reform plank in the platform, having hoped for a straddle, but he could take care of that with moderate, equivocal statements during the campaign. A promise of "sensible" tariff reduction, attacks on Republican misrule, reminders of the "force bill," and a general pledge to cut back on government activity, Cleveland concluded, would carry him to the White House.[40]

One final stroke remained. To manage the campaign Cleveland summoned the cool, efficient William C. Whitney, a wealthy New Yorker who had helped reconstruct the Navy during his first administration. Moving easily between business and politics, Whitney liked to build, and put together political coalitions and the New York City transit system with equal zest. His ability was legendary. As an admirer recalled, "he had the rare gift of doing within a few days the work that would require weeks on the part of the average leader." He also possessed a knack Cleveland did not: he could cooperate comfortably with all elements in the party, reformers and regulars, rural courthouse politicians and Tammany Hall chieftains, anyone who could contribute to a Democratic victory. Working swiftly, Whitney constructed a national organization, built relations with local organizations, wooed dissidents, and spread documents and stump speakers across the country. In September, even David B. Hill came aboard, telling a Brooklyn audience: "I was a Democrat before the Chicago convention, and I am a Democrat still." Whitney's performance was masterful, though assisted, as he knew, by forces beyond his control. Voters clearly preferred the Democrats this year, and Republicans could do little to reverse the trend. They were in confused retreat.[41]

☆☆☆

Harrison had suffered throughout 1891 and 1892. His administration acquired a transitional air, permitted under the American system to rule for another two years, yet damaged and inwardly prepared for further defeats. Harrison did his best to make it otherwise. In December 1890 he delivered an aggressive annual message that defended Republican achievements, asked the nation to withhold judgment on the McKinley tariff until it had had time to function, and urged the Senate to pass the Lodge elections bill. The following Spring, he toured the South and West, displaying once again the speaking style that had been so effective in 1888. In a month he gave 142 speeches outlining his hopes for the nation. Later in 1891 he moved to take closer control of the Republican party. He ousted the recalcitrant Quay as national chairman and replaced him with James S. Clarkson, a shrewd and experienced Iowa Republican. Yet nothing seemed to go quite as planned.

Legislation bogged down, Republican morale dwindled, and party leaders were in open rebellion against the president's leadership. To Harrison the final, greatest blow came on October 25, 1892, just two weeks before the presidential election, when his wife died of tuberculosis after a painful illness.[42]

The second session of the Fifty-first Congress, which now included nearly a hundred lame duck Republicans, was a disappointment. "There are too many corpses and too few mourners," a reporter noted.[43] On December 2, the Senate took up the Lodge bill, amid renewed protests from the Democrats. They need not have worried. Using the recent elections as an excuse, western silver Republicans were eager to side-track the bill in favor of a free coinage measure. On January 5, 1891, eight of them joined twenty-six Democrats to do so. George F. Hoar stared, face pale, disbelieving. "That means the death of the Republican party," those near him thought they heard him mutter. Hoar managed to get the bill back on the calendar, but the end still came quickly, on January 26. Again, western Republicans joined the Democrats to set the bill aside. The long Republican fight was over. "I am too angry to write. . ," Spooner told a friend. "We are fallen upon bad times for the party. The Confederacy and the Western Mining Camps are in legislative supremacy."[44]

Four weeks later the Fifty-first Congress at last adjourned. In the rules it adopted, the measures it passed, and the voting shifts it shaped, it had been historic. Shortly before closing, McKinley offered the House's traditional vote of thanks to the Speaker, but the Democrats, shouting and jeering, refused to support it. For the final time in that Congress, Reed smiled, and told the House that time would vindicate Republican policy. "The highest commendation will be given us in the future, not for what measures we have passed, valuable as they are, but because we have taken so long a stride in the direction of responsible government. [We have] demonstrated to the people that those who have been elected to do their will can do it." The gavel fell. Democrats sang "Home, Sweet Home," a reminder to defeated Republicans where they were headed.[45]

A Republican reporter, eager to refute charges that Reed's rules had stifled debate, estimated that 12,930,000 words had been spoken in the House, with another 10,246,000 in the Senate. It was possible. In all, the Fifty-first Congress had passed 2186 laws, a record number. One law it had not passed, the federal elections bill, and thus signaled the closing of an era. Republicans like Lodge and Hoar and Harrison had clung to the issue of civil rights long after their society had passed them by. People were weary of Civil War issues, indifferent or hostile to blacks, and eager to turn to the new concerns of a nation undergoing rapid urban-industrial growth. Republicans "may clamor about the negro," said the New York *Herald,* "but the plain truth is the North has got tired of the negro." The feeling lasted a long time. It would be half a century before the country again tackled the disfranchisement of millions of black citizens; it would be nearly three-quarters of a century before anything significant was done. When the moment did arrive, between 1957 and 1965, the laws passed resembled the Republican proposals of the late nineteenth century, some consolation perhaps for those who had dared to lead.[46]

For now, Republican spirits fell, and with them, unity. Through 1891 and 1892 the party press turned sour, without the driving, confident mood of earlier days. Republicans sniped at Harrison. Few could fully understand him. Addressing small crowds, he was at his best, informal, expansive, moving, with a sure touch for the right word, the stirring phrase. In individual conversation, on the other hand, he was brusque and cold, like "a dripping cave," Reed said. Collectively he swayed audiences; individually he made enemies. A precise, hard-working administrator, he drove subordinates, but rarely encouraged them. "In his contempt for flattery, he seldom indulged in praise," recalled an official who worked closely with him. To visitors in his White House office, he resembled a "pouter pigeon," anxious for them to be gone. His handshake was like "a wilted petunia," his manner icy and distant. Republican congressmen disliked dealing with him.[47]

By 1891 Quay, Reed, McKinley, Clarkson, Thomas C. Platt, the "Easy Boss" of New York State, and other powerful Republicans were openly rebellious, resentful of this slight or that. Patronage was a particularly touchy matter. A "carefully graded and recognized system of institutional standing," it played a vital role in the period's politics, providing needed jobs for party workers, recognition for party leaders. Harrison heeded the requests of local Republican organizations, usually a politically acceptable formula, but his dour personality, plus new civil service laws that cut into the spoils he could distribute, worked against him. Quay grumbled constantly about patronage slights. McKinley asked Harrison for a promised appointment, said a cold "Good-day" when Harrison reneged, and never visited the White House again during Harrison's term. Reed had already departed, deserting Harrison in October 1890 over the appointment of a bitter enemy to an important post in Portland, Maine, his home city. "I never had but two personal enemies in my life," he remarked. "One of these Mr. Harrison has pardoned out of the penitentiary and the other he has just appointed Collector of the Port of Portland."[48]

Discontent spread like ripples across a pond. Harrison's personal traits, many of which had won praise during the salad days of 1889 and 1890, came under mounting attack. In Republican circles the talk turned more and more to dumping the president in 1892, replacing him with someone who could reverse the party's drift. Harrison knew of the talk, and resented it. His administration deserved better, he thought, and besides, it did the party no good to seek a single scape-goat for its current, complex ills. Harrison resented even more the usual focus of the dump-Harrison discussions, his own secretary of state, James G. Blaine. He had been wary of Blaine from the begin-ning, but wanted to bring his large talents and following into the administration. For his part Blaine had generally honored the tacit understanding through which he had entered the cabinet. He had re-mained circumspect, deferring to Harrison's wishes, acknowledging Harrison's leadership and achievements. The thousands of Blaine loyalists had not. At every opportunity they had hinted that Blaine ran the administration, conceived its policies, and covered for his leader's failings. Why not make him president now in name as well as in fact?[49]

Blaine's own feelings were a mystery, the subject of endless specu-lation by Republican newspapers and politicians. Clearly the White House still tempted, yet he respected Harrison, wanted to avoid any appearance of disloyalty, and enjoyed his duties as secretary of state. The two men made an effective team, with a fruitful balance of ideas and characteristics. Mercurial, Blaine needed Harrison's steadying in-fluence, and in turn provided the spark, the quick flash of insight, that Harrison often lacked. Harrison tended to become testy, especially if he sensed foreign opposition to his policies. In 1891 he quarreled with Italy over the mob lynching of eleven Italian citizens in New Orleans, and during the winter of 1891–92 he came close to war with Chile over the fatal stabbing of two American sailors on shore leave in Valparaiso. Blaine took a moderating hand in both incidents, trying to channel Harrison's stern morality and patriotism into constructive paths. Both men shared a vision of a new era of American power and prosperity, born of commercial supremacy in the markets of the world. "We are great enough and rich enough," said Harrison, "to reach forward to grander conceptions than have entered the minds of some of our states-men in the past."[50]

An enlarged merchant fleet would carry American products around the world, on sea lanes protected by a newly effective Navy that had coaling stations at strategic locations. Harrison and Blaine searched for bases in the Caribbean, nurtured relations with distant Hawaii, a Pacific kingdom with a sizable population of American settlers. Hawaii opened on the markets of Asia, while the Caribbean was the pathway to Latin America, the focus of reciprocity and the Harrison-Blaine vision. Beginning on February 5, 1891, the administration announced a series of reciprocity treaties with Brazil, Cuba, Puerto Rico, Santo Domingo, Nicaragua, Guatemala, and a half-dozen other countries. As planned, the treaties lowered or removed tariff duties on American flour, cereals, pork, farm machinery, and selected manufactured products, in return for undutied sugar, coffee, tea, molasses, and hides.[51]

The results were mixed, thanks partly to an economic depression that was spreading across the hemisphere. But within a year exports to Brazil and Cuba had risen significantly, by 11 percent and 55 percent respectively, and planners hoped for similar gains elsewhere. A few figures were spectacular, including a rise in flour exports to Cuba from only 14,000 barrels in the first half of 1891 to some 337,000 barrels during the same period of 1892. Heartened, Harrison planned to use the figures to soothe discontented western farmers. In January 1893, another part of the vision fell into place, when revolutionists, nearly all American, overthrew the Hawaiian monarchy and proposed annexation to the United States. Harrison moved swiftly to respond, but Blaine was no longer there to help harvest the fruits of their policies. Eight months before, in one of the most dramatic incidents in American political history, he had stunned the country, suddenly resigning as secretary of state.[52]

Harrison had forced the resignation, but so in a sense had age, infirmity, and misunderstanding. Blaine had grown old, almost overnight it seemed to some of those around him. In 1892 he looked older than his 62 years. His hair had whitened, his step grown feeble, and his eyes, once legendary for their hypnotic sparkle, had dimmed. Reporters thought his complexion, always pale, seemed ghostlike. Periodically, gout, headaches, nausea, dizzy spells, and other illnesses kept him away from the State Department. On January 15, 1890, his favorite son, Walker, died suddenly of pneumonia at age 35; barely two weeks later a daughter, Alice, died, also unexpectedly. Blaine never fully recovered. More frequently now, he had to seek rest away from Washington, either at his home in Augusta or his summer cottage at Bar Harbor. Harrison sympathized with Blaine's afflictions, but came to resent the extra burdens he shouldered in Blaine's absences. In the properly mannered 1890s, the two men never discussed their growing estrangement, an unfortunate thing since they could no doubt have worked it out.[53]

As Harrison's standing fell, the pressure mounted on Blaine to oppose him for the 1892 nomination. Blaine alone could reverse the Republican slide, a number of party leaders believed. He could carry New England, the Midwest, and the Pacific Coast—areas where he was traditionally strong—and could win back wavering farmers on the Plains. With reciprocity and his enormous popularity, he might even steal a Border State or two from the Democrats. Politicians like Quay and Platt, caring little for Blaine, wanted simply to use him to oust Harrison. They watched his health for favorable signs, making him sound, sadly, like livestock: "If he winters well at his home this year he certainly ought to be in good condition next spring for the run," one of them said in mid-1891. In September of that year, newsmen polled the delegates at the New York State Republican convention. Startled, they found 16 delegates for Harrison, 639 for Blaine. Similar results at conventions in Massachusetts and other states worried the Harrison camp. "People are like sheep," a Harrison manager wrote in August 1891, "and just about this time they are nearly all jumping over the fence into Blaine's fields."[54]

Still, Blaine declined to run. In December 1891 he apparently wrote a public letter to that effect, but decided to withhold it during the crisis with Chile. The crisis settled, the letter appeared on February 6, 1892, in plenty of time for the Spring's round of Republican state conventions. It also seemed firm enough: "I am not a candidate for the Presidency, and my name will not go before the Republican National Convention for the nomination." Suiting actions to words, Blaine made no attempt to win delegates to the national convention, allowing even his party organization in Maine to endorse Harrison for reelection.[55] But he could not stop all the rumors, and Harrison, tense and upset, would not let the matter go. In early May 1892 Harrison's son, Russell, blundered into the situation, reportedly telling a crowd in a New York City hotel that Blaine could not possibly be a candidate. "He is completely broken down both mentally and physically. He cannot remember the simplest things, and all of the work of the State Department has

been on my father's shoulders for over two years." Explanations quickly followed, but did not thaw the growing chill.[56]

On Friday morning, June 3, with the Republican national convention just four days away, Blaine attended a meeting of the cabinet to
report on current negotiations, then chatted good-naturedly with reporters on the way back to his office. That afternoon he was in for a
surprise. Harrison sent a mutual friend to ask Blaine to clarify his
position on the nomination. Blaine fumed. Gentlemen did not ask
clarifications of someone's word, in this case Blaine's public statement
of February 6. Shortly after noon the next day, he dispatched an aide
with a terse letter of resignation as secretary of state, effective "immediately." Harrison read it, remarking: "Well, the crisis has come."[57]
The news swept through official Washington, emptied government offices, stopped business on the House floor, and went by wire to Minneapolis, the site of the convention. It was staggering, at first hard to
believe. Newsboys hawked extra editions bringing confirmation:
"Blaine has resigned; it is official." A group of leading Republicans
heard the news at a meeting in Philadelphia, and discussed its probable
effect on Republican chances in the election. "Everybody realized that
it meant disaster."[58]

In Minneapolis Blaine badges, crimson and white, suddenly appeared everywhere, as did the familiar white plumes of the Plumed Knight.
Platt, Clarkson, Quay, and others lobbied feverishly, promising lower
tariffs to the Medill Republicans, silver coinage to the silverites, patronage jobs to party workers, anything to anybody who would vote for
Blaine. The Harrison lines trembled, but held firm. Even delegates who
had been with Blaine since the 1870s stood by the instructions of their
state conventions. Quay and Platt switched quickly to McKinley, the
party's brightest young star after his comeback victory in a race for the
governorship of Ohio in 1891. But nothing worked: McKinley naturally
preferred to wait for a more favorable year, and Harrison had the delegates. On Friday, June 10, a hectic seven days after he had decided to
do something about Blaine, the president won renomination on the
first ballot. Blaine promptly issued a call for unity in the campaign,
but there were hard feelings on both sides. "If there was any demand
for plumes in any part of the world," a Harrison man said harshly, "an
export duty on those at Minneapolis, which will never be called for
again in our politics, would pay the national debt."[59]

Harrison appreciated his victory, but sensed its hollowness. As delegates streamed home from Minneapolis, many of them were already talking of 1896 and the prospects for winning that year, not this one. Harrison's renomination "seemed to fall like a wet blanket" on Republicans without personal ties to the administration, noted Marcus A. Hanna, McKinley's close friend and adviser. "There is an utter indifference manifested toward his success." No one wanted to head the campaign. Leading speakers, counted on in the past to rally the party, declined to take the stump. Blaine pleaded fatigue and poor health, and made only one appearance during the campaign. Reed also stayed away, refusing, he said, "to ride in the ice wagon." Harrison himself had to remain by his wife's bedside, capturing the nation's sympathy with a sad vigil that ended just a few days before the election. It was a time, he wrote, of "great anxiety and pain. I was a leader in prison." Bereft of leadership, the campaign was inept, adrift. In July 1892, Republicans reeled under still another blow: a strike, soon bloody, at the Homestead iron and steel works of the Carnegie Steel Company.[60]

The Homestead works, the pride of the steel industry, lay on the left bank of the Monongahela River, ten miles east of Pittsburgh. Employing 4000 people, they turned out 25,000 tons of steel each month, a figure that had recently helped boost the United States into the coveted lead in world steel production. Trouble began in late June 1892, when Andrew Carnegie, the legendary master of the industry, and Henry Clay Frick, his partner and manager, proposed a new wage scale that lowered wages an average of 18 percent, with some cuts as high as 35 percent. The workers struck, and Frick responded by locking them out of the plant. He had already erected a three-mile fence around it, with regularly spaced holes (for "observation," he said) and topped with barbed wire. Reporters converged on Homestead, daily dispatching vivid accounts that seemed to confirm the public's worst fears. For all its benefits, industrialization might carry an intolerable price: social dislocations, class tensions, perhaps even outright warfare. Homestead indicated a growing estrangement between labor and capital, a hardening of attitudes that threatened industrial peace and might undermine society itself.

Controlling the approaches to the plant, the strikers turned back attempts to reopen with nonunion labor. Furious, Frick hired a small private army of Pinkerton detectives, which set out before dawn on July 6 to take the strikers by surprise from the river. The attack failed. Alert strikers spotted the approaching flotilla, gunfire broke out, and Frick's army, pinned down on the river, surrendered. Three attackers and ten strikers died in the battle. A few days later, with local authorities unable to persuade either side to end the warfare, the Pennsylvania governor ordered out the state militia, 7000 strong, to impose peace at Homestead. One final, lurid incident remained. On Saturday, July 23, as Frick sat chatting with a visitor in his office, an Anarchist named Alexander Berkman calmly walked in and shot him. He fired twice, then stabbed him several times. Incredibly, Frick survived, watched police take Berkman away, called in a doctor to bandage his wounds, and stayed in his office until the usual quitting time. "I do not think I shall die," he told the press. "But if I do or not, the company will pursue the same policy and it will win."[61]

Republicans were shocked. For years they had used the iron and steel industry to prove the benefits of tariff protection. The tariff, they had argued, guarded American mills from European competition, created jobs for thousands of workers, raised wages, and boosted production. Wage cuts and strikes sapped the argument badly. Alarmed, Republican leaders sent an emissary to Frick urging him to compromise with his men. "Never, never!" Frick replied, and proceeded to crush the strike. In late July the Homestead works reopened under military protection, with new laborers brought in for the purpose. The strikers held out until November then capitulated. In the meantime, the Democrats had made skillful use of the issue. As Cleveland told a Madison Square Garden audience: "Scenes are enacted in the very abiding place of high protection that mock the hopes of toil, and demonstrate the falsity that protection is a boon to toilers."[62]

Cleveland exploited the issue to woo midwestern Republicans, still unhappy with the high McKinley duties. In October Walter Q. Gresham, a well-known Republican from Indiana, announced for Cleveland, with a blast at the McKinley law. Others followed. More important, Cleveland and the Democrats also courted workingmen, who were clearly restive that summer of 1892. Strikes, sometimes violent, seemed to break out across the country: the steel mills at Homestead; the railroad yards in Buffalo, New York; the coal mines at Coal Creek, Tennessee; the silver mines in the Coeur d'Alene district of Idaho. At one point that summer, the governors of three states called out their militias to deal with violent strikes, while President Harrison sent federal troops into Coeur d'Alene to end bloodshed there. Most workers remained peacefully at their jobs, but observers sensed a hardening of attitudes, a growing militance that might erupt if economic conditions worsened:

I am living in the end of the nineteenth century,
I've been trained and educated like the rest
. . .
For I'm only just a wheel in the machine.

Working in the system,
Working in the system—
'Till a part of which at last I've come to be—
Just toiling to exist,
I never shall be missed,
So I guess I'll make a break for liberty.[63]

☆☆☆

Cleveland spent election day, November 8, 1892, in his New York home, where two special telegraph wires had been installed for the occasion. Shortly after midnight a crowd gathered outside to cheer the new president-elect. Cleveland spoke to them briefly, then returned inside. "It is a solemn thing to be President," he remarked to friends. Through the night the wires brought news of a Democratic sweep across the country. New York State, with its important bloc of electoral votes, fell early in the evening, the South held firm, crucial areas of the Midwest showed signs of breaking away from the Republican party, and there were even encouraging reports from California, which a Democratic presidential candidate had not carried since 1880. Even Indiana, Harrison's home state, seemed about to fall into the Democratic column. Cleveland accepted congratulations from friends and family, and retired at 4 A.M., conscious that he had just won the most decisive presidential triumph in twenty years. "Mr. Cleveland's pleasure was not demonstrative," his wife told reporters the next day. "He seemed to be simply in the enjoyment of a perfect satisfaction."[64]

The final returns sharpened the satisfaction. Cleveland won 5,556,543 votes to Harrison's 5,175,582, a margin of nearly 400,000 votes, large by the era's standards. He carried the South, New York, New Jersey, Connecticut, Indiana, and part of the electoral vote of several other states, including California. He also took Wisconsin and Illinois, the first Democratic candidate to do so since the 1850s. The Democrats won control of both houses of Congress. A large share of the labor vote and increased strength in the cities gave added significance to their achievement. Gaining strikingly among immigrant,

Catholic, and labor voters, they carried New York, Chicago, San Francisco, Milwaukee, Harrison's own Indianapolis, and other cities. Disgruntled Republicans complained that "the slums of Chicago, Brooklyn and New York" had decided the election, but the complaint measured envy as much as anything else. The Democrats had won votes virtually everywhere.[65]

They had done it, significantly, with the help of new campaign techniques. Responding to the growth of a more independent, thoughtful electorate, they had set aside the traditional "army" style of campaigning—with its torchlight parades, brass bands, and party uniforms—in favor of a newer "merchandising" style designed to persuade and educate the voters. The Democrats in Illinois pointed the way, shrewdly stressing education and advertising. In 1892 they put 14,000 workers in the field, distributed nearly 2,000,000 campaign documents in 12 languages among the state's voters, and mailed another 2,000,000 documents to voters in nearby states. Their Chicago office sent 100,000 letters in several languages to Democrats throughout the Midwest urging greater efforts in the campaign. The "merchandising" style, designed to win over the wavering rather than to rally the faithful, paid off handsomely in votes, in Illinois and elsewhere. Soon adopted by both major parties, it took account of the country's changing electorate and marked a new era in American politics.[66]

In this way, and others, the Democrats capitalized skillfully on Republican weaknesses, and beat back the challenge of the People's party in the South. The Populists had opened the campaign with high hopes. At an emotional convention in Omaha, Nebraska, in July, they adopted a spirited platform calling for the free coinage of silver, an improved banking system, a graduated income tax, government ownership of the means of transportation and communication, and stiffer controls over land monopoly. Determined to cut away from the old parties, many of them planned to nominate for president Leonidas L. Polk, the popular and energetic head of the National Farmers' Alliance, who was telling friends that an independent Populist ticket would carry eight southern states and at least fourteen northern ones. But Polk died suddenly in June, and the Omaha convention turned to James B. Weaver of Iowa, a former congressman, Union Army general, and third-party candidate (on the Greenback Labor party ticket) for president in 1880.[67]

An experienced campaigner, Weaver immediately took the stump to make up for the Populists' lack of an extensive organization and party press, much as William Jennings Bryan would do four years later. He found the going difficult, especially in the South where Democrats did not tolerate dissent. Jeers, catcalls, and foot-stomping drowned out his speeches, while nightriders and hired toughs jostled his audiences and intimidated Populist sympathizers. The situation deteriorated as Weaver moved further into the South, until a mob in Macon, Georgia, hurled rotten eggs, tomatoes, and rocks at the candidate and his wife. "The fact was, Mrs. Weaver was made a regular walking omelet by the southern chivalry of Georgia," remarked a companion on the tour. Weaver regretfully called off his southern campaign, and focused on the Plains states and silver mining regions of the Far West where audiences listened more respectfully to the Populist message. "We have a system of [financial] slavery here today as inimical to human life as that which enslaved an emancipated people," Weaver told an enthusiastic crowd in Aspen, Colorado. "We wiped that out and we are on a second crusade today."[68]

The results were only partially satisfying. Weaver won 1,040,886 votes, the first third-party candidate in American history to attract more than a million popular votes. He carried Kansas, Idaho, Nevada, and Colorado, along with portions of North Dakota and Oregon, for a total of 22 electoral votes. A few state and local victories, including the election of Populist governors in Kansas and North Dakota, a handful of congressmen, and a smashing triumph for the entire state ticket in Colorado, further brightened the picture. But for the most part, the returns were cause for disappointment among People's party leaders. Unable to penetrate the South, Weaver had been held to less than a quarter of the vote in every southern state except one, Alabama. He lost heavily in urban areas, with the exception of some mining towns in the Far West; received little support east of the Mississippi; and failed to win over farmers in the Midwest. In Iowa he polled barely 20,000 votes; in Wisconsin he took less than 3 percent of the vote. In no Midwestern state did he win as much as 5 percent of the vote.[69]

Local candidates did no better. The August elections in Alabama and Georgia, both thought to be Populist strongholds, overwhelmed the party's state candidates. The Democrats in both states manipulated the returns to insure Populist defeat. In October, Florida voters turned back a popular Populist gubernatorial nominee by a margin of nearly four to one. Thomas E. Watson, virtually a symbol of the independent movement in the South, lost his Georgia congressional seat. Ignatius

Donnelly ran a distant third in a race for governor in Minnesota. "Beaten! Whipped! Smashed! . . ," Donnelly, discouraged, wrote in his diary. "Our followers scattered like dew before the rising sun."[70]

The rising sun, in truth, appeared to be Democratic. The nation's discontented, those fed up in one way or another with current conditions and Republican rule, had voted for the Democrats, not the Populists, a signal of the basic failure of the People's party campaign. Among the Populists, discouragement set in. Farmers' Alliance membership plunged dramatically in 1892, for the second year in a row. The organization, once the breeding ground of the People's party, was shattered. Still, Populist leaders rallied the forces and pointed hopefully to elections in 1894 and 1896. That was the attraction of politics: another election, another chance, always lay ahead. But the shrewder among them sensed that the disappointing outcome in 1892 might mark the high point of their young party's electoral fortunes.[71]

Harrison took defeat in stride. "For me there is no sting in it," he wrote a friend. "Indeed after the heavy blow the death of my wife dealt me, I do not think I could have stood the strain a re-election would have brought." Harrison blamed defeat on the Homestead strike, economic troubles, and the public's misunderstanding of the tariff's benefits. In his last annual message, in December 1892, he cautioned against Democratic tariff experiments, but acknowledged: "The result of the recent election must be accepted as having introduced a new policy."[72] Early in the new year he prepared for retirement, amid signs that leadership in the party and country was passing to new hands. On January 27, 1893, James G. Blaine died in Washington, and crowds gathered in the streets to mourn. He had been the most popular and imaginative party leader of his time. Within a few days, former president Rutherford B. Hayes and several other members of the Civil War generation also died. The Republican party searched for fresh directions. Battered, divided, it reminded a Republican wit of an old Methodist minister who had a habit of opening his services with the same prayer: "Oh, Lord, I am a mass of bruises, wounds and putrefied sores."[73]

President-elect Cleveland would soon envy the leisure of Harrison's retirement. Within a few days of the election the clamor began: for cabinet appointments, patronage jobs, the adoption of this policy or that. Many Democrats urged Cleveland to call Congress immediately into special session to lower the tariff. Otherwise, tariff reductions would have to await the normal session in December 1893, a full year after the voters' mandate and dangerously close to the midterm elections of 1894. "The sooner the work is begun the better," declared a leading southerner. Sweeping victories, nice as they were, brought their problems. They meant large and diverse coalitions, with each component now expecting enactment of its own program. A thoughtful Republican caught the Democratic dilemma: "The Republican party has been defeated in this election because the Democrats have induced all the people in the country who think that they want something which they have not got, to vote the Democratic ticket in the expectation that that party if in power will give them what they want."[74]

Yet, if the dangers were large, so were the opportunities. The Democrats now had the chance both parties had been seeking for decades. The recent election confirmed 1890's Democratic trend and indicated that a permanent change might have taken place in American politics. For the first time in nearly forty years—since, in fact, the administration of James Buchanan way back in the 1850s—the Democrats controlled the White House and both branches of Congress. On the eve of power, Cleveland saw both the opportunity and the danger. At a dinner in New York he reminded fellow Democrats of their new responsibilities: "When I consider all that we have to do as a party charged with the control of the Government, I feel that our campaign, instead of being concluded, is just begun." Cleveland was right. In the coming years the Democratic party, amid worldwide depression and social upheaval, would face its greatest challenge.[75]

FOUR

The Democrats
in Crisis, 1893-1895

Inauguration day 1893 dawned cold and blustery. Rain had turned to snow during the night. Freezing winds whipped the streets of Washington, shredding flags and ripping the inaugural bunting along the parade route. Spectators shivered in the cold. To their relief, Cleveland kept his inaugural address short, taking fewer than twenty minutes to outline the course of the incoming administration. Under the Democrats, government would be limited, frugal, free from "the unwholesome progeny of paternalism" that had marred the Harrison years. "The lessons of paternalism ought to be unlearned and the better lesson taught that while the people should patriotically and cheerfully support their Government its functions do not include the support of the people." Specifically, the Democrats would pledge a sound and stable currency, measures to restrain the trusts, continued reform of the civil service, and above all, significant reductions in the tariff. The people's verdict was clear, Cleveland said. On this day they turned over control of the government to a party "pledged in the most positive terms to the accomplishment of tariff reform."[1]

A few worrisome incidents jarred the occasion. Economic conditions had deteriorated in the months since the election, and investors at home and abroad saw signs of an approaching financial panic. Alarmed, they began to hoard gold, which drained from the federal Treasury. Discontent lingered in the South and West. The governor of Oregon refused to take part in the inaugural ceremonies, protesting the selection of "a Wall Street plutocrat as President of the United States." But such matters seemed only minor irritants in March 1893, as Cleveland and the Democrats celebrated their ascension to power. The new president still reflected the glow of his extraordinary election victory. He was aggressive and self-assured, more confident than ever before, friends thought. The leader of his party, he somehow stood above it, the focus of a public sentiment that bridged normal political differences. "He has reached the summit of popular favor," remarked a newspaper that March.[2]

Predictions spread that the Republican party, tied to Civil War issues and unable to keep pace with the changing country, would disintegrate into bickering factions, then vanish. A new party—less activist, more attuned to current moods and interests—would take its place. "The 'performers' of the party of energy," as the perceptive *Review of Reviews* put it, the Republicans had finally lost out to the Democrats, "the 'reformers' of the party of inaction." They were finished. "There is a belief in many quarters that the Republican party is about to disappear." The sponsor of actual programs, it had suffered disastrous setbacks, in ways that would never happen to the Democrats. "The Democratic party, of course, is indestructible, because it rests on a basis of permanent principles that make [sic] it the natural enemy of every successive new programme of innovation that comes up demanding accomplishment through active governmental agency."[3]

Cleveland signaled similar thoughts in announcing his new cabinet. Startling Democrats, he named Walter Q. Gresham, the expatriate Indiana Republican, to the premier position, secretary of state. The move pleased independent voters and might encourage additional Republican defections. Woodrow Wilson, a young Princeton University professor, believed the cabinet showed Cleveland's desire for "the infusion of new blood, the disinterested service of men untainted by party management." To some extent it did, but Wilson missed the mark. Other than Gresham, the cabinet consisted largely of veteran Democrats and old Cleveland friends. Cleveland had constructed a highly personal cabinet, filled with men he found sympathetic and congenial: "pure-minded, patriotic, loyal men," he would later say.

Most of them had no constituencies of their own, simply reinforced the president's own views on major issues, and lacked ties to the large numbers of discontented in the country.[4]

John G. Carlisle, the respected Kentucky Democrat whom Cleveland had beaten for the presidential nomination, headed the important Treasury Department. Cleveland liked him, admired his intelligence, and considered him a likely successor in 1896. "He knows all that I ought to know, and I can bear all that he needs to bear," Cleveland remarked. That was good, for the two men would have to bear a great deal in the coming months.[5] "Funny, gruff old" Richard Olney, a corporation lawyer from Boston, took over the Justice Department. Blunt, stubborn, precise, and able, Olney impressed Cleveland with his efficiency and decisive opinions. Others found him "rather a pompous individual, who appears to think that it is a good deal of a concession for him to address anybody." Two other appointments, Hoke Smith of Georgia as secretary of the interior and Hilary A. Herbert of Alabama as Navy secretary, represented gestures to the Democratic South. Neither was outstanding.[6]

Wilson S. Bissell and Daniel S. Lamont, two friends from Cleveland's New York days, became respectively postmaster general and secretary of war. J. Sterling Morton, a conservative Nebraska Democrat whose passion for trees led him to invent Arbor Day, rounded out the cabinet as secretary of agriculture. Attractive in a hearty, growling way, Morton was the administration's major link with restive farmers. That was a blunder. Tactless, he had "a fatal way of saying the wrong thing at the right time and the right thing at the wrong time," as Cleveland would soon discover. In his office he greeted visiting congressmen by pulling out lengthy documents, remarking: "Let me read you a speech I am to make next week." Those who listened had their requests granted. Morton both entertained and edified Cleveland, who liked his frugal, conservative administration of the Agriculture Department. "Legislation can neither plow nor plant," the secretary would say in his 1896 annual report. "The intelligent, practical, and successful farmer needs no aid from the Government. The ignorant, impractical, and indolent farmer deserves none."[7]

The administration underway, Cleveland went to Chicago on May 1, 1893, to open the World's Columbian Exposition, one of the focal events of the entire decade. The Exposition commemorated the four-hundredth anniversary of Columbus' voyage to the New World. It also celebrated modern industrial and technological progress, featuring the latest mechanical inventions in acres of white plaster buildings modeled on Greek and Roman patterns. An opening-day crowd of 200,000 wandered in awe through the White City, the "enchanted city," with its sixty buildings, shimmering lagoons, gilded statues, carved fountains, and most important, machinery. Elaborate in its symbolism, the White City celebrated social harmony, the union of architects, craftsmen, engineers, inventors, businessmen, and laborers to create the industrial society. It fused timeless, classical forms with the hurly-burly progress of the new civilization.

The machinery went far beyond the famous Corliss steam engine that had impressed the world at the Philadelphia Centennial Exposition of 1876, only seventeen years before. It fed on a much more "up-to-date" wonder: the new magic of electricity. To President Cleveland the Exposition showed "the tremendous results of American enterprise" as well as the "progress of human endeavor in the direction of a higher civilization." He touched an ivory telegraph key, and the electric current unfurled flags on the 700 flagpoles, unveiled the central statue of the American Republic, lit 10,000 electric lights, started engines, and powered fountains throughout the grounds. In Machinery Hall, the 37 steam engines started at once, producing, in a reporter's words, "a sound that will thrill every observer." Thirty-five million gallons of water coursed through the fountains each day. The Exposition represented power, modern and complex. It is "a force difficult for the mind to grasp," one dazzled onlooker concluded. "It is the transformation of power into beauty."[8]

Later generations might reach different conclusions, but for a moment in Chicago an era paid homage to its own material and social accomplishments. A moment was all it had. Three days after the opening ceremonies, the stock market in New York broke, rallied, then broke again. The American economy, so lovingly celebrated in the White City in Chicago, was in danger of collapsing.

☆☆☆

Leaving office, President Harrison and other Republicans had pointed again and again to the prosperous conditions in the country. The Democrats could "reform" the tariff, if they wished, but the results of Republican stewardship were clear. "There never has been a time in our history when work was so abundant or when wages were as high," Harrison said, and filled his final annual message with figures measuring the nation's well-being. Business journals also closed 1892, "the most prosperous year ever known," with reports of "strongly favorable indications for the future." The reports were wrong; the figures hid developing troubles. The economy was badly overextended, teetering on the unhappy consequences of a decade of confident expansion.[9]

To head off competitors, railroads had sent tracks into uninhabited areas, gambling on continued growth. Companies had moved beyond their markets, farms and businesses had borrowed heavily for future development, and speculators had boomed "city" lots in towns that scarcely existed. The mood shifted perceptibly early in 1893. Confidence sagged, investors became timid and uneasy. Uncertain currency values, an inadequate banking system, depressed agricultural prices, and declining exports sapped the economy. In mid-February, a sudden flurry of panic selling hit the stock market. In a seven-hour period, investors dumped a million shares of the Philadelphia and Reading Railroad, an industry leader, and the company promptly went under, bankrupt. Business investment dropped sharply, particularly in the critical railroad and construction industries, touching off a cyclical contraction of unprecedented severity.[10]

Frightened, people hurriedly sold stocks and other assets for gold, causing a crisis in the United States Treasury. During January and February of 1893, the demand for gold was overwhelming, at home and in Europe, which was also in the throes of a depression. It flowed out of the Treasury, in exchange for silver coins, greenbacks, and the Treasury notes (or silver certificates) issued to buy silver under the Sherman Silver Purchase Act of 1890. Eroding almost daily, the Treasury's gold reserve slumped toward the $100,000,000 mark, an amount that over the years had become a symbolic measure of the nation's commitment to back its currency in gold. Among gold standard adherents, the blame fell on the Sherman Act, whose silver certificates, redeemed in gold by the Treasury, acted as a constant drain on the reserve. Before taking office, Cleveland worked privately to persuade Congress to repeal the act, but without success. Silverites would not accept repeal without a more liberal silver law. Harrison's Treasury officials hoped just to hold the line until inauguration day. They barely made it. On March 4, as Cleveland delivered his inaugural address, the reserve sank to $100,982,410.[11]

The dwindling reserve worried businessmen, who sensed disaster ahead. "I sit and wonder if you gentlemen in Washington know how very uneasy the legitimate property holders and merchants of the country are about the state of the currency. . . ," a Boston financier wrote Richard Olney in mid-April. "People are in a state to be thrown into a panic at any minute, and, if it comes, and gold is withdrawn, it will be a panic that will wake the dead." Cleveland issued reassuring statements, but there was little he could do. On April 22, for the first time since 1879, the gold reserve fell below $100,000,000.[12]

The news shattered business confidence. Rumors spread that another large gold shipment would leave for Europe in a matter of days, and the stock market panicked and broke. On Wednesday, May 3, railroad and industrial stocks slumped badly, followed the next day by the bankruptcy of several prominent firms. The worst was yet to come. When the Exchange opened that Friday, crowds filled the galleries, anticipating a panic and a flood of selling orders. They were not disappointed. Within minutes, leading stocks plunged to record lows, amid pandemonium on the floor and in the streets outside. A brief rally at the end of the day failed to repair the damage. May 5, 1893, "Industrial Black Friday," was "a day of terrible strain, long remembered on the market."[13]

Quickly, stunningly, the blows piled one on the other. Bankers called in available loans and refused to grant new ones without ample collateral. Unable to get capital, businesses failed, an average of two dozen a day during the month of May. "The papers are full of failures—banks are breaking all over the country, and there is a tremendous contraction of credits and hoarding of money going on everywhere," as one observer noted on May 14. A few days later, the Northern Pacific Railroad announced bankruptcy, another shattering blow to confidence. In June, runs began on Pacific Coast banks and forced several to close. India suspended free silver coinage, paralyzing the American silver market. In four days the price of silver dropped from 81 cents an ounce to 62 cents. Mines and smelters shut down throughout the Mountain States, throwing thousands out of work. Receipts on the Union Pacific Railroad, which had carried much of the ore and bullion, plummeted. On July 26, the fabled Erie Railroad, a legend in railroading history, failed and precipitated another flurry on the stock market. Officials considered closing the Exchange.[14]

August was the worst month. It "will long remain memorable . . . in our industrial history," said the *Commercial and Financial Chronicle,* a leading business journal. Mills, factories, furnaces, and mines shut down everywhere. Hundreds of thousands of workers were suddenly unemployed. In Orange, New Jersey, Thomas A. Edison, the symbol of the country's ingenuity, let go 240 of his 355 employees at the Edison Phonograph Works, grumbling that "the country has resolved itself into a National lunatic asylum." On August 12, *Bradstreet's* reported unemployment at one million people. Some economists guessed two million, or nearly 15 percent of the total labor force.[15] On August 15, a fourth major railroad, the Northern Pacific, went into receivership, Other railroads followed. In mid-October the Union Pacific—with 8950 miles of lines and 22,000 employees—went bankrupt, unable to meet its payroll. In December the Atcheson, Topeka and Santa Fe did the same. Wreckage was everywhere. During 1893, some 15,000 business firms and more than 600 banks failed. At year's end Samuel Gompers, head of the American Federation of Labor, estimated unemployment at three million people.[16]

"There are thousands of homeless and starving men in the streets," a young reporter wrote home from Chicago that ugly December. "I have seen more misery in this last week than I ever saw in my life before." Winter storms swept the city. Hundreds slept in City Hall and other municipal buildings, huddled in hallways and staircases, close by the Columbian Exposition's "enchanted city." Charities, benevolent societies, churches, and labor unions did their best to help, but could not handle the unprecedented numbers. "Famine is in our midst," said the head of the local relief committee. That December, Chicago reported 75,000 unemployed; Boston nearly 40,000; Philadelphia, 47,000; Pittsburgh, 16,000; San Francisco, 35,000.[17]

Washington, D. C., newspapers told of "a vast army of unemployed, and men pleading for food who have never before been compelled to seek aid." In Detroit the needy used vacant lots for "Pingree Potato Patches," named after the city's mayor. In Pasadena, California, they ate at soup kitchens called "Cleveland Cafes," a measure of the speed with which economic hardship turned to political hostility. New York City officials estimated that 100,000 people were out of work, with at least that many more working half-time or less. Newspapers and charities distributed free bread and clothing, until resources ran out. Conditions were little better in farming areas, hit by drought and low crop prices. "The problem is how to live," as one Kansas farmer put it in the summer of 1893.[18]

Continuing through 1897, the depression of the 1890s was the decade's decisive event. It changed lives, reshaped ideas, altered attitudes, uprooted deep-set patterns. The human costs were enormous, even among the prominent. "They were for me years of simple Hell," shattering "my whole scheme of life," said Charles Francis Adams, the heir of two American presidents. "I was sixty-three years old, and a tired man, when at last the effects of the 1893 convulsion wore themselves out." The convulsion renewed doubts about the costs of industrialization, sparked labor unrest and class antagonism, and in pointing up economic interdependencies, shifted the country's focus from the local to the national. Everywhere, older assumptions gave way to newer patterns and nagging doubts.[19]

The depression, vast and unsettling, offered sudden opportunity to the Republicans and Populists, who might lure the discontented and build new coalitions. It strained sectional ties and strengthened complaints of monetary conspiracies—gold in the Northeast, silver in the South and West—to take over the land. Years of crunching hardship made tempers brittle. As a Wisconsin newspaper noted in 1896: "On every corner stands a man whose fortune in these dull times has made him an ugly critic of everything and everybody." Some were uglier than others, and there was talk of revolution and war and bloodshed. Before long, there was also sharp talk about Cleveland and the Democrats, and their apparent inability to "do something" about the depression. It had been their misfortune to be trapped in office as an era's assumptions abruptly collapsed. Later, Cleveland would call the 1890s the "luckless years." For the Democratic party, they were far worse than that.[20]

☆☆☆

For once in his life, Cleveland had trouble making up his mind. Originally he had planned to spend his first summer in office quietly sketching out a tariff bill, to be submitted to a special session of Congress in September. The panic killed that plan and shifted his attention to industrial failures, the shrinking gold reserve, and "the silver business," as he sourly called it. Businessmen pleaded for quick action to shore up the finances and restore confidence, especially for a special session of Congress to repeal the damaging Sherman Act. Several times Cleveland decided to follow the advice, then pulled back at the last moment. Opponents, and some friends, later suggested the delay was intentional, to allow deepening hardship to teach the silver proponents a lesson. Delay might also weaken opposition within his own party, helping to reduce the expected damage from a fight over silver.[21]

By early summer, with panic and unemployment spreading across the country, Cleveland could delay a decision no longer. Besides, the president's doctors had just discovered that he was dangerously ill. On June 18, they found a large cancerous growth on the roof of his mouth and advised an immediate operation. Cleveland swore them to secrecy, aware that a presidential health scare would further drain the economy. Vice-President Adlai E. Stevenson was sympathetic to silver, a fact well known to panicky businessmen and financiers. On June 26, there was more startling news—India had closed her mints to silver—and Cleveland met far into the night with Secretary of the Treasury Carlisle. India's action, which left Mexico the only country in the world with free silver coinage, was the event the two men had been waiting for. It threw silverites on the defensive, illustrated once again the primacy of gold in international money markets, and swung public opinion toward the repeal camp. Even moderate silver journals began to waver, wondering if repeal might help after all.[22]

Cleveland let the momentum gather, then on June 30 summoned Congress into special session for August 7. The current economic crisis, he declared, "is largely the result of a financial policy . . . embodied in unwise laws." Its solution was equally simple: the unconditional repeal of the Sherman Act. Always sure of himself, Cleveland had staked everything on a single measure, a winning strategy if it succeeded, a devastating one if it did not. Characteristically, too, he would brook no opposition and instructed subordinates to withhold patronage from Democrats who "oppose our patriotic attempt to help the country and save our party."[23]

That afternoon he slipped away from Washington, ostensibly to rest at his Buzzards Bay home until Congress met. He boarded a friend's yacht on the East River in New York, and the following day, July 1, as the yacht steamed slowly up the river, surgeons removed much of his upper left jaw and palate. It had been, as Mrs. Cleveland said, a "narrow escape."[24] Fitted with an artificial jawpiece, Cleveland recuperated in secret at Buzzards Bay, seeing only the closest aides, fishing and relaxing, the country thought. Tanned and rested, though still weak, he returned to Washington on August 5, two days before Congress met. The secrecy worked, but at the cost of some criticism of his absence from the capital. Cleveland "is now nursing his fat at Buzzard's Bay," a hostile newspaper complained in mid-July. "He fishes while the country broils."[25]

Fervid silverites were fighting back, stung by the demand for unconditional repeal. To be sure, they had no special affection for the Sherman Act, which had failed to add as much silver to the currency as they had hoped. But repeal without an effective substitute was another matter. "I never did think that the Sherman Bill was a wise piece of legislation," wrote a California senator, "but I believe that if it is unconditionally repealed, . . . silver will be permanently demonetized."[26] That was exactly the point, silverites felt. Eastern and European financiers had joined in a selfish plot to demonetize silver, "a gigantic conspiracy . . . to establish finally and forever the single gold standard, and to extend it over the world." They had subverted the Sherman Act, dictated the closing of the Indian mints, and deliberately caused the collapse of the American economy. Now they had even enlisted the president, who tamely did their bidding.[27]

In such a battle the stakes were high, silverites thought, higher than at any time since the Revolution. The working masses against the parasitic rich, the producers against the speculators, the money of the people against the golden Baal. "The war has begun," Davis H. Waite, the Populist governor of Colorado, told a large rally in Denver on July 11. "Our weapons are argument and the ballot," but should those not succeed, "it is better, infinitely better, that blood should flow to the horses' bridles than our national liberties should be destroyed."[28] The rhetoric, repeated again and again as the repeal struggle approached, alarmed supporters of the gold standard, who in turn ridiculed the "Populist cuckoos" abroad in the land. By the time Congress convened, feelings had hardened on both sides of the currency question. Each side laid sole claim to "sound principles," and respectively blamed the "gold trust" or the "silver inflationists" for the nation's economic ills.[29]

The special session opened on August 7, 1893, with the chaplain's prayer for divine help "in this time of doubt and perplexity, of unrest and agitation among the nations, and in our own land." That day the gold reserve stood at $102,291,395, barely above the critical mark. The Southern Pacific Railroad had just laid off 1000 workers; textile mills in Fall River, Massachusetts, had laid off 7000. In a few days the Northern Pacific Railroad would go bankrupt. On August 8, congressmen and senators heard Cleveland's special message, a calm, reasoned document that reviewed economic troubles, cited the "evil effects" of the Sherman Act, and urged speedy repeal. The message never mentioned the touchy word "gold," and hinted that quick repeal might lead to an international agreement to boost silver. Cleveland had set out to soothe tempers.[30]

The repeal bill moved quickly through the House of Representatives. Outnumbered, the silverites fought a delaying action, but could not withstand the growing public demand for repeal. Democrats—even silver Democrats—wanted to follow the president, who seemed so sure that repeal would benefit the country and party. Cleveland's floor managers played skillfully on the feeling, wooing moderate silver men with appeals to support the president, promises of patronage to ease discontent at home, and assurances that the administration would sponsor some kind of silver measure after repeal. The silver lines bent under the pressure. On August 16, William Jennings Bryan, the rising young Nebraskan, tried to stiffen resolves. The Democrats, he told a crowded, hushed House, "have come to the parting of the ways," the time to choose between arrogant wealth and the "work-worn," "dust-begrimed" people. The country waited for their answer. Will they turn "to the rising sun or the setting sun? Will [they] choose blessings or cursings—life or death—which? Which?"[31]

The speech, eloquent and affecting, established Bryan as silver's chief spokesman, but changed few votes. Headlines that morning had reported the collapse of another railroad, and the pressures for repeal mounted inexorably. House Republicans sat back, tabulating party profits from the Democrats' difficulties. "Let the democrats do the talking and voting," as one Republican put it. "It is their funeral."[32] On August 28, after some final maneuvering, the repeal bill easily passed the House by a vote of 239 to 108, a far larger margin than expected. Most Republicans had supported it, and the Democrats had divided 138 to 78. That was ominous, but Cleveland celebrated, certain that the large vote would ease passage through the Senate.[33]

There, he had chosen Daniel W. Voorhees of Indiana, "The Tall Sycamore of the Wabash," to manage the repeal bill. Voorhees was more of a slippery elm. Just a few months before, he had called unconditional repeal "an outrage," but patronage, dolloped out in lavish quantities, lessened his sense of injustice. As the debate opened, he counted 49 senators for repeal, enough to pass the bill if it reached a vote. But Senate rules provided for unrestricted debate, and the silver senators, who disliked Cleveland intensely, were unlikely to help. Matters stalled through August, September, and early October, angering Cleveland who waved the party lash. If the silver men in the Senate "wanted a fight he would give them one," he burst out to an aide. Actually, the delay strained the public's patience and strengthened Cleveland's hand. "Times are so hard that people sigh for a change, whatever it might be," a discouraged silverite noted.[34]

The continuing discord worried Maryland's Arthur P. Gorman and a handful of other Democratic leaders in the Senate. A senator since 1881, Gorman was a party man, with impeccable credentials. For a time in the 1880s, he had been closely identified with Cleveland. He managed Cleveland's first presidential campaign in 1884, led his try for an equivocal tariff plank in the 1888 Democratic platform, and helped organize his reelection campaign that same year. Since then, the two men had drifted apart. Subtle and sophisticated, Gorman disliked Cleveland's stubborn self-conceit. He resented the way Cleveland claimed to place principle above party. To him, the two were inseparable: the party *was* a principle, and the necessary vehicle to action. Gorman savored organization, preferred quiet work behind the scenes, and labored constantly for Democratic success. Now he saw the party being torn apart, fractured between contending factions, each intolerant of the other. The discord, he was sure, endangered Democratic majorities in at least a dozen states.

Shrewdly, he bided his time, waiting for the proper moment to suggest a compromise that would satisfy both sides. By late October conditions seemed right, and on October 20, Gorman took his compromise plan to Secretary Carlisle and the Senate Democratic steering committee. He proposed to extend the Sherman Act until October 1, 1894, coin the silver seigniorage in the Treasury, and retire all greenbacks and Treasury notes under $10 in denomination. The administration would get repeal, though not for another year; the silverites would get that year's delay, plus a small additional amount of silver currency. Gorman went over the proposal line by line with Carlisle, and left thinking he had the secretary's tacit approval. The following day, 37 of the 44 Democratic senators signed a letter endorsing the plan.[35]

Cleveland was furious. At a cabinet meeting on Monday afternoon, October 23, he pounded the table "so hard that papers flew to the floor," reported one cabinet member, "and I was afraid he would bruise his hand."[36] Within the cabinet, Gresham, Herbert, Hoke Smith, and probably Carlisle favored compromise, but dared not say so. J. Sterling Morton, as always, was unbending. "The President is right," he had declared the day before, the pro-silver coalition "is wrong, and

Right ought to triumph over Wrong, without asking permission from anybody or agreeing to any compromise." Pounding the table, Cleveland vowed to fight until the end, and with that, Gorman's long, patient labors collapsed. Democrats were tired and discouraged. The wily Voorhees seized the moment to cajole the wavering. On October 24, he visited the southern Democratic caucus and, renewing assurances that liberal silver legislation would follow repeal, persuaded a number of southern Democrats to quit. Others decided that they preferred unconditional repeal to compromise, hoping for a backlash in favor of silver.[37]

The end in sight, senators turned back a silverite proposal to restore the 1878 Bland-Allison Act, 37 to 33, then defeated a free silver amendment, 41 to 31. Twenty-two Democrats voted for the free silver amendment, twenty voted against. Ominously, too, the delegations from sixteen states, all in the South and West, voted unanimously for free silver, while the delegations from twenty-one states, almost all in the Northeast and Midwest, voted unanimously against. The lines in the free silver drama were tightening. Early in the evening of October 30, the Senate turned at last to the repeal bill itself, which it passed, 48 to 37. The Republicans voted more than two to one for repeal; the Democrats again divided evenly. The gold reserve that day stood at $84,000,000. Cleveland was pleased, the focus of the victory. "He has brought the entire Senate to his feet," as one newspaper remarked. On November 1, 1893, with Carlisle and Olney looking on, he signed the bill into law, and ordered the mints to stop purchasing silver. The great repeal battle of 1893, an event that would reshape the politics of the decade, was ended.[38]

☆☆☆

At first hopefully, then with mounting impatience, people awaited the promised economic revival. It did not come. The stock market remained listless, even fell a bit the day after repeal. Businesses continued to close, unemployment spread, farm prices dropped. "We are hourly expecting the arrival of the benevolent man who is to pay ten cents a pound for cotton," said the Raleigh *News and Observer* sardonically. Repeal of the Sherman Act was probably a necessary measure. It responded to the realities of international finance, reduced the flight of gold out of the country, and over the long run boosted business confidence. Unfortunately, it also contracted the currency at a time when an expanding money supply might have helped economic recovery. Repeal suffered from the extravagant claims of its sponsors. In the end, it did not even solve the Treasury's gold problem. By January 1894, the reserve had fallen to $65,000,000. A year later it was down to $44,500,000.[39]

Other troubles emerged with time. A tactical error of vast consequence, Cleveland's unrelenting demand for repeal focused national attention on the silver issue, implicitly reinforcing the silverites' belief in the issue's overriding importance. It intensified the silver sentiment Cleveland had intended to dampen. It also ended the Democrats' hopes of submerging their differences on silver in a campaign to lower the tariff. Years later, as the decade drew to a close, Democrats would speculate on what might have happened to the party if Cleveland, as William McKinley would do in 1897, had sidestepped the volatile silver issue and called a special session devoted to the tariff. Many of them angrily recalled their own willingness to subordinate silver to the tariff in the 1892 campaign. Cleveland had chosen instead to stress silver, thereby splitting the party and dimming the prospects for tariff reform. "The very memory is enough to make the heart sick," Henry Watterson, an avid tariff reformer, said in 1904.[40]

Little by little, the Democratic party came apart. A word here, a gesture there, an attempt to explain and conciliate, might have helped reknit the ranks, but Cleveland had no skill at such things. "He did not know what conciliation meant," said a veteran Washington reporter, "and rubbed out sore spots with a brick." Fervent silverites depicted Cleveland as the head of a monetary conspiracy committed to gold and the selfish interests of Eastern financiers. Political moderates, Democrats as well as Republicans, resented the president's negative approach to economic hardship. Relying on the repeal of one law, he had offered no constructive program to remedy the economic situation. "It is not so often what things *really* are, but what they *seem* to be, which controls votes in declaring for or against governmental policy," the governor of Alabama patiently explained to Cleveland. Cleveland seemed rigid and uncaring, mired in outdated doctrines, unable to respond to the plight of the people.[41]

Discontent surfaced quickly. The 1893 elections turned Democrats out of office across the country. The Republicans prospered, as large numbers of Democratic voters either remained at home or voted Republican. Significantly, the Populists again failed to attract the discontented, except in some areas of the South. The Republicans swept

New York and Pennsylvania. In Massachusetts, they ousted Governor Russell, Cleveland's close friend and once the symbol of Democratic hopes in New England. In Iowa, they ousted Governor Boies, a similar symbol in the Midwest and on the Plains. In Ohio, McKinley crushed his Democratic opponent and won another term as governor by 81,000 votes, the largest margin in an Ohio gubernatorial race since the 1860s. Ohio and Massachusetts displayed patterns that delighted Republicans. In both states Republican candidates simply did well everywhere: in rural areas, small towns, and cities, among old-stock and immigrant voters. They made substantial inroads in Boston, Fall River, Cincinnati, Columbus, Cleveland, Dayton, and other urban-industrial areas.[42]

Disgruntled Democrats spoke of their "Waterloo." "I hope it will be the means of putting a little sense into some heads at Washington," wrote a California Democrat. In January 1894, Cleveland issued $50,000,000 in gold bonds to replenish the gold reserve in the Treasury. That month a Republican won a special congressional election in a "safe" Democratic district in New York City. A few months later, Republicans again swept local elections in Ohio, Rhode Island, Michigan, and Connecticut.[43] The Democrats' spirits dwindled, then reeled under a decisive blow in late March, 1894. Looking for a way to soothe silver sentiment and reunite the party, the Democrats in Congress passed a bill authorizing the coinage of the silver seigniorage in the Treasury. The bill was little more than a gesture. It added relatively small amounts of silver to the currency, and found its strongest support among Democrats from pro-silver districts who had rallied to Cleveland's call for repeal the summer before. A seigniorage law, though largely ceremonial, might placate constituents and answer criticism that the Democrats had no positive approach to the depression.[44]

Would Cleveland sign it? Richard P. "Silver Dick" Bland of Missouri, the bill's sponsor and the leader of the House silverites, called on Cleveland to urge him to sign. It would reinvigorate the party, improve the prospects for tariff reform, and help Democrats in the November elections, Bland told the president. Voorhees, Charles F. Crisp, the Speaker of the House, Senator George Gray of Delaware, a respected administration adviser, William Jennings Bryan, Gresham, Hoke Smith, and Herbert carried similar messages to the White House. Voorhees had worked and voted for the bill, a signal, some Democrats thought, that the administration would fulfill the earlier promises to support some silver legislation. On March 29, Cleveland vetoed it, as unwise and inopportune. It would sap business confidence and weaken the benefits of repeal. On Capitol Hill, reporters had never seen congressmen so angry. Silver Democrats clustered in the cloakrooms and lobbies, cursing Cleveland, complaining of a presidential tyranny that violated Democratic precepts of limited executive power.[4 5]

Outside the Northeast, the seigniorage veto was a stunning blow to Democrats, a landmark event in the process of party alienation that led to Bryan's nomination for the presidency in 1896. It further isolated Cleveland, confirmed his apparent rigidity, and renewed charges that he pursued a "purely obstructive" policy toward the depression. Moderate Democrats despaired of ever reuniting the party. Retreating into self-righteousness, Cleveland began to complain of the "misconception and prejudice and ignorance and injustice" around him. "There never was a man in this high office so surrounded with difficulties and so perplexed, and so treacherously treated, and so abandoned by those whose aid he *deserves,* as the present incumbent," he wrote a friend a few weeks after the veto. In Yellowstone Park, guides named a particularly difficult horse after the president. Always in trouble, it led other horses into dangerous situations, and "wouldn't cross the trail but walked into quicksand," the guides explained.[4 6]

The year 1894 was like that. Events flowed into each other, shrill and divisive. Virtually every day people shook open their papers to find news of some fresh crisis or disaster. The gross national product dropped another 3 percent during the year, less than the 5 percent drop of the previous year, but still harsh in its consequences. At midyear the number of unemployed stood at three million, about 20 percent of the labor force. That summer a heat wave and drought struck the farm belt west of the Mississippi River, creating conditions unmatched until the Dust Bowl of the 1930s. Corn and other crops withered in the fields. In the South, the price of cotton fell below five cents a pound, far under the break-even point, and the value of tobacco and other crops slumped badly. Winter storms severely damaged the fruit crops in Florida and California.[4 7]

The papers told of spreading discontent. Tramps wandered the countryside, armies of unemployed crisscrossed the nation. In February 1894, 600 unemployed men stormed the State House in Boston demanding relief. The police ejected them. In April, business journals pointed to a "wave of industrial unrest . . . over the country," including strikes among iron miners in the Mesabi, shoe workers in New England, textile workers in Massachusetts, brickmakers in the Hudson Valley, and others. On April 21, the United Mine Workers struck, ultimately pulling some 170,000 workers out of the coal mines in the Midwest and South. In late June, the American Railway Union struck all the railroads leading out of Chicago, the heart of the nation's transportation network. That October, strikes and warfare raged among workers on the docks in New Orleans. During 1894 there were some 1400 strikes involving more than 500,000 workers. A malaise settled over the land. "Everyone scolds," Henry Adams, the historian, wrote a British friend. "Everyone also knows what ought to be done. Everyone reviles everyone who does not agree with him, and everyone differs, or agrees only in contempt for everyone else. As far as I can see, everyone is right."[48]

On Easter Sunday, 1894, four days before Cleveland's veto of the seigniorage bill, an unusual "army" of perhaps 300 people left Massillon, Ohio. At its head rode "General" Jacob S. Coxey, a mild-looking, middle-aged businessman who wanted to put the nation's jobless to work building roads. Coxey had hoped to lead 20,000 marchers to Washington, to petition Congress to pass the Coxey Good Roads bill, which authorized the printing of $500,000,000 in paper money to finance road construction. Though small, the army drew nationwide attention. Forty-three special newspaper correspondents and four Western Union operators accompanied it, to report every detail of the march. "Never in the annals of insurrection has so small a company of soldiers been accompanied by such a phalanx of recording angels," noted one amused journalist.[49]

Coxey's idea quickly caught on, and other "armies" mobilized around the country. An 800-person contingent left from Los Angeles, "a living petition of want and misery," its leader called it. An army of 600 started from San Francisco and picked up recruits as it moved eastward. When it reached Iowa, it had swelled to some 1500 members. It wanted the government to provide jobs on irrigation projects in the West. The armies commandeered freight trains, or sat in town squares until local citizens raised money and supplies to send them onward. They frightened the well-to-do, who feared a massive upheaval from the bottom of society. "They are mainly of the worst class," James J. Hill, the head of the Great Northern Railway, warned Washington. "Men who do not want to work for a living." Work was in fact what most of the armies sought, but no matter. Cleveland's staff tightened security around the White House, with extra guards housed in barracks on the grounds.[50]

Coxey reached Washington on May 1, after a difficult, tiring march. His daughter, Mame, representing the Goddess of Peace, led the procession, now some 500 strong, up Pennsylvania Avenue. Policemen were everywhere, lining the streets, blocking the approaches to the Capitol where Coxey planned to present his petition. As a crowd of spectators watched, Coxey stepped from his carriage, kissed his wife, and entered the Capitol grounds. He made it to the foot of the Capitol steps, but before he could address the crowd, the police were on him. He and a companion were clubbed, then arrested for trespassing on the grass. Mounted police charged into the spectators, injuring fifty. A week later Coxey was sentenced to twenty days in jail for trespassing. His army disbanded, but in a sense had made its point. It voiced a growing impatience with government inaction, a spreading conviction that government should take a more active hand in stimulating the economy and helping the unemployed.[51]

Discontent seemed contagious, infecting much of the country. Coxey's army was a passing phenomenon, important mainly for its pathos and symbolism. The Pullman strike was another matter. It began just a few days after Coxey's arrest, when the employees of the Pullman Palace Car Company, on the outskirts of Chicago, struck against wage cuts, living conditions, and layoffs. On June 26, the American Railway Union joined the strike, refusing to handle trains that carried Pullman cars. With that, the strike suddenly paralyzed the western half of the nation. Grain and livestock could not reach markets. Factories began to shut down for lack of coal. In California, fruit rotted in boxcars, stranded on the tracks. The strike extended into 27 states and territories, tying up the economy and renewing talk of class warfare. Eugene W. Debs, the young president of the railway union, tried to calm public opinion. He instructed strikers to avoid violence and move the mails, lest the federal government intervene.[52]

In Illinois, the center of the strike, Governor John P. Altgeld carefully monitored the situation, his office virtually a war room, ready to send the state militia wherever needed. Cool and taciturn, Altgeld was accustomed to crises. Since immigrating from Germany, he had worked hard for wealth and power, and enjoyed both. In 1892 he rode the Democratic tide to the governorship, skillfully drawing support from friendly trade unions, fellow German Lutherans, and voters upset with the controversial Edwards school law. The following year, convinced an injustice had been done, he pardoned the anarchists involved in the Haymarket riot of 1886. The pardon set off acrid recriminations. Cleveland and other conservative Democrats distrusted Altgeld, certain he was "soft" on labor. Altgeld rejected the charge. Earlier in 1894 he had dealt firmly with disruptions connected with the coal strike, and he promised similar action against any Pullman-related violence. "If it becomes necessary," he said, "I could and would put 100,000 men into the city of Chicago inside of five days. The whole State would answer to the call as one man."[53]

Cleveland wondered. As the strike developed, alarm swept the administration, fed by inaccurate newspaper reports from the scene. Carlisle feared for the safety of the government's gold stocks in Chicago and New York, the latter far from the strike. The War Department canceled military leaves and ordered officers to their regiments. Cleveland and Attorney General Olney determined to break the strike. Cooperating closely with the railroads, one of the parties to it, they obtained on July 2 a wide-ranging court injunction enjoining Debs and the union from interfering with mail trains or interstate commerce. That day, acting on reports of violence in strike areas, Cleveland ordered federal troops to Los Angeles, and the following day, to Chicago. Altgeld protested vigorously, certain the state could deal with the situation, but to no avail. Cleveland would not listen.[54]

On the morning of Independence Day, cavalry, infantry, and artillery moved into Chicago, which they found calm and peaceful. Violence then broke out. Mobs, apparently made up mostly of non-strikers, overturned freight cars, destroyed railroad equipment, looted and burned. Six buildings in the "enchanted city" burned to the ground. "We have been brought to the ragged edge of anarchy," Olney told reporters, his fears of social upheaval obviously confirmed.[55] In the following days, troops spread through Chicago and occupied the railroad yards at Sacramento and Oakland, California, and other major points. Cleveland "proposes to stand up and stamp this out if it takes the whole army and militia to do it," an aide said after conferring with the president. Hit with soldiers and injunctions, the union never had a chance. By late July the Pullman strike was over, with Debs headed for jail, charged with violating the court order. Much of the country applauded Cleveland's "firmness and courage." "Whilst the struggle is nominally for the expedition of the mails," declared the Washington *Post,* "it is really for the preservation of society."[56]

For a moment, Cleveland enjoyed public acclaim. "The President is in splendid health and spirits," Secretary Morton wrote on July 21. "The riots in Chicago, as he handled them, have proved a sort of political inheritance of vast value." Morton was wrong. Praise came mainly from the comfortable and well-to-do, who lauded Cleveland and voted Republican. Many workingmen turned against Cleveland and the Democrats, particularly as later investigations documented the administration's collusion with the railroad companies in the strike. Federal officers on the Pacific Coast warned Olney of mounting anti-administration feeling, "owing to a conviction among much the larger portion of the people, that the laws of the United States are being enforced with great severity against laboring people and not against the corporations." Altgeld was bitter. Democrats did not send troops into states capable of handling their own affairs. That smacked of centralized power, Republicanism, and Reconstruction. Relentlessly, Altgeld set out to discredit Cleveland, organizing dissident Democrats in a movement to repudiate the president in 1896.[57]

Cleveland had acted conscientiously and for the "people," but in the end had again seemed callous to many people's plight. Increasingly now, the Democratic party took on a ramshackle, almost irrelevant air, without the national outlook and cohesion needed to govern effectively. "We are on the eve of a very dark night," a close friend wrote Cleveland, "unless a return of commercial prosperity relieves popular discontent with what they believe Democratic incompetence to make laws." The Democrats' recent history had suggested that incompetence. The course of the Wilson-Gorman tariff through Congress proved it.[58]

☆☆☆

The Fifty-third Congress, which spanned the years 1893 to 1895, embarrassed even some Democrats. In the House, the Democrats restored the old dilatory rules and promptly bogged down, the victims of their own disappearing quorum. Thomas B. Reed savored the scene, prodding and scoffing, face lit with that cherubic smile. "We must not have any tyranny here," he would occasionally remind Charles F. Crisp, the tense and frustrated Speaker of the House. After months of awkward delay, Crisp and other Democratic leaders had to resort to a version of the Reed quorum-counting rule, a humiliating admission of defeat. The new rule expedited debate but did not improve the party's performance. In this Democratic Congress, only 6 percent of all House votes were party votes, compared with 43 percent during the Republican Fifty-first Congress. The Democrats had never learned to unify diverse followers in behalf of constructive programs. The Fifty-third

Congress repealed the Sherman Silver Purchase Act, passed the seigniorage bill, and repealed the remaining elections laws protecting black voters. It took nearly nine months to pass a tariff bill. "The Democrats have given an exhibition of fairly colossal incompetence," Theodore Roosevelt said happily.[59]

William L. Wilson, the respected West Virginia Democrat who headed the Ways and Means Committee, had reported the tariff bill to the House in late December, 1893. A moderate bill, it balanced the Democrats' sectional interests, offering New England lower duties on raw materials, the South lower duties on manufactured goods and an income tax on corporate and personal incomes over $4000. It expanded the free list to include coal, iron ore, wool, cotton, lumber, salt, sugar, hides, binding twine, and some agricultural implements. The bill satisfied neither ardent tariff reformers nor protected manufacturers, but responded to the business community's plea for quick action to still the tariff debate's unsettling effect on the economy. Wilson skillfully fanned enthusiasm among House Democrats, who in an unusual moment of unity passed the bill on February 1, 1894. "This is not a battle over percentages, over this or that tariff schedule—it is a battle for human freedom," he declared in summoning Democrats to the vote.[60]

The bill encountered tougher going in the Senate, where there were only 44 Democrats to 38 Republicans and 3 Populists. A shift of two votes could defeat it, and one Democrat had already pledged to vote against any measure that included an income tax. Other Democrats had voiced opposition to the drastic reduction in revenues under the Wilson bill. "So we have to cultivate everybody, eat crow and do very many things exceedingly disagreeable," a Democratic senator noted. Resentment still lingered against Cleveland's decision the previous year to give the silver issue priority over the tariff. Democrats squabbled among themselves, fighting to protect home interests. Lobbyists for the sugar, coal, iron, and other industries disliked the Wilson bill and flocked to Washington to do something about it.[61]

The spectacle discredited the bill, and the Democrats. When it was over, the Senate had added 634 amendments, not an unusual number but one that upset the public. Many schedules moved higher. Sugar, iron ore, and coal vanished from the free list, though wool and lumber remained. By placing a duty on sugar, the Senate bill implicitly abrogated the Harrison-Blaine reciprocity agreements with Latin America, an action certain to be unpopular in the Midwest and elsewhere. Experts thought it compared favorably with the House version, especially in its retention of undutied wool, long the heart of the protective system. In ad valorem rates, which measured the duty as a proportion of the invoiced value of the goods, the Senate bill stood at 38.68 percent, higher than the Wilson bill's 35.51 percent, but considerably lower than the 49.58 percent of the McKinley Act. It provided for some genuine reductions in duties, but won few plaudits. It seemed "a beggarly fulfillment of the noisy promises with which the [Democratic] party leaders have so long vexed the nation's ears and misled the nation's confidence," as an angry editorial declared.[62]

Through July the bill stalled in the House-Senate conference committee. Tempers flared amid the turmoil of the Pullman strike, and the public's patience quickly ran out. On July 19, Cleveland intervened, apparently thinking he could bludgeon the Senate as he had in the repeal battle the year before. The bill fell "far short" of desired reform, he wrote in a public letter to Wilson, and amounted to "party perfidy and party dishonor." It was a major blunder, reflecting Cleveland's growing isolation from the party's center. Senate Democrats, including many of his staunchest supporters, erupted in anger and dismay. Cleveland immediately tried to back down, but it was too late. In rapid succession, prominent Democrats took the Senate floor to detail the conditions that had shaped the bill. Gorman was particularly bitter, having worked once again to devise a compromise bill that would hold Democrats together. Cleveland had been consulted at every step, and had himself wavered too often on the tariff issue to speak now of such things as party perfidy and dishonor. "The limit of endurance has been reached. . . ," Gorman said defiantly. "I hurl back the accusation."[63]

The Senate's mood stiffened, and in mid-August Wilson and his fellow House Democrats voted to accept the Senate bill. They looked that day "like a grainfield devastated by a hailstorm," Reed later said. Many of them had spent their lives fighting for tariff reduction, and it had come to this. They salved feelings by passing individual "popgun" bills removing duties from coal, iron ore, barbed wire, and sugar, but knew there was no possibility of Senate passage. Democrats would not get another chance at the tariff for nearly two decades, until the administration of Woodrow Wilson in 1913. Cleveland was "depressed and disappointed," uncertain whether to sign the Wilson-Gorman bill. Finally, on August 28, 1894, he let it become law without his signature, ignoring warnings that such a course would further isolate him from his party. Wilson called the new law "a substantial beginning," but people knew better. It was instead a disheartening end, a dismal conclusion to the Democratic party's tariff reform crusade.[64]

With adjournment, congressmen scattered to their homes, to mend fences for the November elections. Sadness and a sense of impending disaster settled over the Democrats. Voters linked them to the depression, and to the failure of silver repeal, Cleveland's panacea, to cure it. Republicans were confident, certain the tariff fiasco had sealed their opponents' fate. Cleveland was an easy target, the victim of his own sanctimony. "Isn't he funny?" a Republican wrote as the fall campaigns began. "For solemn stupidity, for the wisdom of un-wisdom, he takes the cake."[65] Republican and Populist strategists forecast massive defections among normally Democratic voters. Silverites were unhappy with repeal and the seigniorage veto; businessmen and merchants resented the uncertainties of a year's tinkering with the tariff; sheep growers feared hard times from the removal of the tariff on wool. A story went the rounds about a stranger who came upon a man shearing his sheep backwards, working from the tail toward the head instead of head-to-tail, as usual. "Well, stranger, I'll tell you," the man drawled, seeing the surprise. "I voted for Cleveland in 1892, and since then I just ain't had the nerve to look a sheep in the face!"[66]

Reed, McKinley, Harrison, and other Republicans hammered at the tariff, the depression, and the inability of the Democrats to govern. McKinley spoke to 371 audiences in 16 states, helping Republican candidates and building alliances for a possible presidential bid in 1896. Harrison attacked Democratic incompetence. "Can the country afford to educate that party into a capacity for government?" Democrats had trouble finding candidates for major offices; ambitious leaders preferred private life this year to the certainty of defeat. A half dozen Democrats declined the gubernatorial nomination in New York, and the party turned in desperation to Senator David B. Hill, who also did not want it. Elsewhere, Altgeld and other dissidents urged voters to distinguish between Cleveland and the party, to repudiate the one and vote for the other. "Judas betrayed his master," Altgeld said a week before the election, "but the world did not therefore condemn all twelve of the apostles."[67]

On election night Cleveland followed the returns over a private wire at Woodley, his Washington home. Aides said that he would have no comment on the outcome. It was no wonder. The election buried the Democratic party in state after state. In the largest transfer of congressional strength in American history, the Democrats lost 113 House seats, while the Republicans gained 117. In the Fifty-fourth Congress, the House would contain 244 Republicans, 105 Democrats, and 7 Populists. The Republicans would likely control the Senate as well. The totals were devastating, as was the list of Democratic casualties. William L. Wilson lost by 2300 votes in West Virginia, in a bid for his seventh term. Bland lost in Missouri, William M. Springer in Illinois, William D. Bynum in Indiana. All had been leaders in the House. Prominent senators lost seats. "The truth is," as one said, "there was hardly an oasis left in the Democratic desert."[68]

Twenty-four states elected no Democrats to Congress; six others chose only one Democrat each. A single Democrat (Boston's John F. Fitzgerald, the grandfather of President John F. Kennedy) represented the party's once-bright hopes in New England. As expected, Hill lost badly in New York. The Democrats were decimated in New Jersey and Connecticut, states that were usually closely contested. They lost some of the "Solid South." West Virginia elected 4 Republican congressmen; Maryland, 3; Kentucky, 4; Virginia, 2; North Carolina, 3; Tennessee, 4; and Missouri, 7. Even Texas elected a Republican congressman. In the Midwest, a crucial battleground of the 1890s, the Democratic party was virtually destroyed. Of the 89 congressmen from the region, only three now bore the Democratic standard. Eighty-six were Republicans.

The Republicans swept Illinois, Iowa, Indiana, Wisconsin, and Minnesota. The Michigan returns stunned everyone. The Democrats won no seats at all in the state senate, only one seat in the house. They lost the governorship by 106,000 votes, the largest margin in Michigan's history, and lost all twelve congressional races. The Republicans also did well on the Plains and in the Far West. They ousted Populist governors in Kansas and Colorado, and swept the Dakotas, Idaho, and California. The Republicans gained in farming areas, factory towns, and cities like New York, Albany, Chicago, Milwaukee, and Detroit. Everywhere, from Maine to the Pacific Coast, they recaptured their 1892 losses, built on their 1893 gains, and cut deeply into traditional Democratic sources of support.[69]

The returns discouraged the Populists. Their hopes had again been high as the campaign opened. Hard times might at last break old-party allegiances, moving the large numbers of discontented into the Populist fold. "The People's Party will come into power with a resistless rush," wrote Eugene V. Debs from jail. Working with Debs and others, the Populists wooed labor and the unemployed, particularly in areas where the Pullman strike, the coal strikes, and other summer disturbances had left workers restless and dissatisfied. In the South, they often fused with the Republican party and nominated joint tickets to oppose the dominant Democrats. None of the plans worked quite as the Populists had hoped. Nationwide, they increased their vote by about 42 percent over 1892 totals, an attractive figure but far short of expectations. They made striking inroads in parts of the South, especially in North Carolina, Georgia, and Alabama, and also gained in Nebraska, Minnesota, and California. Encouragingly, they improved in some urban areas, including Chicago and San Francisco, and did well among miners and railroad workers.[70]

Still, it was far from enough. In a year in which thousands of voters were switching allegiances, the Populists elected only four senators and four representatives. They lost Kansas, Colorado, North Dakota, and Idaho, all Populist states in 1892. Governor Waite failed in his bid for reelection in Colorado. Ignatius Donnelly lost his Minnesota state senate seat. Thomas E. Watson lost another race for Congress in Georgia. The Republicans swept Kansas, once a focus of the Populist movement. The Populists had won 37 percent of the Kansas vote in 1890, 39 percent in 1894, a suggestively small increase. Everywhere, the results were disheartening. In Georgia, Alabama, and other southern states, the Democrats continued to use fraud and violence to keep Populist totals down. In the Midwest, the Populists doubled their vote in 1894, yet still attracted less than 7 percent of the vote. From Indiana to California, the discontented had tended to vote for the Republicans, not the Populists. With that, the Populist challenge, once so large with promise and possibility, was over.[71]

The Democrats drifted, torn and discouraged. Administration and anti-administration forces each blamed the other for defeat. Early in 1895, Altgeld declined an invitation to a dinner honoring Jefferson's birthday, certain the celebrants would also praise Cleveland. "Jefferson," he said, "belonged to the American people; Cleveland to the men who devour widows' houses." Administration supporters searched for benefits in their repudiation, enjoying, as one put it, "the spectacle of Hill driven into the ground up to his eyebrows, the picturesque and silver lined hole which Dick Bland pulled in after him, the heap of dust that was once Weaver of Iowa and the shattered prayer wheel which looms on the prairie of Nebraska that was the pious Bryan." William L. Wilson and scores of administration Democrats had also lost, but that drew few reflections. Defeat apparently taught no lessons.[72]

Cleveland retreated into isolation. His mail dwindled, his name evoked jeers at Democratic gatherings outside the Northeast. Former friends in Congress no longer stopped in to chat. Talented young Democrats who had joined the administration in 1893 left for home, disenchanted. Cleveland seldom left the White House, which faithful aides surrounded with guards. There was nowhere to go, except Woodley and Buzzards Bay. "I have been dreadfully forlorn these many months," he wrote in February 1895, "and sorely perplexed and tried." During 1895 and 1896 he twice more resorted to unpopular bond sales to rescue the Treasury's gold reserve. A few of his subsequent actions, particularly his blunt opposition to Great Britain in the 1895 Venezuela boundary dispute, brought praise, but they came too late to reverse the tide. Anti-Cleveland feeling spread through society and infected the Democratic party. For millions of people, Cleveland had become a scapegoat, the purveyor of economic ills, the betrayer of his party's great 1892 victory.[73]

That rising sun, Democratic then, seemed clearly Republican now. The Republicans had learned from defeat. At the decade's beginning, they stretched government power beyond the limits of public tolerance. They intruded too much, tried too hard, as one said, "to carry an ism in one State, and a hobby in another, and a moral idea in some other place." But they learned. By 1894 the Republicans had moved away from pietistic reform, stressing instead an expansive pluralism in which all religions, sections, and classes could take shelter. Showing newfound wisdom, they sidestepped that year the lure of the anti-Catholic American Protective Association.[74] The depression reshaped American politics. It tested party doctrines and shifted voter alignments. The Democrats lost, their tenets of localism and negative government discredited in the crisis. Cleveland unwittingly had seen to that. The Republicans won. The party of activism and national authority, they seemed better suited to the needs of an increasingly interdependent, urban-industrial society. The Republicans mobilized national constituencies, recognized national problems, pursued national programs. They knew how to govern.

Major challenges lay ahead. A depression-torn nation required treatment. The silver issue threatened, like darkening thunderheads on the horizon, and silver Republicans would have to be placated, or ousted. Newly won power in Congress and the states awaited consolidation. And the White House still beckoned.

FIVE

McKinley, Bryan, and 1896

The "battle of the standards," the presidential election of 1896, ranks among the most important elections in American history. Political scientists call it a "critical election," one of a handful (1800, 1828, 1860, and 1932 were the others) that brought fundamental realignments in American politics. New voting patterns replaced the old, a new majority party arose to govern the country, and national policies shifted to suit the new realities. The "battle of the standards" extended the decisive results of the election of 1894 and reshaped politics for decades to come. It was aptly named. Fiercely fought and dramatically staged, the battle matched forces that drew on different traditions and pointed the nation toward different futures. Unfolding, it gathered a charged excitement that sparked a lifetime's memories. Those who lived through it never forgot it.[1]

It began innocuously enough, with the usual chase for the presidential nominations. The Republicans were first in the field, their ranks of contenders swollen by the scent of victory. The November 1895 elections in New York, New Jersey, Ohio, Iowa, Pennsylvania, and Massachusetts had continued the Republican trend, though also registering some minor Democratic gains from the debacle of 1894. The early presidential talk inevitably included former president Benjamin Harrison, now in quiet retirement in Indianapolis. Harrison never encouraged the talk. He had not enjoyed his last year in the White House, and thought it undignified for an ex-president to scramble for a nomination. "I do not like to appear to be in the attitude of the little boy that followed the apple-cart up the hill, hoping the tail-board might fall out!" he wrote a party ally. In February 1896, Harrison formally withdrew from consideration, leaving the important Indiana delegation up for grabs. Privately he threw his support to Senator William B. Allison of Iowa, a venerable Republican who planned to campaign in Harrison's old role as the western candidate.[2]

Allison joined a lengthening list of senatorial candidates, including Cushman K. Davis of Minnesota, Shelby M. Cullom of Illinois, and Matthew S. Quay of Pennsylvania. All had little chance and wished simply to be in the right spot should lightning strike. The powerful Quay, boss of the Pennsylvania party, played the role of favorite son, keeping his large delegation locked up until the time for bargaining arrived. In that strategy he worked closely with his New York counterpart, Thomas C. Platt, the "Easy Boss," known for the deft touch and the stealthy, polished maneuver. Through 1895 and early 1896 Platt sent emissaries to other Republican leaders, suggesting they choose favorite son delegations or back his own favorite son, Levi P. Morton, the septuagenarian governor of New York. The emissaries wheedled, bargained, commanded, in a few cases bribed. Party leaders listened. "T. C. Platt can not turn time backward, make spotted pigs or produce a three-year-old steer in a minute; but there is little else he can not do if he has the nerve," a lieutenant said on a delegate-hunting trip.[3]

Platt and Quay considered supporting Thomas B. Reed, but worried about his temper and independence. For a time Reed was a frontrunner, the focus of endless speculation. He wanted the nomination badly, believed long service in the House had earned it, and thought he spoke for the party's most intelligent elements. Campaigning hard for Republican candidates in 1894 and 1895, he had picked up numerous debts to cash in 1896. He planned to combine solid delegations from New England and the Pacific Coast, plus enough scattering support elsewhere to take the nomination. In December 1895, Reed won reelection as Speaker of the House, a useful base from which to influence policy and attract publicity. Immediately he softened the biting wit, as if to establish his presidential timber.[4]

In newspaper interviews he advised Republicans to avoid a return to prohibitive tariff duties, a telling jab at his main rival, William McKinley. The advice lured western Republicans into the fold and brought important early endorsements from the Chicago *Tribune* and other papers. Still, Reed's momentum flagged as convention time approached. As always, he saw his own handicaps, remarking sardonically that in choosing a candidate, the Republicans "might do worse, and they probably will." A well-intentioned gesture in 1894 toward the silver Republicans had backfired and cost him vital support in New England and the Midwest. Enemies combined against him. Geography undermined him, since Maine, his home state, was safely Republican no matter what the ticket. Worst of all, Reed suffered from his own reputation. He seemed brittle and temperamental, too self-centered, somehow unsuited for presidential leadership.[5]

Geography and temperament both helped McKinley, who took an early lead in the delegate race. Able, calm, and affable, McKinley had seemingly spent a lifetime preparing for the presidency. After a year of college, he had been caught up in the emotion of the Civil War, in which he served with bravery and distinction. Breveted a major, a title he carried for the rest of his life, he left the army in 1865, studied law, and moved to Canton, Ohio, a small industrial town in the northeastern portion of the state. Law turned naturally to politics, and in 1876 McKinley won a seat in Congress. There he devoted himself to the tariff, gradually becoming its chief spokesman. Like Blaine, whom he idolized, he saw the tariff as the path to prosperity and national greatness, a system of beneficent protection for manufacturers, farmers, and laborers. "It is the tax of patriotism, of home and country, of self-preservation and self-development," he said in 1892. "It has made the youngest country on the earth first in agriculture, the first in mining and the first in manufactures."[6]

Congressional service honed the Major's legendary ability to manage people. Unlike Reed, he valued diversity and welcomed constructive dissent. He was charming, moderate, cautious, and thoughtful. "The man's genius was for friendship, for judgment of men, for their management," said the wife of a long-time antagonist. He enjoyed conversation and seldom read books. Philosophies bored him; issues, coalitions, and people instantly awakened his interest. He looked inward for strength. His two children died young, and his wife became a semi-invalid requiring constant attention. McKinley loved cigars, yet refused to be photographed with one for fear of setting a bad example for

Hooray, Ohio!

children. In 1896 he was fifty-three, and his campaign for the presidency was already almost a decade old. Ohio, an important state in a critical region, positioned him nicely for a presidential bid, and had trained him well for the task. Survival in politics there required "the virtues of the serpent, the shark, and the cooing dove," as a contemporary put it. McKinley had learned all three.[7]

McKinley prospered politically in the crises of the 1890s. The depression lent new credibility to the tariff issue and its main sponsor. The labor turmoil of 1894 added to his luster, for as governor of Ohio he dealt openly and even handedly with it, in pointed contrast to President Cleveland. Firm against violence of any kind, he won the respect of both labor and the middle-class. That year he joined Reed and other Republican hopefuls on the stump, traveling some twelve thousand miles and addressing nearly two million people. He visited New Orleans, spoke in the major cities of the Border States, and toured the Northeast and Midwest. Everywhere he stressed the tariff, the depression, and the Cleveland administration: "this tariff-tinkering, bond-issuing, debt-increasing, treasury-depleting, business-paralyzing, wage-reducing" administration. In January 1896, his second term as governor ended, McKinley retired to Canton, to spend time with his wife and nurse his growing boom.[8]

In Canton, a special telephone line connected him directly with the Cleveland, Ohio, office of his trusted friend and ally, Marcus A. Hanna. Contemporaries often misunderstood Hanna. The Democrats lampooned him savagely, using the ally to get at the boss. Caricatures of "Dollar Mark," greedy, gloating, and cruel, filled Democratic newspapers. "Dollar Mark" bribed delegates, bought nominations, and controlled the puppet McKinley. Friends and acquaintances knew better. Hanna was genial, well meaning, and affectionate. He was "a man with a good deal of the boy in him," said an acquaintance, "who would take endless pains to please a child, was sorry when other people were in trouble, [and] liked dispensing happiness under his own roof— and widely elsewhere with his left hand." Hanna was boyish and shrewd, exuberant and hard-headed, energetic, a millionaire businessman who sympathized with labor, a bluff, open man who enjoyed the secrets of politics. Politics absorbed and challenged, especially after he met McKinley, whom he deeply respected. In 1895 he retired from business to devote full-time energies to the McKinley campaign.[9]

They made an effective team. The Major commanded, decided general strategies, selected issues and programs. He stressed ideals.

"Mark," he would say, "this seems to be right and fair and just. I think so, don't you?" Hanna organized, built coalitions, performed the rougher work for which McKinley had neither taste nor energy. They shared a Hamiltonian faith in the virtues of industrialism, central authority, and expansive capitalism. A year before the convention they had settled on strategy: exploit the opposition of Platt and Quay in a campaign of "McKinley against the Bosses" and "The People against the Bosses." Feature McKinley as "The Advance Agent of Prosperity." In the race for convention delegates, hold the Midwest, woo the South, erode Reed's strength in New England, pick up support in the Far West, and wait for others to join the bandwagon. It all worked. By March 1896, the bandwagon had become a steamroller.[10]

Southern Republicans came aboard early. They liked bandwagons, needing a winner in order to share in the federal patronage. In 1895 Hanna bought a vacation home in Georgia, where McKinley visited to meet and talk with southern leaders. The pressure was immense, as worried Reed men reported. In the end, McKinley got nearly 200 delegates from the South, Reed got only 18½. The margin was fatal. During March and April, 1896, critical conventions in Ohio, California, Indiana, Michigan, Minnesota, and Wisconsin instructed for McKinley. "All say there is no sense in trying to stem the McKinley tide," a Platt aide wrote. "At present it is one wide yawp and everybody is joining the yell in order to be on the loaded wagon." On March 31, New Hampshire declared for both McKinley and Reed, a blow to the Speaker. A month later Vermont instructed for McKinley, shattering Reed's New England base. The following day, the large Illinois delegation went for McKinley, and it was all over.[11]

Quay signaled Platt to tone down his statements against McKinley, and himself visited Canton to make peace. On convention eve, Reed's campaign manager, stunned at McKinley's strength, blurted to reporters that McKinley would win on the first ballot. That put the finishing touch to the Reed campaign. On June 16, when the convention opened in St. Louis, McKinley's face and name were everywhere: on banners, posters, hats, badges, drinks, and canes. Hanna had arrived early, to see to last-minute details. The platform troubled him, especially the currency plank. He and McKinley had wanted to emphasize the tariff, play down the gold-silver controversy, and stand for international bimetallism. They had hoped to let McKinley's bimetallic record speak for itself, but silence invited ridicule:

My words have been for silver,
My silence stood for gold,
And thus I show the teaching
Of some great sage of old.
And if there is a question
As to just what I meant,
I'll answer that quite fully—
When I am President![12]

A firm statement might prove useful. It could drive the Democrats toward a divisive stand for free silver, and would win praise in the East and Midwest, both crucial for a Republican victory. Through the spring of 1896, McKinley played a waiting game, letting sentiment gather for an unequivocal plank. Hanna carried the draft to St. Louis. It called for the preservation of "the existing standard" of currency, clear in its intent though not in its precise language. A platform committee tinkered with it in the upstairs hallway of a hotel, and with Hanna's approval added the clinching word "gold." "The Republican party is unreservedly for sound money. . . ," said the final plank. "We are, therefore, opposed to the free coinage of silver, except by international agreement with the leading commercial nations of the earth, which agreement we pledge ourselves to promote, and until such agreement can be obtained the existing gold standard must be maintained."[13]

On Thursday afternoon, June 18, the delegates cheered the plank, then listened as Senator Henry M. Teller of Colorado, an old, white-haired veteran of Republican politics, proposed a free silver substitute. His eyes filled with tears, Teller warned the convention that the gold plank meant distress and disaster. "I cannot subscribe to it, and if it is adopted I must, as an honest man, sever my connection" with the Republican party. The delegates sympathized, respecting Teller's years of service to the party, but defeated the substitute, 818½ to 105½. The vote released emotions. Twenty-three silver Republicans, far fewer than Teller had hoped, marched out of the convention hall. The band struck up "Columbia," and the remaining delegates, angry now, waved handkerchiefs and flags, and shouted "Good-bye," "Put them out," and "Go to Chicago," the site of the upcoming Democratic national convention. In the Ohio delegation, Hanna stood on a chair screaming "Go! Go! Go!" William Jennings Bryan, there as a special correspondent for a Nebraska newspaper, climbed on a desk to get a better view.[14]

Outside the hall, the silverites caucused briefly, and met with a delegation of Populists who had come in anticipation of the walkout. The two groups reached "a perfect agreement as to the future," announced Herman E. Taubeneck, the Populist party chairman, "and henceforth we will work along the same lines." They would try to unite Populists, silver Republicans, and silver Democrats against the money power, possibly with Teller as the combination's presidential nominee. In the convention, meanwhile, the Republicans had returned to business. Speakers placed candidates in nomination, and the balloting started. McKinley listened in by long distance telephone, calmly ticking off states on a pad. Suspense, if any, ended quickly. Ohio's vote put him over the top, an excellent omen, he thought. The totals showed the effect of superb organization, grass-roots support, and accumulating momentum. McKinley won 661½ votes, Reed 84½, Quay 61½, Morton 58, and Allison 35½. Garret A. Hobart, a New Jersey lawyer and fund-raiser, took the vice-presidential nomination, after Reed privately declined it.[15]

Canton celebrated. Church bells, factory whistles, cannon, and fire gongs alerted the countryside to the event. "Major, I congratulate you. . . ," said a friend. "Now you have just a quarter of a minute, before you are mobbed." Townsfolk came to congratulate, visitors flooded in by special trains from nearby cities. Crowds trampled the neat lawn in front of McKinley's North Market Street house, destroyed the flower beds, and tore down fences. Starting late in the afternoon, McKinley addressed nearly 50,000 people before bedtime. He retired about midnight, exhausted. Planning for the campaign would start the next morning. Republicans were pleased and confident. They had a popular, experienced candidate and an attractive platform. The defection of the silver Republicans might cause trouble, but a strong stand for the tariff and sound currency should overcome that. For the moment, the gold plank brought relief, a thankfulness to have the matter settled. Hanna would head the campaign, insuring an energetic and effective organization. The Democrats carried the twin burdens of depression and Grover Cleveland. Surely McKinley would win.[16]

☆☆☆

The Democrats staggered under their burdens. They were tired and discouraged, torn by dissension. Administration Democrats fought anti-administration Democrats. Gold men fought silverites; section battled section; leaders like Gorman and Bryan and Wilson argued over the party's future. Cleveland sulked, alternating between periods of withdrawal and feverish bursts of activity. He fished, protected the gold reserve, and paid careful attention to personal investments. "I find I am developing quite a strong desire to make money," he wrote his financial adviser in 1895, "and I think this is a good time to indulge in that propensity." The nation suffered under depression. Many Democrats in the Midwest, Far West, and South wanted to disavow Cleveland, but recognized the strength of party loyalty and the powers of incumbency. Rarely in American history has a political party repudiated its sitting president. It happened to Cleveland in 1896.[17]

It happened because Cleveland mishandled the depression, and the silver issue. Silver sentiment had grown swiftly after 1894, sweeping through the South and West, appearing even in the rural regions of New York and New England. Pro-silver literature flooded from presses and filled newspaper columns. Pamphlets, some of them distributed by the millions, touted silver's virtues. People read, discussed, and believed. It was a time for solutions, with the economy slumping again. During 1896 unemployment shot up; farm income and prices fell to the lowest point in the decade. "I can remember back as far as 1858," said an Iowa hardware dealer that February, "and I have never seen such hard times as these are." Silverites offered a solution, simplistic but compelling: the free and independent coinage of silver at the ratio of 16 to 1.[18]

Free coinage meant that the mints would coin all the silver offered to them. Independent coinage meant that the United States would coin silver regardless of the policies of other nations, nearly all of which were on the gold standard. The ratio of 16 to 1 pegged silver's value at 16 ounces of silver to 1 ounce of gold, a formulation based on the market prices of the two metals back in the 1830s. Silver had slipped badly in price since then, and the actual ratio was now closer to 32 to 1, but silverites argued that free coinage would boost the price and restore the old relationship. The silverites believed in a quantity theory of money: the amount of money in circulation determined the level of activity in the economy. A money shortage meant declining activity and depression. Silver meant prosperity. Added to the currency, it would swell the money stock and quicken the pace of economic activity. Farm prices would rise. "The blood of commerce will again flow through the arteries of business; industry will again revive; millions of men will find employment; [and] the hand of greed will be stricken from the throat of prosperity."[19]

By 1896 silver was a symbol. It had moral and patriotic dimensions, and stood for a wide range of popular grievances. Cleveland and his fellow gold adherents never understood that. With skillful work, they could have drawn much of the movement's sting, but instead adopted policies that sharpened its symbolism. Cleveland anointed silver in trying to kill it. For many in the society, silver reflected rural values rather than urban, suggested a welcome shift of power away from the Northeast, gave the nation a chance to display its growing authority in the world, and spoke for the down-trodden instead of the well-to-do. It represented the common people, as the vast literature of the movement showed. In article after article, pamphlet after pamphlet, farmers and financiers, thrown together in accidental circumstances, debated the merits of silver and gold, with results obvious to all who knew the virtues of common folk and common sense.[20]

William H. Harvey's *Coin's Financial School,* the most popular of all silverite pamphlets, had the eloquent Coin, a wise but unknown youth, tutoring famous people on the currency. Bankers, lawyers, and scholars came to argue for gold, but left shaken, leaning towards silver. Coin used logic and plain sense. He "was like a little monitor in the midst of a fleet of wooden ships. His shots went through and silenced all opposition."[21] *Coin's Financial School* sold five thousand copies a day at its peak in 1895, with tens of thousands more distributed free by silver organizations. Sequels followed, almost as popular. Frank Baum, a silverite from Chicago, tapped the same themes in an enduring allegory of the silver movement, *The Wonderful Wizard of Oz.* Dorothy (every person) is carried from drought-stricken Kansas to a strange land of riches and witches. On arrival, she disposes of one witch, the wicked Witch of the East (with obvious symbolism), and frees the Munchkins (the common people) from servitude. To return to Kansas, Dorothy must go to the Emerald City (the national capital, greenback-colored).

She wears silver slippers and follows the yellow brick road, thus achieving a proper parity between silver and gold. A kiss from the good Witch of the North (northern voters) protects her on the way. She meets the Scarecrow (the farmer), who has been told he has no brain, but actually possesses great common sense; the Tin Woodman (the industrial worker), who fears he has become heartless, but discovers the spirit of love and cooperation; and the Cowardly Lion (reformers and politicians), who has lost the courage to fight. When the four companions reach the Emerald City, they find that the feared Wizard (the money power) is only a charlatan, a manipulator, whose power rests on myth and illusion. Dorothy unmasks the Wizard, destroys the wicked Witch of the West (those opposing progress there), and with the help of the good Witch of the South (obvious symbolism again), uses the silver slippers to return home to Kansas. Sadly, the slippers are lost in flight. "Oz" was a familiar abbreviation to those involved in the 16 (ounces) to 1 fight.[22]

Like the Wizard, silver itself profited from illusion. It fed on fears and grew with apprehensions. Its supporters, like the "goldolators" they despised, tended to oversimplify issues, appeal to emotions, imagine conspiracies, and cast events in terms of good and evil. They also tried to respond constructively to public need and economic hardship. Silver was a social movement, one of the largest in American history, but its life span turned out to be remarkably brief. As a mass phenomenon, it flourished between 1894 and 1896, then succumbed to defeat, prosperity, and the onset of fresh concerns. But in its time it spoke a mood and won millions of followers. It altered the course of politics. Silver reshaped sectional alignments, changed party outlooks, and helped topple a president. It presided at the birth of a "new" Democratic party.

In 1894 more than twenty Democratic state platforms came out for free silver. That fall, the elections accelerated the trend, decimating the Democrats in the Northeast and Midwest. Power within the party suddenly shifted to the South, where it remained for decades. The party's base narrowed; its outlook increasingly reflected southern views on silver, race, and other issues. Elsewhere, the elections persuaded worried Democrats of the need to move in fresh directions. John P. Altgeld, the head of the Illinois party, led the way. A shrewd and sensitive politician, Altgeld recognized silver's potential. It enabled Democrats to dissociate themselves from the hated Cleveland, disavow past mistakes, and revive their flagging fortunes. It turned dejected Democrats into spirited ones. The fight for silver "has stirred up our people" and "put new life into the Democratic party here," Altgeld told party leaders in other states.[23]

Altgeld moved early, conscious of the need for quick action to head off opposition from the Cleveland Democrats. In June 1895, over a year before the Democratic national convention, he called a special state convention to place the Illinois party on record for free silver.

Party organizations in Texas, Mississippi, and Missouri immediately followed the example. In August, silver Democrats formed a Bimetallic Democratic national committee, a "shadow" group to parallel the Cleveland-run regular committee. It monitored administration activities and lobbied for free silver platforms. In Iowa, Horace Boies, the former governor, eased his party toward silver, hoping to use the issue for a presidential bid in 1896. Richard P. Bland, at 58 the elder statesman of the silver cause, had similar ideas in Missouri. A Jacksonian Democrat, Bland wanted to reunite the West and South in a crusade for silver and the common man.[24]

Out in Nebraska, William Jennings Bryan sensed opportunity. Dissident Democrats had their issue, but they lacked a compelling leader. Boies and Bland would surely stumble, and Altgeld, the most influential among them, could not run for president because of his German birth. Some strategists touted the Republican Teller, but Democratic partisanship made his nomination unlikely. Aside from scattered dark horses, that left Bryan, the "logic of the situation," as he liked to tell close friends during 1895 and early 1896. Few Democratic leaders agreed. Bryan was young, barely 36, and came from a Republican state west of the Mississippi River. He had served two terms in the House of Representatives, and otherwise had little experience for presidential responsibilities. He seemed a man for the future rather than the present. Altgeld thought so, reminding Bryan: "You are young yet. Let Bland have the nomination this time. Your time will come."[25]

Bryan did not relinquish prizes so easily. He dreamed, and had worked tirelessly to turn dream into reality. Growing up in rural Salem, Illinois, he had graduated from Illinois College as valedictorian in 1881. In college, he had studied diligently, become an award-winning orator, and courted Mary Baird, one of the remarkable women of the late nineteenth century. Mary Baird Bryan was winsome and intelligent, most ambitious, a lawyer in her own right, and totally wed to her husband's interests. A few years after marrying, the young couple moved west to practice law in Lincoln, Nebraska. Only moderately successful as an attorney, Bryan discovered himself in politics. He loved people, and won them over by showing it. As in everything he did, he worked hard at politics, polishing his skills, especially his extraordinary speaking ability. Bryan was a captivating public speaker, tall, slender, and handsome, with a beautiful voice that projected easily into every corner of an auditorium. Practicing at home before mirrors, he rehearsed his speeches again and again, as Mary Bryan listened to pick out errors in tone or substance.[26]

In 1890 he won election to the House. A low tariff Democrat who switched to free silver, he symbolized his party's transition during the 1890s. He supported Cleveland in 1892, then broke with him over the depression and the currency. Seeing the mounting public interest in silver, Bryan studied the issue and made it his own. Opponents thought him shallow and unsophisticated, a creation of his own voice, but he attracted a growing following. In 1893 he helped lead the fight against unconditional repeal, and a year later, the object of Cleveland's bitter hostility, retired from Congress to work full time for silver. Between 1894 and 1896, Bryan canvassed the nation, courting editors, wooing potential delegates, and fanning interest in the silver cause. He turned down few invitations and spoke in almost every state. As always, his speeches built on each other, progressively bringing together favorite ideas and sentences from previous efforts. In December 1894 Bryan found a phrase he liked—"I will not help to crucify mankind upon a cross of gold"—and saved it for future use.[27]

Unlike McKinley, Bryan drew on the Jeffersonian tradition of rural virtue, suspicion of urban and industrial growth, distrust of central authority, and abiding faith in the powers of human reason. Jefferson, he once said, "placed man above matter, humanity above property, and spurning the bribes of wealth and power, pleaded the cause of the common people." Bryan pleaded the same cause. He believed in human progress, but unreflective, never thought deeply about its processes or ends. He ably led and only dimly understood. Professionals scoffed at his presidential ambitions, and Bryan himself recognized the distant odds. His prospects depended on silverite control of the party and luck at the national convention. As 1896 approached, he seemed no more than an attractive dark horse, with strong ties to the discontented in the South and West, helpful friends among the Populists, and a broad network of party allies built up during years of relentless campaigning. In retrospect, he was the logical candidate, the embodiment of the forces reshaping the Democratic party.[28]

Tensions mounted through early 1896, as Democrats battled for control of their party. Everything rested now on the state conventions, some forty of them, that would meet between April and June to choose delegates to the national convention. In February, Democrats in Congress voted almost two to one for a free coinage bill, an initial victory for the silverites. Bland, Boies, and Bryan—the "busy bees," J. Sterling Morton sourly called them—redoubled efforts for silver delegations.[29] Cleveland lashed back, determined to hold the party for gold. He was sure the Democrats would lose this year, but wanted a sound money candidate and platform to keep the record clean. Carlisle, Wilson, Morton, Lamont, Hoke Smith, and other spokesmen went west and south to undermine silver and defend administration policy. The experience was sobering. Old friends shunned them; audiences jeered. "I have never seen the masses of the people so wild over a question they know little or nothing about," Wilson said in his diary in May. "To reason with them is as impossible as to talk down an angry cyclone." Morton got a hostile reception on the Pacific Coast, including threats against his life. "The silver sentiment is universal all over the West, and it is growing," he told reporters on his return to Washington.[30]

On April 9, Oregon Democrats, the first to meet, went for silver. A few days later the Alabama party did the same, a blow to administration hopes there. Missouri, Colorado, Washington, and Mississippi followed, while in the East, Pennsylvania and Massachusetts, both important delegations, declared for gold. The Nebraska party split in two, with separate conventions, platforms, and delegations. On April 29, the first break came when Michigan, where Cleveland had made a personal appeal, adopted a sound money platform. Administration spirits soared. "Light out of darkness," Wilson said in his diary. The silver lines wavered, amid fears that Cleveland would win after all. Then, in rapid succession, Iowa, South Carolina, Wyoming, and Tennessee went for silver. "Now we find perverts where we least expected them, and a madness that cannot be dealt with or, indeed, scarcely approached," Wilson said sadly on May 26.[31]

On June 4, Kentucky, Carlisle's own state, declared for silver, a crushing setback for the administration. Silverites elected 24 of the 26 Kentucky delegates to the national convention. The next day, Virginia Democrats voted 1276 to 371 for a free silver platform. It was not even close. Kansas, California, Texas, Georgia, Ohio, Indiana, and North Carolina followed. At the Kentucky, Virginia, and North Carolina conventions, the delegates hissed Cleveland's name. The South Carolina platform denounced him. In Ohio, a delegate called him an "arch traitor," the "Benedict Arnold of the Democratic party."[32] Wisconsin and Minnesota held for gold, but it was not enough. Despairing, Cleveland focused his final hopes on Illinois, one of the last major states to meet. "The 'jig is up'" should Illinois go for silver, Morton had predicted earlier. On June 23, Illinois went overwhelmingly for silver. The convention named Altgeld for another term as governor, attacked Cleveland's actions in the Pullman strike, and demanded free silver coinage. All 48 delegates to the national convention were pledged for silver.[33]

Dazed and angry, Cleveland hurriedly left Washington for Buzzards Bay. There, he fished, hid, and turned away news of party developments. Morton renewed talk of forming a new party, devoted to the proprietors and property owners of the country. In mid-June, William C. Whitney, the legendary organizer of the 1892 victory, canceled a trip to Europe and rallied northeastern Democrats for a last-ditch effort. An international bimetallist, Whitney hoped to subdue the silver Democrats with a mild compromise. He also planned to impress them with his group's dignified dress and demeanor, a measure of his misjudgment of the situation. Collecting David B. Hill, William E. Russell, and others, he chartered a special train which reached Chicago on July 3, four days before the convention opened. The city swirled with excitement. Interested observers outnumbered delegates. Bland still seemed the leading candidate for the nomination, but the silver Republicans were there working for Teller. Taubeneck, Weaver, and Donnelly looked after Populist interests. They joined the Teller camp, aware that the selection of a silver Democrat might lure away enough Populist voters to destroy their party.[34]

Silver delegates, badges, and flags filled Chicago's streets. "At this hour," a Populist leader wrote home, "all that is known is that the silver forces are in full control, and all Chicago rages with universal discussion of the money question."[35] Pleased, Altgeld put the finishing touches on the Bland campaign. Crowds trailed Benjamin R. Tillman, a one-eyed senator from South Carolina who had won notoriety in 1895 by declaring that Cleveland "is an old bag of beef, and I am going to Washington with a pitchfork and prod him in his old fat ribs." Hopeful the nomination might come his way, Tillman buttonholed delegates and sported a lapel pin showing three goldbugs impaled on a silver pitchfork. Bland supporters moved through the crowd distributing "Bland cornfield handshakes," a shake of the right hand, a free glass of whiskey in the left. The scene reminded Whitney's forces of the French Revolution, with resolute, hard-faced men out to overthrow the established order. Hill looked glum, telling one questioner: "I never smile and look pleasant at a funeral."[36]

On the convention's opening day, July 7, the silver Democrats promptly took charge. They defeated Hill for temporary chairman, seated contesting silver delegations, and put together a platform that stunned administration Democrats. "We demand," the financial plank said, "the free and unlimited coinage of both silver and gold at the present legal ratio of 16 to 1, without waiting for the aid or consent of any other nation." The Cleveland Democrats were prepared for that. They were not prepared for planks that denounced nearly every policy Cleveland had pursued since 1893. The platform called for lower tariffs and governmental economy; attacked "arbitrary interference by Federal authorities in local affairs," a slap at Cleveland and the Pullman strike; censured Cleveland's bond issues and his "trafficking with banking syndicates;" and chided the Supreme Court, which in 1895 had declared the income tax unconstitutional. Horrified, some Cleveland men immediately packed their bags and went home. Others drew up a substitute platform, defending the gold standard and praising the administration.[37]

On Thursday, July 9, the delegates listened intently to the platform debate. Tillman misjudged their temper, and alienated most of them with a bitter, sectional speech. Hill, Russell, and William F. Vilas of Wisconsin spoke ably for the substitute platform, but converted no one. "Wait until you hear Bryan," the silver delegates whispered. It was the moment Bryan had spent years getting ready for. Eagerly, he left his seat in the Nebraska delegation and strode to the platform, his face alert, smiling, and confident. "I thought I had never seen a handsomer man," a reporter recalled of that day: "young, tall, powerfully built, clear-eyed, with a mane of black hair which he occasionally thrust back with his hand."[38] Bryan stood for a moment, a hand raised for silence, waiting for the applause and the audience to settle down. He would not contend with the previous speakers, he began, for "this is not a contest between persons. The humblest citizen in all the land, when clad in the armor of a righteous cause, is stronger than all the hosts of error. I come to speak to you in defense of a cause as holy as the cause of liberty—the cause of humanity."

Bryan had the delegates from the start. Almost like a trained choir, they rose, cheered each point, and sat back to listen for more. They were there, Bryan said, "to enter up the judgment already rendered by the plain people of this country." Easterners praised and followed businessmen, but forgot that laborers, miners, and farmers were businessmen, too. "Our war is not a war of conquest; we are fighting in the defense of our homes, our families, and posterity. We have petitioned, and our petitions have been scorned; we have entreated, and our entreaties have been disregarded; we have begged, and they have mock-ed when our calamity came. We beg no longer; we entreat no more; we petition no more. We defy them!" Shouts echoed through the hall, and delegates pounded on chairs. Savoring each cheer, Bryan defended the platform and the primacy of the money issue. Silver would make the masses prosperous, and lead to other reforms.

Then, the famous peroration: "Having behind us the producing masses of this nation and the world . . . we will answer their demand for a gold standard by saying to them: 'You shall not press down upon the brow of labor this crown of thorns, you shall not crucify mankind upon a cross of gold.'" Bryan first moved his fingers down his temples, suggesting blood trickling from his wounds. He ended with his arms outstretched, in a crucifixion stance. Letting the silence hang, he dropped his arms, stepped back, then started to his seat. Suddenly, there was pandemonium. Delegates shouted, cursed, threw hats, coats, handkerchiefs, and other objects into the air. They cheered, laughed, and cried. Clarence Darrow had never seen an audience so moved. "That is the greatest speech I ever listened to," Altgeld said in the midst of the shouting. From the platform, a reporter watched two old men embrace, tears streaming down their cheeks. Delegates seized state banners and paraded around the convention hall. Men who had come to Chicago to nominate other candidates were caught up in the excitement. Outside, crowds danced through the streets.[39]

The silver Democrats had found their leader. To Bryan, it was a moment touched with magic, a rare and perfect union of audience and speaker. He also knew that months of careful groundwork had prepared the way. When the tumult subsided, the delegates defeated the substitute platform and adopted the majority report, 628 to 301. With a sense of happy release, they voted 564 to 357 against a resolution commending the Cleveland administration. The next day, July 10, Bryan won the presidential nomination on the fifth ballot, as Bland withdrew. Hill, Russell, Vilas, and other gold Democrats sat silent through the balloting. Cleveland's repudiation was complete. Bland declined the vice-presidential nomination, and the convention turned to Arthur Sewall, a 61-year-old Maine Democrat and millionaire shipbuilder who favored silver. Sewall's nomination balanced the ticket geographically, and recognized one of the few pro-silver businessmen, but it seemed odd to many Democrats. It would cause serious troubles throughout the campaign.[40]

In Canton, Ohio, a friend called McKinley with news of Bryan's impending nomination. "That is rot," McKinley said, and hung up the telephone. Leaving Chicago, the Cleveland Democrats debated future action, unwilling to accept Bryan's "foul pit of repudiation, socialism, [and] anarchy," as Wilson put it.[41] Bryan's victory reminded them of the crisis of 1860, an attempt to divide the country into sections. Bryan, they thought, intended to divide it into classes, the haves and the have-nots: "to take property from the hands of those who created it and place it in the hands of those who covet it." What should they do? Should they follow the party and somehow swallow Bryan? Should they support McKinley, or name a third ticket? Hill fell back on his famous motto, and told friends: "I am a Democrat still—very still." Cleveland advised caution until tempers cooled enough to plot strategy. "I am so dazed on the political situation," he wrote Olney on July 13, "that I am in no condition for speech or thought on the subject." It would be years before Cleveland could discuss 1896 without obvious rage.[42]

☆☆☆

The Populists were in trouble, and knew it. At the beginning of the year, they had staked everything on the assumption that neither major party would endorse silver. The Republicans seemed safe for gold or cautious bimetallism, and surely Cleveland, with all the powers of the national administration, could keep a silver plank out of the Democratic platform. The assumption dictated Populist strategy, decided at party conferences in January 1896: schedule the national convention for mid-summer, late, after the Republicans and Democrats, in order to gather in the bolting silverites from both parties. Bryan's victory in Chicago destroyed the assumption and the strategy. Now, the Populists were the ones being gathered in. Some angry members charged that Taubeneck and others had been "flimflammed" by the silverites, but in fact, they had simply gambled and lost. After Chicago, the Populists faced a painful choice: nominate an independent ticket, and risk splitting the silver forces; or nominate Bryan, and give up some of their separate identity as a party. Either way, they were certain to lose.[43]

An influential "middle-of-the-road" faction, under Watson in the South and Donnelly in the West, held out for an independent ticket. They played down silver, disliked the notion of cooperation with the Democrats, and wanted to mount a broad reform campaign. The "mid-roaders" were strongest in the South, where tensions between

Populists and Democrats ran high. The Democrats "say we must fuse," declared Watson, "but their idea of fusion is that we play minnow while they play trout; we play June bug while they play duck; we play Jonah while they play the whale."[44] Taubeneck and Weaver, leading the fusionist faction, thought such arguments foolish. The Populists had done poorly in 1894, and needed the kind of additional support Bryan could bring. Silver did narrow the Populist platform, but the "mid-roaders" themselves had often seen the wisdom of that. Why not exploit silver's wide popularity, and then enact other reforms once in office? In the West, Populist leaders reported rank-and-file enthusiasm for Bryan "bordering on hysteria," a sentiment that might be fatal to ignore.[45]

The choice was unpleasant, and it shattered the People's party. "If we fuse, we are sunk; if we don't fuse, all the silver men we have will leave us for the more powerful Democrats."[46] Meeting in St. Louis late in July, the Populists tried to do both, and ended by doing neither. Their convention nominated Bryan, but refused to accept Sewall, the shipping magnate, bank director, and symbol of the financial East. For vice-president it named Watson instead, obviously hoping the Democrats would withdraw Sewall and ratify the Bryan-Watson ticket. Unfortunately, the Populists had little with which to bargain. Bryan ignored them, and his campaign manager promptly announced: "Mr. Sewall will, of course, remain on the ticket, and Mr. Watson can do what he likes." It was awkward and embarrassing, worse perhaps than either of the original alternatives. Watson stayed on the ticket and campaigned in several states until illness forced him home in mid-October. Ill-tempered, he resented his role, and spent the campaign sniping at Populist headquarters and sabotaging efforts at fusion with the Democrats.[47]

Fusion negotiations proceeded slowly, but ultimately produced unified Democratic-Populist tickets in 28 states, mostly in the West. Usually the two parties divided presidential electors on a joint Bryan-Sewall-Watson ticket. In California, Nebraska, Minnesota, the Dakotas, and other states, they also fused on congressional and state races. In Kansas and Colorado, the Populists capitulated to the Democrats and campaigned for the Bryan-Sewall ticket. Fusion fared less well through the South, and in all but four states the Populists simply withdrew the Bryan-Watson ticket. Watson did not appear on the ballot even in Georgia, his home state. In Louisiana, the Populists fused with the

Democrats on national offices and the Republicans on local offices. In North Carolina, they fused with the Democrats on the presidential ticket, the Republicans on the congressional and legislative tickets, and ran a separate ticket for governor, lieutenant governor, and auditor. Populist leaders reeled under the confusion, trying to sort out tickets and mediate between factions. "The uncertainty on Watson & Sewall is tearing our party to pieces," a Tennessee leader said that summer.[48]

The Populist endorsement probably hurt Bryan as much as it helped. It won him relatively few votes, since many Populists—perhaps most—would have voted for him no matter what. It identified him as a Populist, which he was not, and enabled opponents to place him at the head of a ragtag army of malcontents, anarchists, and misguided fanatics. The Sewall-Watson squabble underlined the point, suggesting the fragility of an unnatural alliance. How could such a coalition govern? Would Sewall or Watson be vice-president? Might Donnelly and Taubeneck join Altgeld and Tillman in a jumbled "Demopop" cabinet? The prospect worried moderate voters and highlighted McKinley's program of progress with stability. It also helped unite Bryan's opponents, who set out, as Henry Cabot Lodge declared, to crush "the revolutionary resolutions put forth by the Democratic party, which has passed completely into the hands of the Populists."[49]

☆☆☆

Bryan's victory at Chicago altered Mark Hanna's thinking. "The Chicago convention has changed everything," he warned McKinley. Bryan was a formidable opponent, requiring a far different campaign than the Republicans had planned. He would take the stump and like a modern-day Pied Piper, marshal the discontented. Altgeld had been right. Silver and the Chicago platform rejuvenated the Democrats and diluted the Republicans' chief issues: the depression and the Cleveland administration. "We could have beaten an old-fashioned Democratic nomination and ticket without half trying," a Republican wrote in mid-July, "but the new movement has stolen our thunder." McKinley remained calm and confident, but Hanna fretted. Party leaders from Indiana to California reported growing excitement over Bryan and silver. Hanna moved quickly to recharge the campaign, telling subordinates to "quit blowing, and saw wood." He also urged McKinley to take the stump against Bryan, but McKinley wisely refused. "I might just as well put up a trapeze on my front lawn and compete with some professional athlete as go out speaking against Bryan," he said.[50]

On August 7, after a short rest at home, Bryan set off on a campaign that soon became an American legend. He headed first for New York City, to open his canvass, he said, "in the heart of what now seems to be the enemy's country, but which we hope to be our country before this campaign is over." The phrase "enemy's country," so lightly said, would haunt Bryan through November. Reporters who accompanied him never knew whether to scoff or praise. At the beginning, he had no staff and little organization. He looked up his own train schedules, bought his own tickets, carried his own bags, rode in public cars, and changed trains in the middle of the night to make connections. Often he walked from the station to the hotel. The schedule, such as it was, broke down as soon as the train left Lincoln. Crowds demanded speeches in Iowa and Chicago. Leaving Chicago near midnight, Bryan prepared for bed, but a large crowd waited at the South Chicago station. Another crowd awakened him at Valparaiso, Indiana, and he spoke in his nightgown. By the time he reached New York, he was already tired and hoarse.[51]

On August 12, a sweltering summer evening, twelve thousand people jammed into Madison Square Garden to hear the famous "Boy Orator of the Platte." Significantly, Hill stayed away, and only a handful of the city's Democratic leaders came. Conservatives were apprehensive, fearful that Bryan might rouse the eastern masses with spell-binding oratory. Bryan himself was tense. To rebut charges of wild-eyed radicalism, he had decided to read a calm, closely reasoned speech. He read for nearly two hours, amid the sounds of his departing audience. By the end, more than half the audience had left, and New Yorkers were talking derisively of the "Boy Reader of the Platte." The speech deserved better than that, but it did reflect a critical weakness in Bryan's campaign. It touched only briefly on issues like trusts and the income tax, which appealed to urban voters. Instead, it dwelled on silver, "the paramount question of this campaign." A popular issue in farm areas, silver worried labor, immigrants, and other urban groups. Inflationary, it would likely raise prices, but wages might not keep pace. Bryan recognized the problem, but never fully dealt with it. In the end, it helped cause his defeat.[52]

The New York reception daunted Bryan's closest advisers. How could he possibly win? In severing ties to Cleveland and the "old"

Democratic party, he had cut himself off from many of the traditional tools of Democratic victory. He lacked money, since most party contributors bitterly opposed him. His campaign fund came to about $500,000, a pitiful sum. Across the East and South, major Democratic newspapers refused to endorse him, and in some cases endorsed McKinley. Nearly half the party press opposed him, and party organizations in the Northeast gave only lukewarm support. In early September, the Cleveland Democrats moved decisively against him. Meeting in Indianapolis, they reaffirmed faith in Cleveland and gold, and named a presidential ticket of their own, headed by Senator John M. Palmer of Illinois. Cleveland was delighted, calling the new ticket "a delicious infusion of fresh air." He preferred McKinley to Bryan, and hoped Palmer would divert enough votes from Bryan in the Border States and Midwest to defeat him. Sharing the aim, Hanna secretly subsidized the Palmer campaign in Delaware, West Virginia, Kentucky, and other states where it might tip the balance to McKinley.[53]

Bryan struck back boldly. Skirting party leaders and organizations, he took his campaign directly to the voters, the first presidential candidate in history to do so in a systematic way. He focused on the Midwest, and the key states of Ohio, Indiana, Illinois, Iowa, Wisconsin, and Michigan. There, most strategists believed, the election would be decided. In August and September, he toured the Border States and New England. He spoke to 70,000 people in Louisville, Kentucky, and the crowds through North Carolina were the largest in memory. In rural areas, people stood beside the track, content just to cheer and wave as Bryan's train flashed by. Enthusiastic crowds in New England, including an audience of 75,000 on Boston Common in late September, heartened Bryan, though aides recalled seeing factories with large placards threatening layoffs and closings should he win. "Probably the only passage in the Bible read by some financiers is that about the wise men of the East," he burst out. "They seem to think that wise men have been coming from that direction ever since."[54]

The pace was grueling. In a typical day Bryan might speak twenty or thirty times. Some days he made as many as thirty-six speeches. At stops in major cities, he frequently spoke at least twice in the same evening, once to a large audience outdoors, then again to a different audience in a local meeting hall. On the train, he relaxed as best he could, snatching sleep in a chair or stretched out on the floor of the railroad car. His stamina amazed reporters. "Mr. Bryan has a damnable habit of going to bed at 12 o'clock and getting up at 1:30 for work," as one complained. Aides fanned him in the heat and gave him rub-downs with gin to loosen his muscles. The gin also drove people from the car, another benefit. In October, as the campaign neared its end, Bryan at last got a private car, inaptly named *The Idler,* which increased his comfort and range. Between stops, he tried to rest his voice, a large portion of which, he often told audiences, "has been left along the line of travel, where it is still calling sinners to repentence."[55]

Bryan was an evangelist by nature, and his campaign was a whirl-wind revival meeting. At scheduled stops, people arrived hours or days early, pouring in from nearby towns and farms. To pass the time, they held parades, sang hymns, and listened to speeches from lesser orators. Welcoming committees prepared elaborate receptions based on the 16 to 1 theme. Finally, almost always late, *The Idler* pulled in from the previous rally thirty or forty miles away. Eagerly, the crowd pressed forward to see Bryan, touch him, and take his hand. Women held up babies named after him. A chosen group, often including sixteen girls in white dresses and one boy in a gold-colored suit, welcomed him officially to the town. Warmed by the crowd, Bryan summoned strength for yet another speech, and apologizing for his voice, he would talk briefly of silver and the common people, of justice and righteous-ness, and of the need for the people to reassert control over the affairs of the nation. The talk finished, the crowd pressed forward again, hoping for a last touch or handshake, and *The Idler* pulled out for another town and, somehow, another speech.[56]

October brought the final drive, and Bryan spent much of it in the Ohio and upper Mississippi valleys. The September elections had gone badly, raising fears that his emotional campaign had crested too early, in July and August rather than November. Vermont and Maine went Republican by tremendous margins, and the state elections in the South showed a significant falloff—as much as 20 percent in some areas—in the Democratic-Populist vote. Still, no one could tell. Bryan's audiences remained large and enthusiastic, but did people come simply out of curiosity? While aides worried, Bryan redoubled efforts in Illinois, Indiana, Iowa, and Michigan. To win, he needed to hold the Democratic South, sweep most of the West, and carry at least part of the Midwest. He spent three final days in Chicago, where Democratic hopes were high, and closed out the campaign at home in Nebraska, with a last-minute dash around the state. As if unable to quit, he gave seven speeches in Omaha early in the morning of election day. That evening, exhausted, he collapsed in bed. "If they elect McKinley," he said to a friend, "I will feel a great burden lifted off my shoulders."[57]

It had been an extraordinary campaign. By his own count, Bryan traveled 18,009 miles. He visited twenty-seven states and spoke 600 times to a total of some three million people. He built skillfully on the "merchandising" style of campaign developed in 1892. Like Cleveland and Harrison then, Bryan (and McKinley as well) worked to educate and persuade, to acquaint each voter with the issues at stake in the election. Short of funds, he created a campaign that relied on other weapons. Lacking newspaper support, he took to the stump and forced the press to carry news of his progress, print his speeches, and serve as his spokesman. Circumventing party, he appealed directly to the voters. Bryan summoned voters to an older America: a land where farms counted as much as factories, where the virtues of rural and religious life outweighed the doubtful lure of the city, where common people still ruled, and opportunity existed for all. It was an appealing vision, if parts of it seemed somewhat out-of-date. As the election returns showed, it tapped a deep longing in American society.[58]

☆☆☆

Between June and November, McKinley left Canton for only three days, to fill prior speaking engagements. Suiting tactics to his personality, he chose a front-porch campaign, in the style Harrison had used so effectively in 1888. By staying at home, he could remain fresh and relatively rested, keep careful control of the issues, and using the press, reach fully as many people as Bryan's more strenuous effort. After Bryan's nomination, McKinley also decided to pursue a "blanket" strategy: to focus on Bryan and free silver until October, then switch emphasis to the tariff for the campaign's final month. Throughout, he hammered at three fundamental themes: free silver meant inflation and devalued dollars, and would severely damage the economy; prosperity depended on the tariff to protect the home market and reciprocity to boost the export trade; national unity and progress grew from a policy of tolerance and understanding, not shrill Bryanite divisiveness. McKinley appealed to labor, immigrants, established farmers, businessmen, and the middle class. He spoke for economic nationalism and the advancing urban-industrial society.[59]

Every day except Sunday, delegations of voters flooded into Canton. The railroads provided low excursion rates, as low as $3.50 for the 700-mile round trip from Chicago. It was, as a Democratic news-paper complained, "cheaper than staying at home." On Saturdays, the most popular day, as many as 50,000 people came. Almost always they arrived in large groups, organized as teachers, iron workers, college students, railroad employees, farmers, or hardware salesmen. McKin-ley's skilled staff had arranged each detail. Reception committees met the delegations at the station, and joined the festive march down Main Street, under the ornate plaster McKinley Arch, and up the hill to the candidate's modest North Market Street home. There, amid flags and bunting and curious neighbors, the delegates massed on the front lawn, as the spectators cheered and the bands played. "What poor McKinley has to endure moves my compassion," Reed remarked sympathetically. "I hope he don't hate a brass band." If he did, he never let on. Thanks to his staff, he had advance notice of each delegation, knew the leaders' names, and could chat casually and effectively about affairs in their home district.[60]

Wanting no mistakes, McKinley had cleared each delegation's remarks in advance, and pacing back and forth in his study, had dic-tated his reply. Direct and sincere, his speeches made excellent reading in the next day's newspapers. They stressed good will and national consensus, the tariff, the dangers of free silver, and the Republican pledge to seek an international agreement for silver. Inflation was harmful, and would not help farmers as much as stable growth and a safe domestic market. "That which we call money, my fellow citizens, . . . must be as true as the bushel which measures the grain of the farmer, and as honest as the hours of labor which the man who toils is required to give." After a handshake and a last farewell, the visitors left for home with a souvenir piece of the fence or lawn, and exciting stories about meeting the handsome, genial McKinley. Delegations passed through Canton at an impressive rate, enabling McKinley at home to rival the impact of Bryan on tour. In the four months of the campaign, he spoke more than 300 times to 750,000 people from 30 states.[61]

While McKinley voiced the issues, Hanna organized the campaign. He did it brilliantly, assembling a team of talented individuals to staff a highly efficient organization. He established twin headquarters in New York and Chicago, and shuttled between them. "I will be in the saddle, so to speak, and be found at both places at different times." The New York office oversaw operations in the Northeast and raised money. At first, money only trickled in, but the growing fear of Bryan among business and the well-to-do increased the trickle to a torrent. In 1896 the Republicans raised $3,500,000, twice as much as Harrison had spent four years before. Hanna enlisted Platt and Quay in the eastern campaign, and persuaded Reed to stump in New England and the Pacific Coast. In the Chicago office, the more important of the two, Charles G. Dawes, a young Chicago banker and McKinley friend, supervised efforts in the vital Midwest. Known as "The General" among his subordinates, Dawes rivaled Hanna in energy and efficiency. Together, they constructed an educational campaign that has never been matched in American politics.[62]

To do it, Dawes dispensed almost $2,000,000, four times as much as Bryan's entire campaign. He spent nearly $500,000 on printing, another $150,000 on speakers. In mid-September he was supporting 250 speakers in 27 states. Each week his Bureau of Publication and Printing distributed boiler plate (preset type) and other materials to newspapers reaching five million families. Dawes targeted voting groups and assigned specific subordinates to work on them. Besides a Literary Bureau and a Speakers' Bureau, his Chicago office had a "Colored Voters' Department," a Woman's Department (though women could not vote in the election except in Wyoming, Utah, and Colorado), and a German office. There were even departments to deal with bicyclists and traveling salesmen. A group of Union Army generals, assembled in a "Patriotic Heroes Battalion," toured in a flag-draped train to rally veterans. During the last two weeks of the campaign, Dawes dispatched 1400 orators to complete McKinley's strategy: to "talk tariff, think tariff, dream tariff."[63]

Dawes also assembled a team of writers who turned out campaign pamphlets in a dozen languages, including German, French, Spanish, Italian, Swedish, Norwegian, and Hebrew. In all, he sent out over 200,000,000 pamphlets, ample reading matter for the country's 15,000,000 voters. The New York headquarters added another 20,000,000 pamphlets, distributed mostly in the Northeast. The mailing room in Chicago employed 100 workers, and boxcars loaded with literature left the city daily. There were 275 different pamphlets, nearly all of them tailored to a specific voting group and locale. Pamphlets treated the impact of free silver and the tariff on coal miners, ranchers, iron and steel workers, wool growers, wheat farmers, and a host of other groups. From Chicago, they went to state Republican committees, which in turn sent them on to county and precinct workers for distribution among the voters. Apparently they were read and reread, discussed, and passed from hand to hand. By election day, the Republicans had distributed more literature than in all their presidential campaigns since the founding of the party in the 1850s.[64]

Cleverly, the Republicans varied their appeal to suit the tastes of particular regions. Everywhere they stressed prosperity, the need, as Reed put it, to "re-build out of the ruins of the last four years the stately mansions of national happiness, prosperity and self-respect." In the Northeast, they emphasized sound money, confident of a large turnout against Bryan. In the Midwest, they touted the home-grown McKinley, the Advance Agent of Prosperity, and the benefits of the tariff and a stable currency for the region's developing urban-industrial system. A similar strategy prevailed in the Border States, where Republicans hoped to capitalize on widespread doubts about Bryan and silver. Farther west, campaigners mixed the tariff and currency, adroitly using the tariff issue to woo moderate silverites who feared Democratic low tariffs. Emphasizing McKinley's commitment to international bimetallism, many Republicans in the West campaigned openly for silver, a tactic that held some silverites in the McKinley fold and kept the western campaign from becoming a clear-cut contest between silver and gold.[65]

By September, McKinley had clearly blunted the Bryan drive. In October, he built skillfully on the advantage, taking a comfortable lead in most of the important states. "The election is going to be a tremendous landslide in our favor," Dawes predicted on October 1. Thorough organization and a campaign of education had done the job. In the end, Bryan's single-minded silver crusade had faltered, as crusades often do. It won new voters, but alienated many others, who preferred McKinley's calm pluralism. While Bryan spoke of class, ethnic, and sectional divisions, McKinley stressed broad, positive programs in which everyone could share. "We are all dependent on each other, no matter what our occupation may be," he said. "All of us want good times, good wages, good markets; and then we want good money always." United, the nation could turn with renewed vigor to the critical tasks at hand, a process in which farmers, laborers, and manufacturers—city and country, East and West, natives and foreign-born—all had vital roles to play.[66]

To buttress the point, Hanna closed the campaign with a national "flag day" on Saturday, October 31. In cities and towns across the North, thousands upon thousands of marchers paraded through flag-decked streets, cheering and shouting for McKinley. The demonstrations countered Democratic charges that businessmen had coerced employees into supporting McKinley. In San Francisco, the parade lasted four hours. In Chicago, it lasted five hours and involved 100,000 marchers. In New York, more than 100,000 people marched, and 750,000 lined the streets to cheer. McKinley presided over a large rally in Canton, complete with forty brass bands. American flags hung everywhere. "No flag represents as much as it does," McKinley declared; "it represents liberty, it represents equality, it represents opportunity, it represents possibilities for American manhood obtainable in no other land beneath the sun." On November 2, the day before the election, Hanna and Dawes reviewed final details and forecast overwhelming victory. At home, McKinley waited patiently, his porch and lawn a wreck, himself tired and confident, pleased that the taxing "battle of the standards" was nearly over.[67]

☆☆☆

Bryan and his wife rose at 6:30 on election day and voted at a local fire station. Reporters joked with the weary candidate, trying in pantomime to persuade him to vote for McKinley. McKinley walked four blocks to his polling place and waited in line to vote. Hanna arrived early in the afternoon with favorable reports. "You are all right; everything is going swimmingly," he said. Across the nation, voter turnout was extraordinarily high, a measure of the intense popular interest in the issues and the candidates. Observers called it the most important election since 1860. In hotly contested Illinois, Indiana, Iowa, Michigan, and Ohio, turnout reached 95 percent of the eligible voters, a figure that would rarely be approached again. That evening, huge crowds gathered around newspaper offices to watch the returns. By nightfall the outcome was clear. William McKinley had won the greatest presidential victory in twenty-four years.[68]

He won a great swath of states from Maine to North Dakota, took Oregon and California, and carried four Border States: Maryland, Delaware, Kentucky, and West Virginia. For the first time in twenty years, a Republican presidential candidate had broken into the Solid South. Nationwide, McKinley won 271 electoral votes to 176 for Bryan. He took 7,111,607 votes (50 percent of the total) to Bryan's 6,509,052 (46 percent), the largest margin for either party since Ulysses S. Grant's victory in 1872. Palmer and the Cleveland Democrats got only 134,645 votes, a dismal total, but helped swing several close states into the McKinley column. Thousands of Cleveland Democrats voted directly for McKinley. Reflecting the turnout, both Bryan and McKinley received more votes than any previous candidate of their respective parties. Even in defeat, Bryan won 750,000 more votes than Cleveland had in 1892. But McKinley won nearly 2,000,000 more votes than had Harrison. Bryan carried 26 states and territories, most of them in the sparsely populated Rocky Mountain, Plains, and Deep South regions. He failed to hold the Democratic South, did not sweep the West, and carried no states at all in the Midwest.[69]

Disgruntled, Bryan's campaign manager promptly charged that the outcome stemmed from "every kind of coercion and intimidation on the part of the money power, including threats of lockouts and dismissals, and impending starvation."[70] Hanna and the money power, in short, had bribed and threatened their way to victory. Such legends, understandably attractive to defeated candidates, die hard. Suasion and coercion certainly took place on both sides: among some employers who pressured workers to support McKinley, and among some Democrats who used fraud and intimidation in the cities and against black voters in the South. But coercion did not determine the outcome in 1896. Bryan lost because in a campaign of education, he failed to lure the critical voters: the labor, farm, immigrant, middle class, and other voters who were sure they had a stake in urban-industrial America. McKinley won precisely because he attracted those voters, and seemed in step with a nation preparing to move into the twentieth century.

McKinley swept the densely populated Northeast and Midwest, including the eight states—New York, New Jersey, Pennsylvania, Ohio, Indiana, Illinois, Michigan, and Wisconsin—in which one-half of the country's total vote was polled. In the two regions, he won a clear majority of the rural vote and took the urban centers, which had generally gone for Cleveland in 1892. McKinley crushed Bryan in the cities, extending the pattern of Republican gains there that emerged two years before. Bryan carried only one midwestern city with more than 45,000 inhabitants, lost San Francisco, Philadelphia, Baltimore, and other cities, and won only seven of Boston's twenty-five wards. He lost both New York and Kings (Brooklyn) counties, the first Democratic candidate to do so since the 1840s. He also lost Chicago, where McKinley piled up 58 percent of the vote. In Newark, New Jersey, McKinley won fourteen of the fifteen wards. In Trenton, he won a startling 68 percent of the vote. In eighty-five midwestern cities, where

Cleveland's plurality in 1892 had been 162,000 votes, McKinley out-polled Bryan by 464,000.[71]

Dwelling on free silver, Bryan had failed to create a labor consti-tuency. In northern cities, he lost votes in working-class as well as middle-class and silk-stocking districts. In New England, he took less than one-third of the vote. He carried only one county in all of New York State, and none of the industrial cities of the South. Bryan tried to ally the South and West, but lost crucial portions of each. He did well in the once-Republican Plains and Mountain States, and fell just a few thousand votes short in California, Kentucky, Indiana, and other needed states. On the other hand, he carried Nebraska, his home state, by barely 13,000 votes. McKinley also pressed him in Tennessee, Virginia, Kansas, South Dakota, and Wyoming, a sign of the effective-ness of the Republican campaign. A rise in crop prices before the election, related to crop failures abroad, hurt Bryan in wheat and corn producing areas. He had linked wheat prices to the price of silver, a connection now disproven. In the Midwest, thousands of German Lutherans and Catholics, attracted by sound money and McKinley's pluralism, helped tip the region to McKinley. Ironically, Bryan, the crusading moralist, lost votes in the same way the Republican pietists had earlier in the decade.[72]

On election night, Bryan sadly studied the returns, looking, said a newsman who was with him, like "a General reading the reports of some great battle in which whole armies were swept away." He retired early, and the next day wired McKinley his congratulations, the first losing candidate ever to do so: "We have submitted the issues to the American people and their will is law." Although disappointed, Bryan was justifiably proud. At the age of 36, he had taken control of a major political party and won more than six million votes. He made numer-ous errors, but brought the Democrats closer to victory than any other candidate could have done. In part, his loss reflected a continuation of 1894's devastating anti-Democratic trend. Bryan's emotional crusade for silver capitalized on agrarian discontent, buoyed disheartened Democrats, and attracted voters who otherwise would not have sup-ported the Democratic ticket. His terse explanation for his defeat— "I have borne the sins of Grover Cleveland"—oversimplified the out-come, but made considerable sense. The nominee of a divided and discredited party, he had come remarkably close to winning. Bryan promptly called 1896 the "First Battle" and prepared for 1900. "The fight has just begun," he told followers the night after the election.[73]

For the Populists, the election marked an end rather than a beginning. The Bryan-Watson ticket got only 222,583 votes (less than 2 percent of the popular vote), and Populist totals were down nearly everywhere. McKinley's victory dazed party leaders. Deeply embittered, Watson left politics for law, saying: "Our party, as a party, does not exist any more." Donnelly was despondent. "Will the long lane never have a turning?" he wrote in his diary. "Will the sun of triumph never rise?" It never did. Vestiges of the party lingered into the new century, but only as shadows. Fewer than 80 delegates attended its 1898 national convention, and the elections that fall sped the downward slide. In 1900, 1904, and 1908, it mounted weak presidential campaigns that came to nothing. The Populist heyday had passed quickly, and was over by 1894. The Bryan campaign was simply a final flourish. In its time, the party won some successes, but not the ones that mattered most. It could not preserve the small independent farmer in an era of consolidation and complex growth. It could not restore agrarian power in a nation that hurried toward city and factory. In a political system that built on majorities, it never won a majority of the country's voters. It never even came close, and failing, declined as swiftly as it had arisen.[74]

Cleveland spent election night with his cabinet at the White House, following the returns. Long after midnight they parted, satisfied that McKinley had won. There was sadness in the occasion, and thoughts turned naturally to what might have been. At the start of the decade Democratic hopes had been high. Successive elections in 1890 and 1892 repudiated the Republican party and seemingly established permanent Democratic rule. It was not to be. Within a short time, amid depression, internal dissension, and glaring inability to govern, Cleveland and the Democrats had squandered their hard-won gains. Cleveland never quite understood what had happened. He left office in March 1897, the most unpopular president since Andrew Johnson. A few old friends gathered at the ceremony marking the inauguration of his successor. McKinley had the presidency, Bryan had the party, and for Cleveland there was only bitter retirement. William L. Wilson, himself a sad victim in the decade's drama, caught the mood that inaugural day. "I felt very much like I had been to a funeral," he said.[75]

In Canton, election night brought giant celebrations. Workers tied down the switches on factory steam whistles, boys yelled through megaphones, and crowds shouted around the McKinley house. The din

End of Populists

mounted through the early night. "Pandemonium is let loose," said a reporter. "Canton is beside itself with joy." In his study, McKinley was already turning his attention to devising a cabinet and policy for the new administration. The prospects seemed exciting. The election of 1896 cemented the voter revolution of 1894, and together the two elections closed a distinct era in American political history. They terminated the politics of equilibrium and laid the foundation for a generation of Republican rule. For more than three decades after 1896, with only a brief Democratic resurgence under Woodrow Wilson, the Republicans remained the country's majority party. They had won the decade's crucial battle for party mastery, and now, at last, they could govern.[76]

A blend of piety and pragmatism, the president-elect prayed for guidance, yet did not neglect to consult key Republican leaders. Fashioning his administration, he planned to move vigorously on the tariff and international bimetallism, work to restore relations with Congress, so badly deteriorated under Cleveland, and hope for prosperity. Foreign affairs required sensitive attention. There were troubles in Cuba, which threatened war with Spain. In the aftermath of the election, the country relaxed, happy to leave behind the tart divisiveness of the mid-1890s. People thronged to see the president-elect, who once again was a symbol of national unity. The decade so far seemed a kaleidoscope of change and flashing movement, with little opportunity for planning or reflection. Perhaps now the pace of change could slow, and tempers mellow. If all went well, the next four years would carry McKinley and the nation triumphantly into the twentieth century.

The Years of Power, 1897-1901

In 1897 the White House, like the presidency itself, was caught between eras. Built a century before, rebuilt after the British burned it during the War of 1812, it badly needed repair. Inside, the paint was dull and cracked, the wallpaper peeling. Carpets, curtains, and furniture were old and decaying. So was the flooring. For large receptions, aides placed extra posts in the basement to shore up the floor, and prayed that no foreign delegation would suddenly disappear through it. The mansion had some "modern" conveniences, including running water, telephones, and an elevator: the last, a groaning, creaking contraption, powered by water pressure from a tank on the roof. Harrison had installed electric lights, but disliked to turn them on and off for fear of shock. The staff fit the decor. Many dated from Reconstruction, or before. One had first been hired as Lincoln's bodyguard. The doorkeeper had held the door the last time for Lincoln and James A. Garfield, and took pride in it, though others might have thought it a bad omen. Along Pennsylvania Avenue in front, an automobile occasionally chugged past, signaling the coming of a new era. During his term McKinley became the first president to ride in an automobile, reaching the handsome and frightening speed of eighteen miles an hour.[1]

The president earned $50,000 a year, a princely sum, but out of it had to pay some of the employees and expenses of the mansion. The presidency itself was still rooted in the people, not yet the august, forbidding force it became in the twentieth century. The public roamed freely through the White House grounds, though fears for Cleveland's life had closed off some portions. Visitors had access to all of the mansion's first floor, except the dining room. Three times a week, the downstairs filled up with tourists, politicians, and townspeople, who had come to greet the president. At state receptions as many as four thousand guests passed through the receiving line, with practiced greeters like McKinley moving them skillfully along, shaking 1800 hands an hour. For privacy, the president's family retreated to the west wing of the second floor, whose five bedrooms and two dressing rooms made up the private living quarters. The rest of the second floor was open to newsmen, official callers, cabinet officers, and others. Even as McKinley took office, ex-president Harrison complained strongly in the *Ladies' Home Journal* about the difficult working conditions at the White House.[2]

Moving in on March 4, 1897, the McKinleys established themselves quickly in the country's fancy. Mrs. McKinley was an invalid, requiring her husband's constant attention. Several times a day he left meetings and work to look in on her in the family living quarters. The new president himself seemed open and accessible, a pleasant contrast to Cleveland's forbidding isolation. He rode the Washington street cars, walked the streets, and enjoyed looking in department store windows. Children lay in wait for him in the avenues around the White House, anticipating his smile and ready greeting. In the afternoons he walked with aides in "the yard," as a homespun administration called the White House grounds. Evenings he relaxed on the back piazza of the mansion, puffing contentedly on a cigar and chatting with congressional and party leaders as the evening traffic flowed by. An activist president, McKinley ran the administration and set its policies. Conscious of the limits of power, he maintained close ties with Congress and worked hard to educate the public on national choices and priorities.[3]

The days were full and busy. McKinley soon abandoned the crowded presidential office on the mansion's second floor, and took over the cabinet room next door. Seated in a swivel armchair at the head of the long cabinet table, he met visitors, dictated letters, and conducted the business of the administration. A short distance away stood a large globe, around which the president and cabinet would soon gather to locate distant and little-known places like Guam and the Philippines. An exceptional administrator, McKinley chose a capable staff, especially George B. Cortelyou, his assistant personal secretary. Bright and talented, frosty in manner, Cortelyou seemed to hurtle through work. He supervised the staff, typed McKinley's major speeches and state papers, saw to his personal safety, helped organize his day, managed relations with the press, and performed a host of other functions. McKinley started with a staff of six, the number Cleveland had used, but soon found it inadequate to keep up with the heightened pace of the new administration. By the end of the first term, the staff numbered eighteen, and still over-worked, reflected some of the important changes McKinley had wrought in the presidency.[4]

The cabinet was average in ability, sound in reputation, and advanced in age. Its youngest member was 54. Its oldest, at 74, was John Sherman, who had consented to serve as secretary of state. McKinley revered Sherman, whom he had known for years, and thought his decade's service on the Senate Foreign Relations Committee qualified him for the post. A well-intentioned gesture, designed to honor Sherman at the close of his long career, it did not turn out well. Sherman had little taste for the job and insufficient energy for its mounting demands. He suffered lapses in hearing and memory that embarrassed McKinley and the foreign diplomats he dealt with. McKinley also erred in the selection of Russell A. Alger of Michigan as secretary of war. A Civil War general and midwestern timber magnate, Alger was popular and affable, and his appointment satisfied westerners, Union Army veterans, and influential Republicans like Platt and Quay. He was also indecisive, lazy, and in frail health. In older, more placid times, Sherman and Alger would have been perfectly satisfactory, but the coming years would test cabinet officials as they had not been tested in decades. "He is a sanguine, generous man," as a fellow cabinet member later said of Alger, "but the task—and it is a tremendous one—is too much for him."[5]

McKinley offered Hanna the postmaster generalship, but Hanna preferred to wait for Sherman's vacated Senate seat. For secretary of the treasury, one of the most important posts, McKinley turned to Lyman J. Gage, the president of the First National Bank of Chicago. Cautious and respected, Gage was an excellent choice that pleased midwestern Republicans and gold Democrats, and signaled the administration's commitment to the gold standard. John D. Long, a popular former governor of Massachusetts and old McKinley friend, became secretary of the Navy, another of the positions that assumed sudden importance in 1898. McKinley's cabinet measured his ability to grow in the presidency. As the need became apparent, he found better men for the vital posts, and in two years replaced all but three of the original cabinet. The appointment of John Hay as secretary of state in 1898 and Elihu Root as secretary of war a year later showed his growing strength. The cultured and witty Hay, whom McKinley had first appointed ambassador to Great Britain, had the taste, energy, and experience Sherman had lacked. Root was brilliant and tough, a tight-lipped driving lawyer with the right qualities to help McKinley through the difficult crises ahead.[6]

McKinley turned the administration easily to his wishes. "He was a man of great power," Root said, "because he was absolutely indifferent to credit . . . but McKinley *always had his way.*" He preferred to persuade rather than dictate, cajole rather than command, and sometimes had difficulty making up his mind. His patience and tact were legendary. As Cortelyou, who knew him well, said: he was "the strong man," "the dominating force," yet he acted with "a gentleness and graciousness" that bound men to him and masked his triumphs. McKinley restored the pulse of leadership lost under Cleveland. Unlike Cleveland, he trusted the people and kept close watch on public opinion. He consulted Congress, struck new relations with the press, and traveled far more than previous presidents. In four and a half years, he made more than forty trips outside the capital, including major speaking forays in 1898, 1899, and 1901. He, not Theodore Roosevelt, established the presidency as the nation's focus, its "bully pulpit." McKinley consolidated the Republican victories of the mid-1890s and in some sense began the modern presidency. Though the flamboyant Roosevelt overshadowed him after death, McKinley ranks among the most important presidents.[7]

☆☆☆

Once in office, McKinley moved swiftly to implement pledges from the 1896 campaign. His inaugural address reaffirmed support for international bimetallism, proposed a commission of experts to study the coinage, banking, and currency laws, and summoned Congress into special session for March 15, 1897 to revise the tariff. The Republican members of the House Ways and Means Committee, under Nelson

Dingley, Jr., of Maine, a renowned master of the tariff's intricacies, had been working on a tariff bill since the previous December. McKinley consulted closely with his friend Dingley, and through him, Hanna, and others, leaked hints that the administration wanted a moderate tariff law. It also wanted a fresh start on reciprocity, ended by the Democrats in 1894. Reciprocity boosted trade, provided markets for surplus farm and manufactured products, and benefited foreign policy, McKinley said in his inaugural address and again in speeches during the summer and fall of 1897. "Good trade insures good will," he told a Cincinnati commercial group. "It should be our settled purpose to open trade wherever we can, making our ships and our commerce messengers of peace and amity."[8]

The Dingley bill was ready when Congress met. A moderate measure, it left hides and copper on the free list, took raw wool off the list, placed high duties on woollens, silks, and linens, and left the main iron and steel schedules largely untouched. In the most important change, it almost doubled the duty on sugar, an effective revenue-producing item, in order to end the Treasury deficits that had existed since 1893. The Republicans had Speaker Reed and ample margins in the House, and the bill passed easily on March 31, after only two weeks of debate. Conditions were different in the Senate, where they had a shaky one-vote margin. The Finance Committee moved many duties lower, but in the party caucus, Senate leaders had to soothe and conciliate, working especially with western Republicans, most of them still-bitter silverites, who demanded a duty on hides and much higher duties on wool, lead, lead ore, and beet sugar. That summer, with McKinley and others in the audience, the annual Gridiron Club dinner spoofed the process. A House member carried a large scroll, labeled "the Dingley bill," off-stage to the Senate. He returned, the bill in shreds, his hat awry, clothes torn and battered. "Mr. Speaker," he reported simply, "I have been there." McKinley, Reed, and Dingley roared with laughter.[9]

In the end, the Senate added 872 amendments, most of them unimportant, and passed the bill on July 7. A smaller number of amendments had split the Democrats in 1894, but the Republicans moved amicably to iron out the differences. In conference committee, the Senate retained the duty on hides, though at a lower rate, and the other concessions made to the westerners. The House won most of the major battles, and the final bill closely resembled Dingley's original measure. It raised average duties to a record level, but largely because of the new sugar duty. On products like cotton and tinplate, it imposed lower duties than the 1890 McKinley Act. Iron ore, pig iron, and steel rails stayed at the rates of the Wilson-Gorman Act. But if many rates moved downward from the McKinley levels, the sugar, wool, and silk schedules moved average duties higher than ever before. An old hand at the tensions of tariff making, Dingley was pleased. Out of conference, his bill quickly passed the House and Senate, and McKinley signed it on July 24, 1897. In four months the Republicans had passed their tariff law, a heady contrast to the Democrats' performance in 1894.[10]

Before long, the Dingley Act would trouble the Republican party. The final burst of nineteenth century protectionism, it reflected the flush of the 1896 victory, the thought that higher rates might cure the depression, and the culmination of a generation of Republican tariff doctrines. It tried to balance high rates with reciprocity provisions, but adopted a form of reciprocity less effective than the 1890 version. It authorized the president to lower duties on art works, brandy, and wine, a concession designed to enlist France in the fight for international bimetallism; to use the threat of penalty duties on coffee and tea to win trade benefits from Latin America; and most important, to negotiate treaties reducing the Dingley rates as much as 20 percent in exchange for similar reductions on American products. McKinley had hoped for more. The treaties, for example, had to be negotiated within two years, could run for only five years, and needed ratification by Congress. But he acted speedily after signing the law. He began reciprocity negotiations in August 1897, and in October named a veteran congressman and diplomat, John A. Kasson, to head a special reciprocity team in the State Department.[11]

In two years Kasson negotiated seventeen treaties, including major pacts with France, Argentina, Jamaica, and Ecuador. McKinley submitted them to Congress in late 1899, and tried gently to move the Republican party toward lower tariffs and reciprocity. Both trade and politics, he thought, demanded it. Through 1897 and 1898 he spoke frequently for reciprocity. In February 1899, he told the Boston Commercial Club: "We have quit discussing the tariff, and have turned our attention to getting trade wherever it can be found. . . . [We] are seeking our share of the world's markets." On his cross-country tour that year, he again stressed the need for outside markets. McKinley, the symbol of "McKinleyism," had changed his views during the 1890s. He kept his faith in the tariff, but came to favor greater sophistication in its use. The modern world claimed a new unity, with once-vast distances shortened by telegraph, telephones, steamships, and trains. "God and man have linked the nations together. . . ," he said in his last speech at Buffalo, New York, in 1901. "Isolation is no longer possible or desirable. . . . The period of exclusiveness is past."[1 2]

Individuals changed more easily than parties, and for McKinley's party, the issue was fraught with trouble. Since the Civil War the Republicans had demanded unswerving loyalty to the protective system. Now, many of them found it difficult to modify lifelong views. Others saw reciprocity as a threat to domestic enterprise and a denial of patriotic virtues. With the return of prosperity, midwestern Republicans renewed pleas for lower duties, and soon won attractive newcomers like Jonathan P. Dolliver, Senator Albert J. Beveridge of Indiana, and Governor Robert M. La Follette of Wisconsin. In Iowa, another up-and-coming Republican, Albert B. Cummins, helped popularize the "Iowa Idea," a proposal to remove or lower tariffs that sheltered trusts and monopolies. By the decade's end, consumers, critics, and the Republicans themselves were asking tough questions about the tariff. Had it outlived its usefulness in the maturing American economy? Did it foster monopolies, squeeze out small businesses, raise prices, and provide artificial profits for giant grasping combinations? Did it stand, as William Jennings Bryan soon charged, "at the cradle" of the trusts?[1 3]

McKinley responded, but because he usually moved quietly, many in the country did not know how far he had traveled. High-tariff advocates knew, and were stunned. His death in 1901 stilled the movement, clouded the issue, and brought to power a president less conscious of the growing tensions over the tariff. Roosevelt and the party repressed the issue for several years, but in 1909, when a tariff bill again came before Congress, Republican unity dissolved in a bitter fight. The tariff and reciprocity debate of 1897 to 1901 foreshadowed the fight, and also reflected larger questions of national and party policy. In part, the Republicans in the late nineteenth century had built their consensus on a pledge to *promote,* to use the varieties of state and national power to develop the country's full potential. By 1900, with the industrial system firmly in place, the focus had shifted. The need to *regulate,* to control the effects of industrialism and large-scale enterprise, became a central public concern of the new century. McKinley prodded the Republicans to meet that shift, but died before his plans matured. It became another of the important transitions over which he presided.[1 4]

☆☆☆

To everyone's relief, the economy began to revive during 1897. Unemployment remained disturbingly high—15 percent that year and 10 percent as late as 1899—but most indices showed the swift flood of returning confidence. In April the stock market rose. Investment blossomed, as businessmen, suddenly optimistic, started to plan and build. Farmers prospered. Farm prices climbed sharply during 1897, reflecting bumper crops of wheat, cotton, and corn. Farm exports also rose, especially to Europe where crops were poor. On August 21, wheat sold at $1 per bushel in Chicago, the highest price since 1891. Iron and steel production reached record highs, and American furnaces turned out 30 percent of the world's pig iron. Exports in 1897 passed the billion-dollar mark, another record. Soft spots remained, and the economy did not reach full capacity again until about 1901. But for the first time since 1890, the 1897 Treasury statements showed a net inflow of gold. The gold reserve stood at a comfortable $160,-000,000, well above the level that Cleveland had sacrificed so much to maintain.[15]

The Republicans basked in the glow. They were the party of progress and prosperity, an image that built victories until the 1930s and Herbert Hoover. McKinley's popularity soared. Crowds cheered wherever he went, and the press praised the fresh sense of national unity and purpose. Congress and the president worked together. Enjoying political talk, McKinley met frequently with key congressmen, Democrats as well as Republicans, over small dinners or in private chats. He quietly molded legislation and vetoed only fourteen bills in his entire term. During 1897 he acted decisively. In March he tightened the civil service rules and called Congress into special session for the tariff. In April he named a three-member commission, headed by Senator Edward O. Wolcott of Colorado, a leading silver Republican, to work with European governments for international bimetallism. In the early summer, he pressed Congress to form a commission to reform the banking and currency laws. In June he signed a treaty of annexation with Hawaii, and submitted it to the Senate, where it languished amid growing concern about the situation on the island of Cuba.[16]

Cuba: the word stirred complex emotions. Long a center of Spain's vast empire in the New World, it had once housed royal governors who oversaw dominions stretching across two continents. Now, the dominions were mostly gone, and Cuba itself, the rich and fertile "Ever

Faithful Isle," was in rebellion. Decades old, the rebellion began in the 1860s, flickered, then burst out again in 1895. Americans followed it closely, most of them keenly sympathetic to the revolutionary cause. They admired the Cuban struggle for independence and wanted somehow to help the suffering people, especially after 1896 when a new Spanish general, Valeriano Weyler, arrived to stamp out the rebellion. Adopting drastic measures, including a reconcentration policy that swept Cubans from the countryside into diseased and crowded camps near the cities, "Butcher" Weyler won battles against the insurgents, but lost the decisive campaign for American public opinion. In the end, he convinced Americans that something had to be done.[17]

Some Americans needed little convincing. Talk of expansion had grown for years, feeding on racial doctrines, a sense of national mission in the world, the example of European colonial expansion, and other considerations. Many people—perhaps most—resisted the idea, but still, Americans in the 1890s showed greater interest in outward involvements, particularly in Asia and Latin America. Controversies involving Chile, Hawaii, Samoa, Haiti, Venezuela, Brazil, and Cuba illustrated the trend. Harrison and Blaine looked outward to the Caribbean and Pacific. Cleveland squabbled with Great Britain over the Venezuela boundary. Captain Alfred T. Mahan, an influential naval theorist, stressed the importance of enlarged markets, an efficient merchant marine, and a swift, powerful Navy to protect both. By the late 1890s Americans had a new consciousness of their position in the world, a sense that the Cuban situation sharpened.

The so-called "yellow press," a group of circulation-hungry New York newspapers, fanned emotion over Cuba, printing lurid tales of Spanish cruelty. Pro-Cuban sentiment grew and spilled across party lines. Congress, the 1896 Republican platform, many silver Republicans, most southern Democrats, and William Jennings Bryan all favored a free Cuba. "It is to our direct interest to get Spain out of the island," a Republican senator wrote. "The less of Europe we have over here the better."[18] Clinging to silver, Bryan warmed slowly to the Cuban cause, but by early 1898, had taken to waving small Cuban and American flags during speeches. The issue was popular, and Republican leaders warned that the Democrats might use it to recoup their recent losses. "Free Cuba" and "Free Silver" could make attractive slogans in 1898 and 1900. Seizing the advantage, the Democrats flooded the 1897 special session with speeches, memorials, and resolutions on Cuba. Republicans responded with resolutions of their own. Reed, who thought the whole agitation dangerous, headed off action in the House, but the congressmen had made their point. Somehow the turmoil and killing must cease.[19]

Though sympathetic to the Cuban struggle, McKinley wanted a solution that would stop short of war. "War," he said at his inauguration, "should never be entered upon until every agency of peace has failed; peace is preferable to war in almost every contingency." Cuba worried him from the start. The lengthening stalemate inflamed opinion, damaged American investments, and invited foreign intervention, particularly from Germany, whose ambitious young Kaiser coveted naval bases in the crumbling Spanish empire. Determined to end the conflict, McKinley in July 1897 settled on a two-pronged policy: persuade Spain to accept American mediation, "civilize" the war, and ultimately relax or relinquish her hold on the island. Meanwhile, win breathing space from an impatient public in order to give Spain an opportunity to comply. Courageous, the policy braved opinion at home, but included a fatal condition. McKinley respected the Cubans' right to self-determination and early decided not to impose a settlement on them. Since they demanded independence, which Spain would never grant, the McKinley policy had scant chance of success.[20]

McKinley knew that, but clung tenaciously to both peace and the Cubans. The important thing was time: time to let the Cuban situation develop, time above all to let Spain adjust to the painful new realities. Even in the final days before the war, McKinley was still fighting for time, hoping for a last-minute shift in Spanish policy. In October 1897, a new ministry in Madrid announced substantial concessions, including the recall of Weyler, an end to the reconcentration policy, a release of American prisoners in Cuba, and a promise of more humane methods of warfare. There was even a plan of autonomy for the Cubans, though under Spanish control. Pressing for more, McKinley used the concessions to keep intervention-minded opponents off balance. Reed held a tight rein on the House, while Hanna, Lodge, George F. Hoar, John C. Spooner, and William B. Allison worked to cool ardor in the Senate. In December McKinley devoted more than a third of his annual message to Cuba, pointing to the "hopeful change" in Spanish policy and urging continued patience.[21]

Time and patience suddenly ran out in the middle of February, 1898. In late January, Spanish Army officers opposed to autonomy helped sack newspaper offices in Havana, and a flurry of pro-Cuban resolutions again swept Congress. Soon after, McKinley sent the battle-ship *Maine* to Havana as a gesture of strength and good will. On February 9, the New York *Journal,* a leader of the "yellow press," published a letter stolen from Enrique Dupuy de Lome, the Spanish minister in Washington, in which he called McKinley "weak," "a would-be politician," and "a bidder for the admiration of the crowd." Head-lines flared the insult, though the president ignored it. He worried more about other sections of the letter, which revealed Spanish in-sincerity in the negotiations. By coincidence, the next day's mail brought an official note from Spain, stiffening her position. Five days later, at 9:40 in the evening of February 15, as the *Maine* rode at anchor in Havana harbor, an explosion ripped through her hull. The ship, a trim symbol of the new steel Navy, sank quickly, with the loss of 260 lives.[22]

McKinley got the news at 3 A.M., shaking his head in disbelief. After dawn, looking tired and careworn, he conferred with the cabinet and leading members of Congress. There would be an immediate in-vestigation of the sinking, he told them, and again urged patience. Spain had expressed regrets. Crowds gathered quietly on Capitol Hill and outside the White House, mourning the lost men. Soon there was a new slogan: "Remember the *Maine* and to Hell with Spain!" and a new bitterness. "I can't see how the explosion could have been the result of an accident," Shelby M. Cullom, a Republican senator, said to a reporter, "and I think the time is rapidly approaching when this country should do something."[23] Most people seemed willing to wait for the investigation, as McKinley requested, but patience clearly was wearing thin. Republicans feared defeat in the important Novem-ber elections and perhaps even a revival of free silver. Lodge reported conversations with dozens of Massachusetts Republicans, supporters of the president's Cuban policy, who thought the time had come to act. "If the war in Cuba drags on through the summer with nothing done," Lodge warned, "we shall go down in the greatest defeat ever known before the cry: 'Why have you not settled the Cuban ques-tion.'"[24]

Still, McKinley delayed. Through February and March he pressed Spain for the crucial concessions of armistice and, implicitly, inde-pendence. In early March, wanting to be ready for war if it came, he asked Congress for $50,000,000 in emergency defense appropriations. On March 27, with the report of the investigating board at last in hand, he cabled Spain his final terms. The following day he released the report, which blamed the sinking on an external, and thus, to the public, presumably Spanish explosion. Tempers snapped, and for a few weeks McKinley's popularity plummeted. Theater audiences cheered the Star-Spangled Banner and hissed the president's picture. In Virginia and Colorado, he was hanged or burned in effigy. Theodore Roosevelt, assistant secretary of the Navy, who believed a war with Spain would strengthen character, shook a fist at Mark Hanna and called for war.[25]

Bryan summoned reporters to say, "the time for intervention has arrived. Humanity demands that we shall act."[26] Democrats took up the cry, urging a speedy recognition of Cuban independence. Influential business and Republican party journals swung over to intervention, eager to end the uncertainty. Congressmen shouted threats to act without McKinley. "Congress will declare war in spite of him," fretted Secretary of War Alger, shaken out of his easygoing manner. "He'll get run over and the party with him." In the Senate, Cullom, Joseph B. Foraker of Ohio, William P. Frye of Maine, and other Republican interventionists taunted the administration. Nearly fifty Republicans in the House caucused to protest Reed's control and assert Congress's power to declare war. Saddened, Reed agreed to give way, and Vice-President Hobart took McKinley for a long drive to report that the Senate could not be restrained much longer.[27]

McKinley waited tensely for the final Spanish answer. When it came, it conceded some things, but not the important ones, and reluctantly, he prepared his war message, which Congress heard on April 11. The message was calm, reasoned, almost dull. Congress listened in silence, applauding only the phrase: "In the name of humanity, in the name of civilization, in behalf of endangered American interests which give us the right and the duty to speak and to act, the war in Cuba must stop."[28] McKinley asked for an ultimatum to Spain and a few more days. On April 21, the ultimatum rejected, Spain severed diplomatic relations. The following day McKinley proclaimed a blockade of Cuba, and on April 23, called for 125,000 volunteers. On Monday, April 25, Congress passed a declaration of war, and late that afternoon, McKinley signed it. He was confident, but sad. Years before he had seen war and death at first hand, and disliked the memory. Now, despite all he had done, the country was at war again. Looking out the White House windows, McKinley could see cavalry and baggage wagons already en route to the Florida coast.[29]

Ten weeks later most of the fighting was over: ten glorious, dizzying weeks, with victories to fill every headline, slogans to suit every taste. On May 1, with the war barely a week old, Commodore George Dewey crushed the Spanish fleet in Manila Bay, and suddenly, Manila and the Philippines lay within grasp. Dewey portraits, songs, and poems blossomed everywhere, and his calm order to the flagship's gunner— "You may fire when ready, Gridley"—hung on every tongue. Instantly people talked of Dewey for president in 1900, though no one, including Dewey himself, knew much about his politics. In the White House, a visitor found McKinley poring over a small map of the Philippines cut from a schoolbook. Aides quickly set up a "War Room" in a corner office on the second floor, complete with giant wall maps, troop and fleet pins, and dozens of special telegraph and telephone lines. McKinley spent a great deal of time there, dispatching orders and watching the red and white pins that marked the Spanish and American fleets. Reporters were given space nearby, for the country clamored for news. Every day Cortelyou distributed a typed press release, becoming in effect the first presidential press secretary.[30]

No sooner had the Dewey fad begun than the country buzzed about the daring voyage of the great battleship *Oregon* around Cape Horn to join the Atlantic Squadron; the gameness of General Joseph "Fighting Joe" Wheeler, an old Confederate cavalryman, who led troops in the hard fighting around Santiago; the eagerness of Captain Henry Taylor, of the *Indiana,* who, spotting the Spanish fleet, shouted: "Get to your guns, lads, our chance has come at last"; the piety of Captain Jack Philip, of the *Texas:* "Don't cheer, boys, the poor devils are dying"; the patriotism of Colonel William Jennings Bryan, in charge of a regiment of Nebraska Volunteers; and the compelling gall of Lieutenant Colonel Theodore Roosevelt, who, blue polka dot handkerchief streaming in the wind, led the Rough Riders in a gallant charge up Kettle Hill. People chuckled when Wheeler, forgetting which war he was in, yelled: "We've got the damn Yankees on the run!" On July 4, Independence Day, they cheered the destruction of the main Spanish fleet off Santiago Bay. Two weeks later Santiago itself surrendered to the American Army, and the war was almost over.[31]

It had been, in John Hay's well-known phrase, "a splendid little war." It ended quickly: in 113 days, as McKinley noted again and again in the election campaign that Fall. It took relatively few lives, most of them the result of accident, yellow fever, malaria, and typhoid in Cuba. Of the 5500 men killed in the war, only 379 died in battle. The Navy lost one man at Santiago Bay, none at all in the tremendous victory at Manila Bay. Alger's War Department bungled badly in equipping, feeding, and moving the troops, but blame fell on Alger, not on McKinley or the war. Late on a rainswept Friday afternoon, August 12, 1898, representatives of Spain and the United States met in McKinley's office to sign the preliminary instrument of peace. William R. Day, who had replaced Sherman as secretary of state, beckoned Cortelyou over to the large globe, remarking: "Let's see what we get by this." What the United States got, then and later that year in the formal treaty of peace, was the Philippines, Puerto Rico, Guam, and independence for Cuba. As the representatives signed, McKinley looked on proudly. Less than four months had passed since that other Washington afternoon, when sadly he had approved the declaration of war.[32]

More than any other event in the 1890s, the war with Spain changed the country. It built confidence, altered assumptions, and reshaped the way Americans saw themselves and the world. When it was over, American possessions stretched into the Caribbean and deep into the Pacific. American influence went further still. The war established the United States as a world power, a dominant force for the new century. It brought colonies and millions of colonial subjects, imperial dreams and responsibilities. It strengthened the presidency, swept the nation together in a tide of emotion, and confirmed old traditions that democracy could defeat monarchy, the New World drub the Old. Afterward, Americans looked outward as never before, touched, they were sure, with a special providence. "My countrymen," McKinley said to a Chicago audience that October, "the currents of destiny flow through the hearts of the people. Who will check them? Who will divert them? Who will stop them?"[33]

The "currents of destiny": it seemed a happy phrase for a chosen people, as Mr. Dooley pointed out to his friend Hennessy over his Archey Road bar. "We're a gr-reat people," said Hennessy, in his rolling Irish brogue. "We ar-re that," replied Mr. Dooley. "We ar-re that. An th' best iv it is, we know we ar-re."[34]

☆☆☆

The Democrats had spent 1897 and 1898 in uneasy squabbles. From retirement ex-president Cleveland continued to fight Bryan's "bogus" leadership, "cursing," as he later said, "the animals who have burglarized and befouled the Democratic home." Equally unyielding,

Bryan turned aside advice to unify the party and play down free silver. "The gold Democrats, if they come back to the Democratic party, must come as silver men," he said bluntly.[35] Slowly the Democrats resumed their role as the party of opposition. The "system of 1896," as political scientists have called the electoral alignments that emerged from the 1894 and 1896 elections, worked against them. They were the minority party, with significant strength only in the South, a handful of northern cities, and a few Border and western states. Of the 26 Democratic senators in office after the 1898 election, none came from the Northeast, Midwest, or Pacific Coast. Twenty-two came from the South. Between 1896 and 1928, the South provided almost 85 percent of the Democrats' electoral votes.[36]

At the top Bryan remained firmly in charge, the object of fierce devotion among an army of followers. On election night in 1896 he opened his campaign for 1900. In the next three years he traveled over 92,000 miles, speaking countless times to a total of several million people. Few Democratic leaders were left to rival him. Bland, Boies, and Altgeld slumped in popularity after 1896, Tillman and other southern Democrats had difficulty attracting a national following, Hill worked to rebuild his power in New York, Carlisle quit politics to practice law, Whitney went back to making money on Wall Street, and William L. Wilson became a university president. Cleveland Democrats dominated the party in the Northeast, but in November 1897, lost badly in key races in Kentucky, Iowa, and Nebraska. In mid-1898 the head of their national committee resigned to stump for the Republicans. Gorman and others remained powerful figures in Congress, but the Democrats lacked major national leaders, a problem that lasted until 1912 when Woodrow Wilson took command.[37]

Intensely moral and patriotic, Bryan was troubled by the war. He applauded the effort to free Cuba, but feared the lure of conquest, especially in the Philippines. "Is our national character so weak that we can not withstand the temptation to appropriate the first piece of land that comes within our reach?" he asked in June 1898, just after enlisting in the Army. Cleveland and Carlisle also spoke out against expansion, indicating that the Democrats might find common ground.[38] Anti-imperialism could be popular among voters, including immigrants, who saw unhappy parallels with the European experience. Expansion meant centralized government, a growing bureaucracy, and a standing army. In areas like Puerto Rico and the Philippines, it embraced "alien" peoples of different races, an issue that worried southern

Democrats, among others. In July, in the midst of the war's excitement, Congress passed the joint resolution annexing Hawaii, a signal of events to come. Loyally Bryan kept silent in the Army, but resigned in December to campaign against imperialism. "I believe our country is in more danger now than Cuba was when I enlisted," he wrote his wife.[39]

Many in the country agreed. Andrew Carnegie, labor leader Samuel Gompers, the aging mugwump Carl Schurz, prominent Republicans like Reed, Hoar, and Sherman, the presidents of Harvard and Stanford universities, Mark Twain, and a host of others raised nagging questions about expansion. Was it constitutional? Was it right? Did a colonial empire fit with American traditions of freedom and self-government? What about ultimate statehood for the new possessions and their polyglot populations? How could the country, a meddler in Asia, uphold the Monroe Doctrine against meddling in Latin America? In November 1898, opponents of expansion formed the Anti-Imperialist League to lead the fight. Membership centered in New England, fell off in the West and South. The cause enlisted more Democrats than Republicans, though never a majority of either. The anti-imperialists lacked a coherent program. Some, like Bryan, favored keeping naval bases in the conquered areas. Some wanted Hawaii and Puerto Rico. Others wanted to give up everything. Most simply wished that Dewey had sailed away after beating the Spanish at Manila Bay.[40]

McKinley had occasionally had the same thought. If only Dewey had sailed away. Puerto Rico offered no difficulty: close to the mainland, it appealed even to anti-imperialists like Bryan. Guam, small and unknown, escaped attention. The Philippines were the problem: huge, sprawling, and distant. What should the administration do with them? It could annex them, grant them independence, give them back to Spain, or let them go, undoubtedly to be snapped up by another power. McKinley liked none of the alternatives. He could not give the islands back: Spanish power was broken there, and besides, American opinion would not allow it. If he let them go, they would fall, as he later said, "a golden apple of discord, among the rival powers."[41] Germany, Japan, Great Britain, and Russia had all expressed interest. McKinley leaned to independence for the islands, but nearly everyone who had been there thought the people were not ready. He considered a protectorate, but discarded the idea, convinced it would bring responsibilities without control. That left annexation, with an eye perhaps to future independence after a period of tutelage.[42]

Public opinion, at first hesitant, was swinging to the same conclusion. Religious and missionary organizations appealed to McKinley to keep the Philippines in order to Christianize them. Merchants and industrialists saw them as the key to the fabled China market and the wealth of Asia ("Barbarians are no customers," Carnegie retorted hotly.)[43] McKinley prodded public sentiment in October, setting off on a speaking tour through Iowa, Nebraska, Missouri, Indiana, Illinois, Ohio, and Pennsylvania. In eleven days he gave fifty-seven speeches, talking eloquently of victory and prosperity, justice, humanity, and national unity. The country had new duties and responsibilities. "In this age of frequent interchange and mutual dependence, we cannot shirk our international responsibilities if we would. . . ," he said to great applause in Omaha early in the tour. "The war was no more invited by us than were the questions which are laid at our door by its results. Now as then we will do our duty."[44]

For McKinley the tour was a heady experience. "Everywhere," he wrote a friend afterward, "there were the most enthusiastic demonstrations and the Government seemed to have the hearty support and encouragement of the people." The receptions were large, almost worshipful. Audiences cheered loudly. Local dignitaries crowded aboard the train, eager to shake hands, talk politics, and share in the president's luster. Newspapers compared him to Lincoln, the acclaimed leader of another war, whose early restraint had also won respect once the fighting began. McKinley returned to Washington heartened, more confident than ever, stiffened in his resolve to keep the Philippines. Shortly after his return, the Fall elections added to his spirits. As expected, the Republicans lost seats in the House, but fewer than usual for a mid-term election. They kept control of the House and increased their margin in the Senate.[45]

Outside the South, the Democrats did well only in the Northeast, and even there Theodore Roosevelt, the hero of Kettle Hill, took the governorship of New York. They recaptured New York City and cut into Republican totals in Pennsylvania, New York, and Massachusetts. The Republicans swept the West, ostensibly Bryan country, where the war and prosperity had sapped discontent. "Good crops and a successful war will, I imagine, prove too much for the demo-pops," a Republican had predicted in June. He was right. Kansas, Wyoming, Michigan, and California registered Republican wins. The Democrats there had stressed free silver, but voters no longer seemed interested. (Bryan stubbornly refused to admit the point: "It is a mistake to suppose the financial issue is a dead issue," he told reporters a month after the election.) Eight silver senators lost their seats, leaving the Senate in the hands of the gold men. Republicans were jubilant, looking ahead to 1900. McKinley was also pleased. For the final two years of his term, he would have a comfortable majority in both houses of Congress.[46]

One final hurdle remained. The treaty of peace with Spain, signed in Paris on December 10, 1898, needed two-thirds of the votes in the Senate for ratification. At first McKinley anticipated little difficulty. He had carefully appointed three senators to the five-member Peace Commission that negotiated the treaty. He had consulted closely with Senate leaders, who knew that to vote against the treaty meant to continue the war, an unpopular stance at best. But the issues were large, and troubles lay ahead. It had been almost three decades since the Senate had ratified an important treaty. Sixty votes were needed, and a number of thoughtful Democrats and Republicans hung back. Gorman, Hoar, William E. Mason of Illinois, Eugene Hale of Maine, George G. Vest of Missouri, and others balked at taking the Philippines. Hoar, conscientious and respected, spoke the mood of the group just before McKinley left Washington for a Christmas swing through the South. How was he feeling, McKinley asked his old friend. "Pretty pugnacious, I confess, Mr. President," Hoar replied.[47]

Pugnacious himself, McKinley was an old hand at counting up votes. In mid-December, hoping to blunt the opposition of several southern senators, he attended the Atlanta Peace Jubilee, and used the event to show the extent of pro-treaty sentiment in the South. In style and emotion, the trip almost matched his recent tour of the Midwest. McKinley was at his best, firm and eloquent, dwelling on a newly favorite theme: sectional reconciliation. The Union Army major took along General Joseph Wheeler, stood solemnly when the bands played "Dixie," reviewed parades of Confederate veterans, promised to care for the graves of Confederate dead, and proclaimed that the Spanish war had united the sections. "Sectional feeling no longer holds back the love we bear each other," he told a joint session of the Georgia legislature. At every stop, audiences cheered allusions to the war's results. The flag now waved in two hemispheres, McKinley said to loud applause in Atlanta. "Who will withdraw from the people over whom it floats its protecting folds? Who will haul it down? Answer me, ye men of the South, who is there in Dixie who will haul it down?"[48]

Debate opened in the Senate on January 4, 1899. Gorman, a shrewd strategist, led the opposition, mostly Democrats and a handful of Republicans. At the start he counted 36 votes against, five more than needed to defeat the treaty. Worried, McKinley worked both sides of the aisle, calling wavering senators to the White House for lunch, cigars, and a private chat. Lodge, Hanna, and Nelson Aldrich of Rhode Island rallied forces on the Hill. Bryan was in Washington, now an ex-colonel of Volunteers and ironically a supporter of ratification. His stand exasperated anti-expansionists like Carnegie and Gorman, who urged him to rally the Democrats and Populists to defeat the treaty. Once ratified, they argued, the treaty would acquire a sanction difficult to reverse. Bryan took a different view. He disliked the treaty, but wanted an end to the war. Then, Congress could deal separately with the question of Philippine independence, and the Democrats, the imperialism issue dead, could focus on the money and trust issues in 1900.[49]

On the final weekend before the vote, the White House could count 58 senators for ratification. All the Republicans except Hoar and Hale had come into camp, with John C. Spooner, who detested the thought of acquiring the Philippines, actually leading the constitutional debate for the treaty. That Saturday night, news came that armed conflict had broken out between American troops and Filipino insurgents under Emilio Aguinaldo, who demanded immediate independence. The news increased pressure to ratify the treaty. The following Monday, February 6, the Senate voted for the treaty 57 to 27, one vote to spare. Absent senators lowered the number needed to ratify. Ten Democrats—two of them won over at the last moment by promises of patronage—three Populists, and two Silverites joined the majority. Vice-President Hobart then cast the deciding vote against the Bacon resolution, a Bryan device, which pledged independence to the islands as soon as they had a stable government. The battle over, Hanna dashed out of the Senate chamber, hands clasped over his head. Excited crowds surged through the corridors, conscious of the historic moment. Lodge, exuberant, called it "the closest, hardest fight I have ever known."[50]

The next day Hoar appeared at the White House for a friendly talk with the president. He had lost, and now renewed assurances of loyalty and respect, which McKinley beamingly returned. The scene would have mystified some observers, but good Republicans were like that. McKinley was delighted with the treaty victory, though the Filipino revolt tempered his pleasure. On February 15, the first anniversary of the sinking of the *Maine,* he journeyed to anti-expansionist

Boston to speak to the Home Market Club. The speech was among the best he ever made, a blunt defense of the administration's Philippine policy. Stirringly, McKinley spoke of those who had wanted the war but shrank from its results; of those like himself who had dreaded war but lived with its responsibilities; of the uncertainties of war and the requirements of peace; and of the process by which he had concluded that the United States, under God's providence and "in the name of human progress and civilization," must keep the islands.

"No imperial designs lurk in the American mind," he said. Rousing, the speech reflected the era's assumptions of American destiny and superiority. At its best the feeling was broadly generous, a conviction that Americans could help other peoples toward prosperity and independence. At its worst, it was smugly paternalistic and drew on attitudes of racial dominance. To listeners in 1899 it made sense. McKinley, who was tolerant and generous, closed to prolonged applause. "I do not prophesy," he said. "The present is all-absorbing to me. But I cannot bound my vision by the blood-stained trenches around Manila—where every red drop, whether from the veins of an American soldier or a misguided Filipino, is anguish to my heart,—but by the broad range of future years, when . . . [the Filipino] children and children's children shall for ages hence bless the American republic because it emancipated and redeemed their fatherland, and set them in the pathway of the world's best civilization."[51]

On the way back to Washington, McKinley must have reflected on the changes the year had wrought. The country was expansive, prosperous, and confident. The issues of the Civil War had faded, as had the shrillness of the recent depression. People seemed genial and self-assured, moderate in outlook, prepared again to count on a better tomorrow. The year since the *Maine* had changed McKinley, too. Matured by the war, he was tougher, less compliant, more imperious. He had grown used to giving orders and controlling events. His party, despite the treaty fight, was united. The Democrats as usual were in disarray, divided over policy, in danger of fumbling the promising issue of imperialism. With any luck in the election of 1900, the Republicans could look forward to four more years of power.[52]

☆☆☆

On his Christmas swing through the South in 1898, McKinley visited the Tuskegee Institute in Alabama, Booker T. Washington's industrial school for black students. Tuskegee was a mandatory stop for Republican politicians, a place to reaffirm both the vigor and limits of the party's commitment to black rights. After a tour of the grounds, McKinley spoke to the students, advising them: "Patience, moderation, self-control, knowledge, character will surely win you victories and realize the best aspirations of your people." Though he did not mention it, the elections a month before had brought fresh outbreaks of racial violence in Illinois and across the South. The situation was particularly bad in North Carolina, where blacks held a number of offices. In November 1898, lynchings, shootings, beatings, and fraud drove blacks and their supporters from the polls. Rifle-toting mobs burned black newspaper offices in Wilmington and other towns. Dozens of blacks were killed or injured. At a Peace Jubilee in Chicago, Booker T. Washington pointed sadly to the growing signs of race prejudice, "a cancer gnawing at the heart of the republic."[53]

Southern Democrats warned blacks to pay heed. "The negro must take a subordinate place," South Carolina's Tillman said, "and he will be treated with consideration and kindness in proportion as he is peaceable and well behaved and makes friends of his white neighbors." Observers noted troubling ironies. Negro troops had fought in Cuba and the Philippines, ostensibly to "free" native populations from oppressive rule. The Republicans, long prevented from acting on civil rights, now had the needed majorities, but somehow lacked interest and commitment. McKinley, a stout supporter of the Lodge elections bill earlier in the decade, was busy stressing sectional unity, a laudable goal, yet one that came partly at the expense of black citizens. Harrison and other Republican presidents had spoken out forcefully against violence and fraud, but McKinley said nothing. People noticed. A cartoon in the New York *World* showed the president studying a map of the Philippines, as a figure drew back a curtain revealing lynchings and murders. "Civilization Begins at Home," the caption said.[54]

In the Philippines, the sad bloody war against Aguinaldo stretched on, not ending until several years after his capture in March 1901. A later generation found similar dilemmas in Vietnam. American troops chased an elusive foe, who fought, then vanished into a friendly population. Reports of American atrocities outraged anti-imperialists, who in turn were accused of encouraging the enemy. In August 1899, the respected Root replaced Alger in the War Department, but Democrats kept up their attacks. That summer Democratic platforms in the Northeast assailed the "wanton and needless" war, fought against the nation's own principles of self-government.[55] In the Midwest, Democrats worked hard among German-American voters, who disliked expansion, opposed standing armies, and suspected an anti-German bias in McKinley's foreign policy. "We lost the last campaign because we lacked the foreign vote," Bryan told a meeting of party leaders in Des Moines. "They did not understand the silver issue. But they will understand what a standing army means. They know what expansion and imperialism mean, and will vote against them."[56]

Bryan tested the theory in the 1899 elections, particularly in his own Nebraska and McKinley's Ohio. Stumping both states, he stressed the blend of free silver, anti-trust, and anti-imperialism issues he hoped might win in 1900. Hanna and others rushed to Ohio, fearful of defeat in the president's home state. Expansion was popular in much of the West, but in some areas, Republican leaders reported that German voters, "who have been with us on the issue of 16 to 1, in a large majority are against us and many of them wavering."[57] Hard work and a presidential tour through the Midwest and Plains in October stiffened the lines. McKinley spoke feelingly of the future of the Philippines, while local campaigners took Bryan to task for clinging to free silver. The combination proved effective. In the end, Bryan could point to Democratic victories in Nebraska, Kentucky, and Maryland, but little else. The Republicans won comfortably in Ohio, and in two-thirds of the states with elections. Privately, some of them welcomed Bryan's win in Nebraska, wanting no obstacles to his renomination in 1900.[58]

Afterwards, Bryan heard conflicting advice. Silverites pressed for another silver campaign and a "loyalty test" to determine admission to the next national convention. Late in 1899, the Democratic national committee, a Bryan group, voted unanimously to make silver the main issue in 1900. Aghast, Democrats like Hill, Hoke Smith, Altgeld, Henry Watterson, Tammany boss Richard Croker, and James K. Jones, Bryan's campaign manager in 1896, urged Bryan to compromise. Defeat, prosperity, and new discoveries of gold in Alaska, Australia, and South Africa had undercut the silver issue. Imperialism and the trusts were the coming questions. At the least, would Bryan not agree to a brief reaffirmation of the 1896 platform, with no direct reference to silver or a specific ratio? "We cannot, cannot, cannot, and will not, will not, take up 16 to 1 in the East," said an emissary from William Randolph Hearst. But Bryan refused to bend, saying that to do so would be "ignorant or cowardly." "If the Democratic party wants somebody to lead a retreat," he had declared a few months before, "they must find someone accustomed to walking backwards."[59]

As 1900 began, conservative Democrats toyed with the idea of beating Bryan for the nomination, but soon gave it up. Gorman won early support among anti-imperialists and southern Democrats, yet attracted few Cleveland Democrats, who remembered the 1894 tariff squabble. He dropped out quickly. Croker advanced the prospects of Augustus Van Wyck, a relatively obscure New York judge, whose candidacy deservedly went nowhere. Recognizing a winner, Croker then threw his support to Bryan, with an eye to future favors and a better nomination in 1904. In April 1900, Dewey at last tossed his Admiral's hat into the ring, and watched in embarrassment as no one noticed. By then Bryan had the nomination well in hand. When the Democratic national convention opened in Kansas City on July 4, it was his from the start. Still hoping to head off a free silver campaign, Hill visited Lincoln for a three-hour talk with Bryan, and returned chastened. "I have a reputation for being somewhat cold at times myself, but I am not an iceberg," he remarked privately.[60]

On the third day, the convention unanimously named Bryan for the presidency. In a dramatic gesture for party unity, Hill seconded the nomination. Bryan had stayed in close telephone contact with the convention, at one point threatening to decline the nomination if the platform did not include a forthright silver plank. ("Bryan would rather be wrong than President," Reed promptly quipped.) By one vote—a delegate from the new territory of Hawaii—the platform committee gave way and declared for free coinage at 16 to 1. More than half the platform covered imperialism, militarism, and Republican policy in Cuba and the Philippines. "We recognize imperialism as the paramount issue of the campaign," it said, in a compromise Bryan accepted. Other planks called for "unceasing warfare" against trusts and denounced the Dingley tariff, "a trust breeding measure." The convention over, the Populists and Silver Republicans, only shadows now, added their endorsements to the Bryan ticket. At home in Lincoln, Bryan was already telling friends that he took the nomination out of duty, since victory seemed impossible this year.[61]

Four years older, and heavier, with a receding hairline, Bryan still showed signs of the exuberant youth who had burst on the presidential stage in 1896. Troubled by gold and the money power then, he was worried now, concerned about the trend toward wealth, material gains, and imperial adventure. He spoke his worry at Indianapolis on August

8, a month after the nomination, in a sparkling address that became the keynote of his campaign. The address made no mention of silver. "The contest of 1900," Bryan said, "is a contest between democracy on the one hand and plutocracy on the other." Imperialism, a tool of plutocracy, profited no one except the wealthy and powerful, army contractors, colonial officials, and shipowners "who would carry live soldiers to the Philippines and bring dead soldiers back." It distorted traditions and subverted values. "We cannot repudiate the principle of self-government in the Philippines without weakening that principle here." Bryan jabbed shrewdly at McKinley's trade argument: "It is not necessary to own people in order to trade with them." Closing with a plea for human rights and against bloodshed everywhere, he pledged if elected to call Congress into special session to provide a stable government and independence to the Philippines.[62]

The speech, an effective one, angered McKinley, who pointedly referred to the "exaggerated phrase-making" of a presidential campaign. Bryan's pledge differed little from his own policy, which also called for stable self-government once the insurgents laid down their arms. There were too many inconsistencies in the Democratic position. The Kansas City platform tacitly accepted the annexation of Hawaii and Puerto Rico. Bryan himself had never questioned the acquisition of Puerto Rico. Were nearby colonies "good," distant ones "bad"? And how could a party resting on the oppression of black voters in the South speak so forcefully about equal rights abroad? Surely voters would see the absurdity. McKinley welcomed the imperialism issue, confident he would win. "It is no longer a question of expansion with us," he had said on his midwestern tour late the previous year; "we have expanded. If there is any question at all it is a question of contraction; and who is going to contract?"[63]

Renominated in June, McKinley looked like an easy winner. Republicans catalogued his accomplishments, starting with prosperity, reciprocity, and the Dingley tariff. True, the president's reciprocity treaties still sat in the Senate, the victims of conservative opposition and wartime distractions, but he planned to push them again after the election. In March 1900, he signed the Gold Standard Act, which made gold the standard of currency and closed the silver controversy that had so dominated the 1890s. Like Roosevelt after him, he respected talented people, and brought many into his service, including Root, Hay, Gage, Attorney General John W. Griggs, and a federal judge named William Howard Taft who agreed to set up a civil government in the Philippines. In foreign policy, the administration negotiated the Hay-Pauncefote treaty (later renegotiated, and signed at the end of 1901), to get Great Britain's consent to American control over an isthmian canal; established the celebrated Open Door policy in China; and pressed successfully for a Permanent Court of International Arbitration, at The Hague, to settle disputes equitably and without conflict.[64]

Hanna again took charge of the campaign. His friendship with McKinley had cooled—the president never consulted him quite as much as he wished—but his loyalty had not. "There is only one issue in this campaign, my friends," he told voters, "and that is, let well enough alone." As in 1896, the national committee relied on speakers and reading material. It printed 70 pamphlets on issues such as "Imperialism," sent out 125,000,000 copies, mailed 21,000,000 postcards, and distributed twelve columns of reading matter each week to 6,000 Republican newspapers.[65] On July 1, with the campaign barely underway, Republican strategists already gave McKinley 206 electoral votes, with another 64 leaning his way. He needed only 224 to elect. To worriers, it all seemed too safe, too secure. "When parties get to be so prosperous and harmonious," an onlooker wrote, "they tempt Providence." "I wisht the campaign was over," said Mr. Dooley in September. "I wisht it'd begin," replied Hennessy. "I nivver knew annything so dead. They ain't been so much as a black eye give or took in th' ward, an it's less thin two months to th' big day."[66]

The only scare came in September, when Bryan, on another of his whirlwind tours, suddenly switched from imperialism to the trusts. Republicans were defensive on the issue, not quite sure what to make of it. Business consolidations increased rapidly between 1895 and 1905, at the pace of nearly 300 a year. Some Republicans praised the trend, certain it led to greater efficiency and lower prices. Others, including McKinley, hesitated. Like most of his generation, the president had been brought up to welcome business growth. Seeking middle ground, he tried to distinguish between "good" trusts and "bad," and hoped that publicity, tariff reciprocity, and other mild prescriptions might solve the problem. In December 1899, he urged Congress to take action, but announced no program. As always, the war in the Philippines distracted. Privately, McKinley discussed strengthening the Sherman Antitrust Act and pledged action after the election. Bryan's thrusts hurt, but not enough to make the difference. That would come in 1901, as J.P. Morgan, in a few dramatic strokes, formed the United States Steel Corporation, the first billion-dollar trust.[67]

The election, as expected, was not even close. McKinley won 7,219,525 votes (52 percent of the total) to Bryan's 6,358,737 (45 percent). He won 292 electoral votes to 155 for Bryan. McKinley's plurality of 860,000 votes was the greatest for any presidential candidate since 1824. Turnout reached 72 percent of the eligible voters, well below the 1896 figure, but the last time it ever exceeded 70 percent. Of the states McKinley had carried in 1896, he lost only Kentucky, and he added Kansas, Nebraska, Wyoming, Utah, South Dakota, and Washington. Bryan carried the South, the Border, and a handful of silver states. He won nothing in the Northeast and Midwest, and only four states in the West, though he did somewhat better in the cities and among labor voters than in 1896. Embarrassingly, McKinley carried Bryan's state, county, city, and precinct. The Republicans kept control of Congress. At Bryan's home, the mood was somber, depressed. "At the close of another presidential campaign it is my lot to congratulate you on a second victory," he wired McKinley.[68]

Bryan had wanted a solemn referendum on imperialism. To some extent, he got it, but inevitably the election of 1900 turned on other issues as well. Prosperity, the war, expansion, sound money, the tariff, and a general satisfaction with Republican rule all played a role in McKinley's victory. Using the imperialism issue, Bryan managed to lure back some Cleveland Democrats, including Wilson, Smith, Watterson, and Olney. Others, like Cleveland himself, could not bring themselves to support Bryan. Democrats like J. Sterling Morton agreed with Bryan's stand on imperialism, detested his position on social and economic issues. "It is a choice between evils," Morton wrote of the McKinley-Bryan contest, "and I am going to shut my eyes, hold my nose, vote, go home and disinfect myself." He voted for McKinley. Carl Schurz, a leading anti-imperialist, voted for Bryan, but called it "the most distasteful thing I ever did." His anti-imperialist ally, David Starr Jordan, the president of Stanford University, wound up voting for McKinley. So did Andrew Carnegie.[69]

Following the election, most Democratic leaders thankfully set Bryan aside as presidential timber. Seizing on defeat, the Cleveland Democrats tried again to bind the South and Northeast in a conservative alliance. In 1904 they won and nominated a conservative Democrat for the presidency, but lost badly in the election. Four years later, for lack of anyone better, Bryan ran again, losing for a third time. Through the first decade of the new century, the Democrats withered under the warm sun of Republican supremacy. Only a split among

Republicans in 1912 enabled Wilson to win, and afterward, the Republicans regained control through the 1920s. In states where politics had once been closely contested, the Democrats barely went through the rituals. California was an example. In the seven elections from 1880 through 1892, twenty-two Republicans and nineteen Democrats won seats from California in the House of Representatives. In the seven elections from 1898 through 1910, fifty-two Republicans and five Democrats won seats. Across the West, Midwest, and Northeast, the Republicans had come to stay.[70]

McKinley had taken the returns at home in Canton. Friends found him sobered by the outcome, "more impressed with his responsibilities than with his triumph." Congratulations flowed in. A week after the election McKinley shared credit for the victory with his cabinet and asked them all to remain into the second term. Only Griggs, the attorney general, planned to leave. There was one new member of the administration. Vice-President Hobart had died in 1899, and the Republican national convention had turned for a replacement to the dashing young governor of New York, Theodore Roosevelt. "Teddy," with his flashing grin and falsetto voice, had strengthened the ticket, but was uncertain about his prospects. He would become "a dignified nonentity for four years," he jokingly told friends. That, given the Roosevelt temperament, was unlikely. Besides, McKinley made use of the office, adding substantially to its attractions. The vice-presidency placed Roosevelt in line for 1904 and associated him with McKinley, who ranked, the new vice-president thought, next to Lincoln "during the whole 19th century in point of great work worthily done."[71]

☆☆☆

The new year, 1901, began brightly, with the customary round of events and receptions. On New Year's Day, as usual, McKinley opened the White House to the public, and shook 5350 hands in three hours. On January 25, the McKinleys celebrated their thirtieth wedding anniversary. Happily, the president made plans to refurbish the mansion, still in acute disrepair. In March, he gave his second inaugural address, sounding the themes he had made familiar: prosperity, reciprocity, an end to sectionalism, and American responsibilities at home and in the world. It rained most of the day, a much-noted change from the famous "McKinley weather." That month, Aguinaldo surrendered, promising an end to the unfortunate trouble in the Philippines. Negotiations toward independence were moving rapidly in Cuba, which cleared the way for the removal of American troops early in 1902. In May and June, McKinley planned a six-week speaking tour to the Pacific Coast, with swings through the South and Northwest. The trip, with half the cabinet along, marked another departure for the McKinley presidency.

McKinley wanted to talk to the people about reciprocity and the trusts, his two major concerns at the start of the second administration. He would need popular support to work both issues through a reluctant Congress, and he got it. The trip became a triumphal procession, a continuous round of crowds, cheers, and applause. "No President," said a reporter who was along,"—certainly no president since the days of Lincoln—has been so close to the hearts of the people as Mr. McKinley." Through the South, he talked about the benefits of foreign markets, the possibilities for southern cotton in the Far East, and the way in which trade tied nations together. In California he stressed similar themes, saying in San Francisco, "There is nothing in this world that brings people so close together as commerce." Trade promoted social stability, making people hopeful parts of a developing system. McKinley planned to end the tour with a major policy address at the Pan-American Exposition in Buffalo, but his wife's sudden illness on the Coast changed that. Instead, he returned with her to Washington and accepted a substitute date, September 5, at the Exposition. There, he would make clear his break with simple, old-fashioned Republican protectionism.[72]

Although few people knew it, the war with Spain had further altered McKinley's thinking on the tariff. Before, one obstacle had always blocked serious revision: the government needed revenue, and tariff duties were one of the few publicly sanctioned methods of taxation. The war, McKinley saw immediately, swung public opinion toward acceptance of greater federal power, and with it, new forms of internal taxation. In November 1898, McKinley quietly aired this view with a visiting British statesman, who signaled his government to expect important departures in administration tariff policy.[73] A year later the president submitted Kasson's reciprocity treaties to the Senate, but waited for reelection to press them. By the summer of 1901 he was ready to move. Trial balloons appeared in the New York *Tribune,* Philadelphia *Press,* and other Republican papers, and visitors to Canton, including Hanna and Cullom, the head of the Senate Foreign Relations

Committee, found him adamant for reciprocity. "I feel I am representing his ideas," Cullom told reporters afterward, "when I say that
there are . . . some things we ought to do which will amount to a
partial revision of the tariff."[74]

On September 5, a crowd of 50,000 listened at the Pan-American
Exposition as McKinley explained his ideas. The occasion, a fair cele-
brating hemispheric unity, was perfect for his purpose. Progress had
knit the world together, in ways the United States, with its "almost
appalling" prosperity, must share. "We must not repose in fancied
security that we can forever sell everything and buy little or nothing."
Sensible trade agreements offered outlets for surplus production,
while at the same time protecting home industry. "Isolation is no
longer possible or desirable." As the crowd cheered, McKinley left
for a tour of the Exposition, and the next day, Friday, visited Niagara
Falls before returning to the fair for a public reception. Despite warnings, he wanted to meet as many people as possible, and in his well-
known style, shake their hands. The line was long, and near the front
waited Leon Czolgosz, a twenty-eight-year old unemployed laborer and
anarchist. McKinley moved the line along with practiced speed, until
suddenly, his outstretched hand was struck aside. Then, there were
two loud pistol shots.[75]

McKinley stared in astonishment, and was led to a chair. Seeing
blood on his stomach, he whispered to Cortelyou: "My wife—be
careful, Cortelyou, how you tell her, oh, be careful." Guards wrestled
Czolgosz to the floor. "Don't let them hurt him," McKinley said. Only
one bullet had struck home, and surgeons quickly probed the wound,
without result. A recent discovery called the X-ray was on display at
the Exposition, but was not used. Vice-President Roosevelt, Hanna,
and most of the cabinet rushed to Buffalo, but McKinley rallied, and
doctors announced he was out of danger. Relieved, Roosevelt pulled a
McKinley friend aside to discuss his 1904 presidential prospects, and
left for his summer retreat in the Adirondack Mountains of New York.
Meanwhile, McKinley was slowly dying, the victim of misdiagnosis and
spreading internal infection. On September 13, a week after the shoot-
ing, he collapsed. Telegrams urged Roosevelt and others to return.[76]

The vice-president, characteristically, was out hiking, and the news
of McKinley's relapse reached him on the side of a mountain. Coolly,
he dashed by horse and train to Buffalo, but arrived almost a dozen
hours too late. Shortly after two o'clock in the morning of September
14, McKinley had died. "The great life was ended," said Charles G.

Dawes, who was there at the close. A funeral train carried the body to Washington and on to Canton, amid a vast outpouring of grief. There was a worshipful tone about it, and a sense that an era had ended. A new century, another era, had begun, but the passage was not abrupt, and the connections were clear. Something called "progressivism" was taking shape, with its roots deep in the 1890s and before. Had McKinley lived, he would have claimed it, though in gentler, less energetic fashion than Roosevelt did. By 1904, drawing on his enormous popularity, he could have dealt with the tariff and trust issues, and made way for Roosevelt. A mild McKinley progressivism, no Roosevelt-Taft split, no election of Wilson—and the course of politics in the twentieth century might have changed. But McKinley did not live.[77]

In a dim library in a Buffalo home, Roosevelt took the oath of office and pledged: "it shall be my aim to continue, absolutely unbroken, the policy of President McKinley for the peace, the prosperity, and the honor of our beloved country."[78] He meant it, and tried, but in the end took the country in some substantially different directions. That was right. It was a time for change, just like the 1890s. Still, the Roosevelt departures—both at home and abroad—owed a great deal to McKinley, Blaine, Reed, and Harrison, and to the party doctrines and struggles of the 1890s. Out of years of stalemate, the Republicans had built a national party system, using strong national government, activist policies, and energetic leadership to govern an expanding urban-industrial society. Now, the twentieth century, so long and eagerly awaited, had arrived, and the 1890s were over.

Appendix

TABLE 1

Popular Votes in Presidential Elections, 1884–1904

Year	Republicans		Democrats		Populists		Other	
1884	4,851,981	(48%)	4,874,986	(49%)			325,739	(3%)
1888	5,439,853	(48%)	5,540,329	(49%)			396,441	(3%)
1892	5,175,582	(43%)	5,556,543	(46%)	1,040,886	(9%)	277,373	(2%)
1896	7,111,607	(50%)	6,509,052	(46%)	222,583	(2%)	316,298	(2%)
1900	7,219,525	(52%)	6,358,737	(45%)			394,809	(3%)
1904	7,628,785	(56%)	5,084,442	(38%)	114,546	(1%)	695,335	(5%)

Source. The information in this table is derived from Arthur M. Schlesinger, Jr., editor, *The Coming to Power: Critical Presidential Elections in American History,* Chelsea House, New York, 1972.

TABLE 2

Party Strength in Congress, 1886–1904

Congress and Year Elected		Republicans	Democrats	Other
		Senate		
Fiftieth	(1886)	39	37	
Fifty-first	(1888)	39	37	
Fifty-second	(1890)	47	39	2
Fifty-third	(1892)	38	44	3
Fifty-fourth	(1894)	43	39	6
Fifty-fifth	(1896)	47	34	7
Fifty-sixth	(1898)	53	26	8
Fifty-seventh	(1900)	55	31	4
Fifty-eighth	(1902)	57	33	
Fifty-ninth	(1904)	57	33	
		House		
Fiftieth	(1886)	152	169	4
Fifty-first	(1888)	169	161	
Fifty-second	(1890)	88	235	9
Fifty-third	(1892)	127	218	11
Fifty-fourth	(1894)	244	105	7
Fifty-fifth	(1896)	204	113	40
Fifty-sixth	(1898)	185	163	9
Fifty-seventh	(1900)	197	151	9
Fifty-eighth	(1902)	208	178	
Fifty-ninth	(1904)	250	136	

Source. The information in this table is derived from *The Statistical History of the United States,* Fairfield Publishers, Stamford, Conn., 1965.

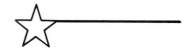

Suggestions for Additional Reading

The decade of the 1890s has attracted considerable study. The following suggestions are not intended as a comprehensive bibliography, but instead point out the most useful sources on the politics of the decade.

The best interpretive study of political life in the late nineteenth century is H. Wayne Morgan, *From Hayes to McKinley: National Party Politics, 1877-1896,* Syracuse University Press, Syracuse, 1969, which is also a pleasure to read. It replaces Matthew Josephson, *The Politicos, 1865-1896,* Harcourt-Brace, New York, 1938. Harold U. Faulkner, *Politics, Reform and Expansion, 1890-1900,* Harper, New York, 1959, is now dated. David P. Thelen, "Social Tensions and the Origins of Progressivism," *Journal of American History,* 56 (1969), 323–41, and Thelen's *The New Citizenship: Origins of Progressivism in Wisconsin, 1885–1900,* University of Missouri Press, Columbia, 1972, point up the enduring importance of the 1890s.

Other volumes that advance challenging interpretations include Robert H. Wiebe, *The Search for Order, 1877–1920,* Hill and Wang, New York, 1967; Samuel P. Hays, *The Response to Industrialism, 1885–1914,* University of Chicago Press, Chicago, 1957; Walter T. K.

Nugent, *From Centennial to World War: American Society, 1876–1917,* Bobbs-Merrill, Indianapolis, 1976; Morton Keller, *Affairs of State: Public Life in Late Nineteenth Century America,* Harvard University Press, Cambridge, 1977; and Richard Hofstadter, *The Age of Reform: From Bryan to F.D.R.,* Knopf, New York, 1955. Edward C. Kirkland, *Industry Comes of Age: Business, Labor, and Public Policy, 1860–1897,* Holt, Rinehart and Winston, New York, 1961, is a mine of information, while Charles Hoffman, *The Depression of the Nineties: An Economic History,* Greenwood, Westport, Conn., 1970, examines economic developments during the decade.

Historians and political scientists have investigated the decade's electoral alignments, with fruitful results. Walter Dean Burnham, *Critical Elections and the Mainsprings of American Politics,* Norton, New York, 1970; Lee Benson, "Research Problems in American Political Historiography," in Mirra Komarovsky, ed., *Common Frontiers of the Social Sciences,* Free Press, Glencoe, Ill., 1957, 113–83; Samuel P. Hays, "The Social Analysis of American Political History, 1880–1920," *Political Science Quarterly,* 80 (1965), 373–94; and Paul T. David, *Party Strength in the United States, 1872–1970,* University Press of Virginia, Charlottesville, 1972, are especially illuminating. See also, the helpful essays in William Nisbet Chambers and Walter Dean Burnham, eds., *The American Party Systems: Stages of Political Development,* Oxford University Press, New York, 1967.

Arthur M. Schlesinger, Jr., ed., *History of American Presidential Elections,* 4 vols., Chelsea House, New York, 1971, Volumes II and III, examines each presidential election in the period. Studies of individual elections are needed, except the 1896 contest, which can be followed in Stanley L. Jones, *The Presidential Election of 1896,* University of Wisconsin Press, Madison, 1964; Paul W. Glad, *McKinley, Bryan, and the People,* J.B. Lippincott, Philadelphia, 1964; and Robert F. Durden, *The Climax of Populism: The Election of 1896,* University Press of Kentucky, Lexington, 1965. The article literature on 1896 is also immense. George Harmon Knoles, *The Presidential Campaign and Election of 1892,* Stanford University Press, Stanford, 1942, covers that election, as does Donald M. Dozer, "Benjamin Harrison and the Presidential Campaign in 1892," *American Historical Review,* 54 (1948), 49–77. Carl N. Degler, "American Political Parties and the Rise of the City: An Interpretation," *Journal of American History,* 51 (1964), 41–59, looks at the entire decade, with a special eye to the decisive election of 1894.

State and regional studies shed light on the workings of politics. Among the best are Richard J. Jensen, *The Winning of the Midwest: Social and Political Conflict, 1888–1896,* University of Chicago Press, Chicago, 1971; Paul John Kleppner, *The Cross of Culture: A Social Analysis of Midwestern Politics, 1850–1900,* Free Press, New York, 1970; and Samuel T. McSeveney, *The Politics of Depression: Political Behavior in the Northeast, 1893–1896,* Oxford University Press, New York, 1972. For political studies of individual states, see Geoffrey Blodgett, *The Gentle Reformers: Massachusetts Democrats in the Cleveland Era,* Harvard University Press, Cambridge, 1966; Lewis L. Gould, *Wyoming: A Political History, 1868–1896,* Yale University Press, New Haven, 1968; Raymond H. Pulley, *Old Virginia Restored: An Interpretation of the Progressive Impulse, 1870–1930,* University Press of Virginia, Charlottesville, 1968; and R. Hal Williams, *The Democratic Party and California Politics, 1880–1896,* Stanford University Press, Stanford, 1973.

For a brief analytical treatment of the Republican party, the best place to start is Lewis L. Gould, "The Republican Search for a National Majority," in H. Wayne Morgan, ed., *The Gilded Age,* revised edition, Syracuse University Press, Syracuse, 1970, 171–87. Vincent P. DeSantis, *Republicans Face the Southern Question: The New Departure Years, 1877–1897,* Johns Hopkins Press, Baltimore, 1959, traces Republican efforts to break the "Solid South," as does, with less understanding, Stanley P. Hirshson, *Farewell to the Bloody Shirt: Northern Republicans and the Southern Negro, 1877–1893,* Indiana University Press, Bloomington, 1962. Robert D. Marcus, *Grand Old Party: Political Structure in the Gilded Age, 1880–1896,* Oxford University Press, New York, 1971, looks at Republican party organization over several decades.

On the Democratic side, J. Rogers Hollingsworth, *The Whirligig of Politics: The Democracy of Cleveland and Bryan,* University of Chicago Press, Chicago, 1963, has less to offer. For interpretive studies of the Democrats, see R. Hal Williams, "'Dry Bones and Dead Language': The Democratic Party," in H. Wayne Morgan, ed., *The Gilded Age,* cited above, 129–48; Paolo E. Coletta, "Bryan, Cleveland, and the Disrupted Democracy, 1890–1896," *Nebraska History,* 41 (1960), 1–27; C. Vann Woodward, *Origins of the New South, 1877–1912,* Louisiana State University Press, Baton Rouge, 1951; J. Morgan Kousser, *The Shaping of Southern Politics: Suffrage Restriction and the Establishment of the One-Party South, 1880–1910,* Yale University

Press, New Haven, 1974; and Dewey W. Grantham, *The Democratic South,* University of Georgia Press, Athens, 1963. John J. Broesamle, "The Democrats from Bryan to Wilson," in Lewis L. Gould, ed., *The Progressive Era,* Syracuse University Press, Syracuse, 1974, 83–113, ably carries the story into the twentieth century.

On Populism, the literature is vast, and varies considerably in quality. John D. Hicks, *The Populist Revolt: A History of the Farmers' Alliance and the People's Party,* University of Minnesota Press, Minneapolis, 1931, is the standard work; Lawrence Goodwyn, *Democratic Promise: The Populist Moment in America,* Oxford University Press, 1976, is the most recent. Robert C. McMath, Jr., *Populist Vanguard: A History of the Southern Farmers' Alliance,* University of North Carolina Press, Chapel Hill, 1975, is good on the Alliance. There are studies of Populism in virtually every state, among them: Walter T. K. Nugent, *The Tolerant Populists: Kansas Populism and Nativism,* University of Chicago Press, Chicago, 1963; Sheldon Hackney, *Populism to Progressivism in Alabama,* Princeton University Press, Princeton, 1969; James E. Wright, *The Politics of Populism: Dissent in Colorado,* Yale University Press, New Haven, 1974; O. Gene Clanton, *Kansas Populism: Ideas and Men,* University Press of Kansas, Lawrence, 1969; and Stanley B. Parsons, *The Populist Context: Rural Versus Urban Power on a Great Plains Frontier,* Greenwood, Westport, Conn., 1973.

Biographies of Populist figures include Martin Ridge, *Ignatius Donnelly: The Portrait of a Politician,* University of Chicago Press, Chicago, 1962; C. Vann Woodward, *Tom Watson: Agrarian Rebel,* Macmillan, New York, 1938; Peter H. Argersinger, *Populism and Politics: William Alfred Peffer and the People's Party,* University Press of Kentucky, Lexington, 1974; and Michael J. Brodhead, *Persevering Populist: The Life of Frank Doster,* University of Nevada Press, Reno, 1969. Robert F. Durden, "The 'Cow-Bird' Grounded: The Populist Nomination of Bryan and Watson in 1896," *Mississippi Valley Historical Review,* 50 (1963), 397–423, is helpful on that event. Fuller bibliographies of Populism are in Sheldon Hackney, ed., *Populism: The Critical Issues,* Little, Brown, Boston, 1971; and Allen J. Going, "The Agrarian Revolt," in Arthur S. Link and Rembert W. Patrick, eds., *Writing Southern History: Essays in Historiography in Honor of Fletcher M. Green,* Louisiana State University Press, Baton Rouge, 1965, 362–82.

Cleveland and Bryan led the changing Democratic party. On Cleveland, one of the most important figures in the party's history,

Allan Nevins, *Grover Cleveland: A Study in Courage,* Dodd, Mead, New York, 1932, is thorough and sympathetic, while Horace Samuel Merrill, *Bourbon Leader: Grover Cleveland and the Democratic Party,* Houghton Mifflin, Boston, 1957, is very critical. Robert McElroy, *Grover Cleveland: The Man and the Statesman,* 2 vols., Harpers, New York, 1923, is still useful. Cleveland's letters, some of which are conveniently printed in Allan Nevins, ed., *Letters of Grover Cleveland, 1850-1908,* Houghton Mifflin, Boston, 1933, say much about his personality and policies.

On Bryan, Paolo E. Coletta, *William Jennings Bryan,* 3 vols., University of Nebraska Press, Lincoln, 1964-69, is the best multivolume biography. Louis W. Koenig, *Bryan: A Political Biography of William Jennings Bryan,* G. P. Putnam's Sons, New York, 1971, is also useful, though readers must look elsewhere for analysis of the Republican opposition and the workings of politics in the decade. Paul W. Glad, *The Trumpet Soundeth: William Jennings Bryan and His Democracy, 1896-1912,* University of Nebraska Press, Lincoln, 1960, is helpful. Bryan offers his own interpretations, in three works: *The First Battle: A Story of the Campaign of 1896,* W. B. Conkey, Chicago, 1896; *The Second Battle,* W. B. Conkey, Chicago, 1900; and, with Mary Bryan, *Memoirs of William Jennings Bryan,* John C. Winston, Philadelphia, 1925.

Other Democrats can be followed in Mark D. Hirsch, *William C. Whitney: Modern Warwick,* Dodd, Mead, New York, 1948; James A. Barnes, *John G. Carlisle: Financial Statesman,* Dodd, Mead, New York, 1931; John R. Lambert, *Arthur Pue Gorman,* Louisiana State University Press, Baton Rouge, 1953; Herbert J. Bass, *"I Am a Democrat": The Political Career of David Bennett Hill,* Syracuse University Press, Syracuse, 1961; and Festus P. Summers, *William L. Wilson and Tariff Reform,* Rutgers University Press, New Brunswick, 1953.

Harrison, Blaine, and McKinley are crucial to an understanding of the Republicans. Harry J. Sievers, *Benjamin Harrison,* 3 vols., University Publishers and Bobbs-Merrill, New York and Indianapolis, 1952-68, is the place to start on Harrison, though Volume III, on the administration, is thin. A full-length study of the administration is still needed. Blaine awaits a biographer, although David Saville Muzzey, *James G. Blaine: A Political Idol of Other Days,* Dodd, Mead, New York, 1934, is useful. Gail Hamilton, *Biography of James G. Blaine,* Henry Bill, Norwich, Conn., 1895, reprints some Blaine letters. Albert T. Volwiler, ed., *The Correspondence of Benjamin Harrison and James*

G. Blaine, 1882-1893, American Philosophical Society, Philadelphia, 1940, shows the developing relationship between the two.

McKinley, the decade's most important political figure, has received skilled treatment in H. Wayne Morgan, *William McKinley and His America,* Syracuse University Press, Syracuse, 1963; and Margaret Leech, *In the Days of McKinley,* Harper, New York, 1959. For a sense of McKinley's authority and style, read his masterful presidential speeches, in *Speeches and Addresses of William McKinley,* Appleton, New York, 1900. William A. Robinson, *Thomas B. Reed: Parliamentarian,* Dodd, Mead, New York, 1930, is intriguing on the "Czar," but Reed, like Blaine, needs an up-to-date biography. Hanna is covered in Herbert Croly, *Marcus Alonzo Hanna: His Life and Work,* Macmillan, New York, 1912; and Thomas Beer, *Hanna,* Knopf, New York, 1929.

On other Republican figures, Dorothy Ganfield Fowler, *John Coit Spooner: Defender of Presidents,* University Publishers, New York, 1961; Thomas Richard Ross, *Jonathan Prentiss Dolliver: A Study in Political Integrity and Independence,* State Historical Society of Iowa, Iowa City, 1960; Leland L. Sage, *William Boyd Allison: A Study in Practical Politics,* State Historical Society of Iowa, Iowa City, 1956; Bingham Duncan, *Whitelaw Reid: Journalist, Politician, Diplomat,* University of Georgia Press, Athens, 1975; and John A. Garraty, *Henry Cabot Lodge,* Knopf, New York, 1953, are helpful. The alluring young Roosevelt, a peripheral figure until the end of the decade, can be seen in Elting Morison, et al., eds., *The Letters of Theodore Roosevelt,* 8 vols., Harvard University Press, Cambridge, 1951-54.

Some of the period's most significant issues have only recently come under serious study. Tom E. Terrill, *The Tariff, Politics, and American Foreign Policy: 1874-1901,* Greenwood, Westport, Conn., 1973, is very helpful on the tariff. Frank W. Taussig, *The Tariff History of the United States,* G. P. Putnam's Sons, New York, 1910; and Edward Stanwood, *American Tariff Controversies of the Nineteenth Century,* 2 vols., Houghton Mifflin, New York, 1903, contain useful data. William Letwin, *Law and Economic Policy in America: The Evolution of the Sherman Antitrust Act,* Knopf, New York, 1965, is excellent. The "force bill" gets perceptive coverage in Richard E. Welch, Jr., "The Federal Elections Bill of 1890: Postscript and Prelude," *Journal of American History,* 52 (1965), 511-26. Also, Richard B. Sherman, *The Republican Party and Black America from McKinley to Hoover,* University Press of Virginia, Charlottesville, 1973; and

Lawrence Grossman, *The Democratic Party and the Negro in Northern and National Politics, 1868–1892,* University of Illinois Press, Urbana, 1976.

On foreign policy, Walter LaFeber, *The New Empire: An Interpretation of American Expansion, 1860–1898,* Cornell University Press, Ithaca, 1963; and the stimulating essays in John A. S. Grenville and George Berkeley Young, *Politics, Strategy and American Diplomacy: Studies in Foreign Policy, 1873–1917,* Yale University Press, New Haven, 1966, are excellent. Charles S. Campbell, *The Transformation of American Foreign Relations, 1865–1900,* Harper & Row, New York, 1976, is stimulating. The literature on Cuba, the Philippines, and the Spanish-American War is large, but consult Ernest R. May, *Imperial Democracy: The Emergence of America as a Great Power,* Harcourt, Brace, and World, New York, 1961; David F. Healy, *The United States in Cuba, 1898–1902: Generals, Politicians, and the Search for Policy,* University of Wisconsin Press, Madison, 1963; and the good bibliography in Robert L. Beisner, *From the Old Diplomacy to the New: 1865-1900,* AHM Co., Northbrook, Ill., 1975. A forthcoming book by Glenn A. May, on *Social Engineering in the Philippines, 1900–1913,* will enhance our understanding of American colonial policy. On particular foreign policy issues, Paul S. Holbo, "Presidential Leadership in Foreign Policy: William McKinley and the Turpie-Foraker Amendment," *American Historical Review,* 72 (1967), 1321–25; and Michael H. Hunt, *Frontier Defense and the Open Door: Manchuria in Chinese-American Relations, 1895–1911,* Yale University Press, New Haven, 1973, are revealing.

The 1890s are one of our most intriguing and exciting decades. Readers interested in additional literature on the decade should consult the bibliographical listings in Vincent P. DeSantis, *The Gilded Age, 1877–1896,* AHM Co., Northbrook, Ill., 1973; and Arthur S. Link and William M. Leary, Jr., *The Progressive Era and the Great War, 1896–1920,* Appleton-Century Crofts, New York, 1969.

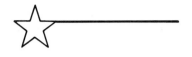

Footnotes

CHAPTER ONE

[1] Richard J. Jensen, *The Winning of the Midwest: Social and Political Conflict, 1888-1896* (Chicago, 1971), pp. 34-57; John A. Garraty, *The New Commonwealth, 1877-1890* (New York, 1968), p. 224.

[2] Entry for Nov. 9, 1888, in Charles Richard Williams, ed., *Diary and Letters of Rutherford Birchard Hayes,* 5 vols. (Columbus, Ohio, 1924), 4, 421; Chicago *Tribune,* Nov. 7-8, 1888; New York *Tribune,* Nov. 8, 1888.

[3] Allan Nevins, *Grover Cleveland: A Study in Courage* (New York, 1932), pp. 367-403, 413-39; *The Nation,* 45 (Dec. 8, 1887), p. 447; Cleveland to Chauncey F. Black, Sept. 14, 1888, Grover Cleveland Papers, Manuscript Division, Library of Congress.

[4] Cleveland to S. B. Ward, Nov. 6, 1888, in Allan Nevins, ed., *Letters of Grover Cleveland, 1850-1908* (Boston, 1933), p. 191.

[5] Robert McElroy, *Grover Cleveland: The Man and the Statesman,* 2 vols. (New York, 1923), 1, 300–301; New York *Herald,* Nov. 15, 1888.

[6] A. B. Farquhar to Cleveland, Nov. 15, 1888, in Nevins, *Letters of Grover Cleveland,* p. 192; Herbert J. Bass, *"I Am a Democrat": The Political Career of David Bennett Hill* (Syracuse, N.Y., 1961), pp. 121–26.

[7] Harrison to Morton, Oct. 29, 1888, Levi P. Morton Papers, New York Public Library; Harry J. Sievers, *Benjamin Harrison. II. Hoosier Statesman, 1865–1888* (New York, 1959), pp. 371, 423–25.

[8] Charles Hedges, ed., *Speeches of Benjamin Harrison* (New York, 1892), pp. 108–10, 160–61; Mary R. Dearing, *Veterans in Politics: The Story of the G.A.R.* (Baton Rouge, 1952), pp. 372–74.

[9] Blaine to Harrison, Nov. 7, 1888, Harrison to Blaine, Nov. 14, 1888, Blaine to Harrison, Nov. 9, 1888, Benjamin Harrison Papers, Manuscript Division, Library of Congress.

[10] George F. Hoar, "Are the Republicans In to Stay?" *North American Review,* 149 (Nov., 1889), 617–19; New York *Tribune,* Nov. 8, 11, 1888.

[11] Julia B. Foraker, *I Would Live It Again: Memories of a Vivid Life* (New York, 1932), p. 151.

[12] Paul F. Boller, Jr., *American Thought in Transition: The Impact of Evolutionary Naturalism, 1865–1900* (New York, 1969), p. 150; Paul H. Buck, *The Road to Reunion, 1865–1900* (Boston, 1937), pp. 44–114; Robert B. Beath, *History of the Grand Army of the Republic* (New York, 1888), p. 695.

[13] W. Dean Burnham, *Presidential Ballots, 1836–1892* (Baltimore, 1955), pp. 118–58; Walter Dean Burnham, "The Changing Shape of the American Political Universe," *American Political Science Review,* 59 (March, 1965), 7–28.

[14] Samuel J. Tilden, in Robert Kelley, *The Transatlantic Persuasion* (New York, 1969), p. 270.

[15] New York *Evening Post,* Aug. 9, 1892. Also, Geoffrey Blodgett, *The Gentle Reformers: Massachusetts Democrats in the Cleveland Era* (Cambridge, Mass., 1966), pp. 91, 147.

[16] William L. Wilson, *The National Democratic Party: Its History, Principles, Achievements, and Aims* (Baltimore, 1888), pp. 222-36; New York *Times,* Oct. 4, 1888; Chicago *Tribune,* March 4, 1889.

[17] C. Vann Woodward, *Origins of the New South, 1877-1913* (Baton Rouge, 1951), p. 65; Dewey W. Grantham, Jr., *The Democratic South* (Athens, Ga., 1963), p. 23; William J. Cooper, *The Conservative Regime: South Carolina, 1877-1890* (Baltimore, 1968), pp. 105-106.

[18] Alexander Clarence Flick, *Samuel Jones Tilden: A Study in Political Sagacity* (New York, 1939), p. 169; Paul Kleppner, *The Cross of Culture: A Social Analysis of Midwestern Politics, 1850-1900* (New York, 1970), pp. 35-91. Also, Melvyn Hammarberg, "Indiana Farmers and the Group Basis of the Late Nineteenth-Century Political Parties," *Journal of American History,* 61 (June, 1974), 91-115.

[19] Foraker, *I Would Live It Again,* p. 140; Hoar, "Are the Republicans In to Stay?" pp. 619-21; Lewis L. Gould, "The Republican Search for a National Majority," in H. Wayne Morgan, ed., *The Gilded Age* (Syracuse, N.Y., 1970), pp. 171-76.

[20] Hedges, *Speeches of Benjamin Harrison,* p. 59; New York *Weekly Mail and Express,* April 30, 1890, in scrapbooks in Harrison Papers.

[21] New York *Tribune,* Oct. 25, 1890; *Beatrice Webb's American Diary, 1898* (Madison, Wis., 1963), pp. 54-55.

[22] *Iowa State Register,* quoted in *The Nation,* 46 (Jan. 26, 1888), pp. 64-65; interview with James S. Clarkson, in New York *Times,* Feb. 12, 1888; Vincent P. DeSantis, *Republicans Face the Southern Question: The New Departure Years, 1877-1897* (Baltimore, 1959), pp. 160-90.

[23] Daniel W. Crofts, "The Blair Bill and the Elections Bill: The Congressional Aftermath to Reconstruction" (unpublished Ph.D. dissertation, Yale University, 1968), p. 226; Grantham, *The Democratic South,* pp. 23-26.

[24] Hedges, *Speeches of Benjamin Harrison,* p. 22; Walker Blaine, "Why Harrison Was Elected," *North American Review,* 147 (Dec.,

1888), 687; John G. Sproat, *"The Best Men": Liberal Reformers in the Gilded Age* (New York, 1968), pp. 29–44.

[25] Horace Samuel Merrill, *Bourbon Leader: Grover Cleveland and the Democratic Party* (Boston, 1957), pp. 79–134.

[26] Foraker, *I Would Live It Again*, p. 132; entry for April 19, 1880, Garfield Diary, James A. Garfield Papers, Manuscript Division, Library of Congress; David Saville Muzzey, *James G. Blaine: A Political Idol of Other Days* (New York, 1934), pp. 225–367; Gail Hamilton, *Biography of James G. Blaine* (Norwich, Conn., 1895), pp. 479–645.

[27] New York *Tribune,* Dec. 8, 1887; Joseph J. Mathews, *George W. Smalley: Forty Years a Foreign Correspondent* (Chapel Hill, 1973), p. 97; entry for Dec. 6, 1887, in Reed Diary, Thomas B. Reed Papers, Bowdoin College Library.

[28] New York *Times,* June 5–8, 1888; Eugene T. Chamberlain to Daniel S. Lamont, June, 1888, W. W. Ivins to Lamont, Aug. 10, 1888, Cleveland Papers; John R. Lambert, *Arthur Pue Gorman* (Baton Rouge, 1953), pp. 138–41.

[29] New York *Times,* Oct. 14, 1888; Tom E. Terrill, *The Tariff, Politics, and American Foreign Policy, 1874–1901* (Westport, Conn., 1973), pp. 7–13; Edward P. Crapol, *America for Americans: Economic Nationalism and Anglophobia in the Late Nineteenth Century* (Westport, Conn., 1973), pp. 4–17.

[30] Hedges, *Speeches of Benjamin Harrison,* pp. 157–58; Congressman Julius C. Burrows, in New York *Tribune,* Feb. 10, 1888; A. T. Volwiler, "Tariff Strategy and Propaganda in the United States, 1887–1888," *American Historical Review,* 36 (Oct., 1930), 76–96.

[31] Blaine speech, in New York *Times,* Oct. 14, 1888.

[32] William Henry Wood to Harrison, June 30, 1888, Harrison Papers.

[33] John F. Dezendorf to Harrison, June 26, 1888, A. E. Bateman to Harrison, July 17, 1888, Harrison Papers; Fitzhugh Lee to Cleveland, Feb. 12, 1888, James Phelan to Lamont, April 8, 1888, Cleveland Papers.

[34] New York *Times,* Aug. 11–12, 1888; New York *Herald,* Aug. 11, 1888; James S. Clarkson to Harrison, July 25, 1888, Harrison Papers.

[35] New York *Times,* Aug. 14–26, Sept. 30, Oct. 4–12, 26, 1888; Whitelaw Reid to Harrison, Nov. 3, 1888, Harrison Papers; remarks by Murat Halstead, in Brooklyn *Standard-Union,* July 21, 1890, in scrapbooks in Harrison Papers.

[36] Harrison to Reid, Sept. 27, 1888, Reid to Harrison, Sept. 25, 1888, Reid to Harrison, Oct. 6, 1888, Harrison Papers; Hedges, *Speeches of Benjamin Harrison,* p. 112; R. C. Buley, "The Campaign of 1888 in Indiana," *Indiana Magazine of History,* 10 (Jan., 1914), 32; A. P. Miller, *Relation of the Colored Race to the Republican Party* (n.p., 1888), campaign pamphlet in Yale University Library.

[37] Burnham, *Presidential Ballots,* pp. 140–45; Jensen, *Winning of the Midwest,* pp. 30–31; Samuel McSeveney, *The Politics of Depression: Political Behavior in the Northeast, 1893–1896* (New York, 1972), pp. 22–24, 28.

[38] Blaine to Harrison, Nov. 9, 1888, Harrison Papers; New York *Tribune,* Nov. 8, 1888; Chicago *Tribune,* Nov. 8–9, 1888; San Francisco *Chronicle,* Nov. 8–9, 1888.

[39] Blaine to Harrison, Nov. 9, 1888, Harrison Papers.

[40] Harrison to Margaret Peltz, Nov. 17, 1888, in Sievers, *Benjamin Harrison: Hoosier Statesman,* p. 427; Henry L. Stoddard, *As I Knew Them: Presidents and Politics from Grant to Coolidge* (New York, 1927), pp. 173–74; S. B. Elkins to Harrison, Feb. 19, 1889, Harrison Papers.

[41] Harry J. Sievers, *Benjamin Harrison. III. Hoosier President, the White House and After* (Indianapolis, 1968), pp. 27–31; Baltimore *American* and Richmond *Dispatch,* undated, 1889, articles in scrapbooks in Harrison Papers.

[42] New York *Tribune,* Feb. 15, 1889; Matthew S. Quay to Harrison, Feb. 15, 1889, Harrison Papers.

[43] Foraker, *I Would Live It Again,* p. 134; Harrison to Blaine, Jan. 17, 1889, Blaine to Harrison, Jan. 21, 1889, Harrison to Blaine, Feb. 11, 1889, Blaine to Harrison, Feb. 13, 1889, Harrison Papers.

[44] Harriet S. Blaine to James G. Blaine, Jr., March 5, 1889, in Harriet S. Blaine Beale, ed., *Letters of Mrs. James G. Blaine,* 2 vols. (New York, 1908), 2, 249; New York *Times,* March 5, 1889; Washington *Post,* March 5–6, 1889.

[45] Chicago *Tribune,* March 4-5, 1889; Chicago *Inter-Ocean,* March 5, 1889.

[46] James D. Richardson, ed., *A Compilation of the Messages and Papers of the Presidents,* 11 vols. (Washington, 1897), 7, 5440-49; St. Louis *Globe-Democrat,* March 6, 1889, in scrapbooks in Harrison Papers.

[47] Richardson, *Messages and Papers of the Presidents,* 7, 5448.

[48] Cleveland to Wilson S. Bissell, April 13, 1889, in Nevins, *Letters of Grover Cleveland,* p. 203; William H. Crook, *Memories of the White House* (Boston, 1911), pp. 176-77; Foraker, *I Would Live It Again,* p. 135.

[49] Arthur Meier Schlesinger, *The Rise of the City, 1878-1898* (New York, 1933), pp. 1-2, 53-77; Edward C. Kirkland, *Industry Comes of Age: Business, Labor, and Public Policy, 1860-1897* (New York, 1961), pp. 163-80, 280-85; Fred A. Shannon, *The Farmer's Last Frontier: Agriculture, 1860-1897* (New York, 1945), pp. 125-267.

[50] Milwaukee *Sentinel,* Oct. 22, 1892, in David P. Thelen, *The New Citizenship: Origins of Progressivism in Wisconsin, 1885-1900* (Columbia, Mo., 1972), p. 43; Hedges, *Speeches of Benjamin Harrison,* p. 257; Thomas G. Shearman, "The Owners of the United States," *The Forum,* 8 (Nov., 1889), 269-73; C. B. Spahr, *An Essay on the Present Distribution of Wealth in the United States* (New York, 1896).

[51] Richardson, *Messages and Papers of the Presidents,* 7, 5448-49.

CHAPTER TWO

[1] Dolliver to Gay Dolliver, Feb. 14, 1889, in Thomas Richard Ross, *Jonathan Prentiss Dolliver: A Study in Political Integrity and Independence* (Iowa City, Iowa, 1958), p. 89; Chicago *Tribune,* March 4, 1891; David J. Rothman, *Politics and Power: The United States Senate, 1869-1901* (Cambridge, Mass., 1966), pp. 2-42.

[2] Washington *Post,* Dec. 5, 1889; New York *Herald,* April 23, 1889; Redfield Proctor to Harrison, Aug. 30, 1889, Harrison Papers.

[3] New York *Tribune,* May 28, 1889; James A. Barnes, *John G. Carlisle: Financial Statesman* (New York, 1931), pp. 146, 166-67;

David W. Brady and Phillip Althoff, "Party Voting in the U.S. House of Representatives, 1890-1910: Elements of a Responsible Party System," *The Journal of Politics,* 36 (Aug., 1974), 762.

[4] Henry Cabot Lodge, "The Coming Congress," *North American Review,* 149 (Sept., 1889), 294; Philadelphia *Press,* April 26, 1889, in scrapbooks in Harrison Papers; New York *Herald,* April 23, 1889.

[5] John A. Garraty, *Henry Cabot Lodge: A Biography* (New York 1953), p. 109; William A. Robinson, *Thomas B. Reed, Parliamentarian* (New York, 1930), pp. 6-78.

[6] Champ Clark, *My Quarter Century of American Politics,* 2 vols. (New York, 1921), 1, 278; Omaha *Bee,* Dec. 1, 1889; New York *Tribune,* Dec. 3, 1889; Washington *Post,* Sept. 11, 1890.

[7] Omaha *Bee,* Dec. 1, 1889; Robinson, *Reed,* pp. 147, 271; Arthur Wallace Dunn, *From Harrison to Harding,* 2 vols. (New York, 1929), 1, 300-02; O. O. Stealey, *Twenty Years in the Press Gallery* (New York, 1906), p. 401.

[8] Baltimore *American and Commercial Advertiser,* June 2, 1890, in scrapbooks in Harrison Papers; Thomas B. Reed, "Rules of the House of Representatives," *Century Magazine,* 15 (March, 1889), 795; entries for Jan. 3, 10, 1889, Reed Diary.

[9] New York *Tribune,* Dec. 10, 1889; New York *Herald,* Dec. 3, 1889.

[10] New York *Tribune,* Jan. 21, 1890; Joseph G. Cannon, "Dramatic Scenes from My Career in Congress. II. When Reed Counted a Quorum," *Harper's Monthly,* 140 (March, 1920), 433-41.

[11] *Cong. Rec.,* 51st Cong., 1st sess. (Jan. 29, 1890), pp. 948-49; Chicago *Tribune,* Jan. 30, 1890; Washington *Post,* Jan. 30, 1890; New York *Evening Post,* Jan. 30, 1890. The quorum had become 165, reduced because of the death of a member after Congress opened.

[12] *Cong. Rec.,* 51st Cong., 1st sess. (Jan. 29, 1890), pp. 949-60; Washington *Post,* Jan. 30, 1890; New York *Tribune,* Jan. 30, 1890.

[13] *Cong. Rec.,* 51st Cong., 1st sess. (Jan. 30, 1890), pp. 978-79, 993-95; New York *Tribune,* Jan. 31-Feb. 1, 1890; Chicago *Tribune,* Jan. 31-Feb. 1, 1890.

[14] *Cong. Rec.,* 51st Cong., 1st sess. (Jan. 31, 1890), pp. 998-99; Philadelphia *Press,* Jan. 30, 1890; New York *World,* Jan. 31, 1890; New

York *Times,* Jan. 31, 1890; Buffalo *Express,* Jan. 31, 1890, clipping in scrapbooks in Harrison Papers.

[15] Tom L. Johnson, *My Story* (New York, 1911), pp. 63–64; Chicago *Tribune,* Jan. 30, 1890. Johnson privately congratulated Reed, who told him that a number of other Democrats had also done so.

[16] Chicago *Tribune,* Feb. 4, 1890; Philadelphia *Press,* Feb. 6, 1890; New York *Tribune,* Feb. 5, 1890; Augusta [Georgia] *Chronicle,* Jan. 31, 1890, in scrapbooks in Harrison Papers.

[17] Ross, *Dolliver,* p. 92; *Cong. Rec.,* 51st Cong., 1st sess. (Feb. 6, 1890), pp. 1105–08, (Feb. 14, 1890), p. 1347; New York *Tribune,* Feb. 6–7, 15, 1890.

[18] Roosevelt to James Brander Matthews, Feb. 10, 1890, in Elting E. Morison, et al., eds., *The Letters of Theodore Roosevelt,* 8 vols. (Cambridge, Mass., 1951), 1, 213–14; Roosevelt to Reed, Sept. 15, 1889, Reed Papers; Washington *Post,* Feb. 1, 1890.

[19] Richardson, *Messages and Papers of the Presidents,* 7, 5472–74; Chicago *Tribune,* Dec. 5, 1889.

[20] Chicago *Tribune,* Nov. 7–9, 1888, Dec. 3–4, 1889; Plumb to Harrison, July 3, 1888, Joseph Medill to Harrison, Sept. 16, 1888, Harrison Papers; *The Nation,* 46 (Jan. 12, 1888), 21–22; Washington *Post,* Feb. 15, 1890.

[21] New York *Tribune,* Dec. 7, 1889; Blaine to Harrison, Feb. 13, 1889, Harrison Papers; James G. Blaine, "Free Trade or Protection," *North American Review,* 150 (Jan., 1890), 46; Festus P. Summers, *William L. Wilson and Tariff Reform* (New Brunswick, N.J., 1953), pp. 49–68.

[22] *Cong. Rec.,* 51st Cong., 1st sess. (April 16, 1890), p. 4253; New York *Tribune,* March 21, April 1–7, 17, 1890; Chicago *Tribune,* March 19–20, April 1–2, 17, 1890; San Francisco *Examiner,* April 2, 1890; Baltimore *Sun,* April 2, 1890; *The Nation,* 50 (March 27, 1890), 249–50.

[23] Chicago *Tribune,* March 20, April 2, 17, May 22, 1890; Blaine to McKinley, April 10, 1890, in *The Nation,* 64 (May 13, 1897), 349; Washington *Post,* June 7, 1890; St. Louis *Republic,* April 8, 1890; New York *Journal of Commerce,* April 8, 1890.

[24] Blaine to Daniel A. Cony, June 14, 1890, in New York *Times,*

June 17, 1890; New York *Herald,* June 23, 1890; James Laurence Laughlin and H. Parker Willis, *Reciprocity* (New York, 1903), pp. 185–87.

[25] New York *Times,* Feb. 12, 1890; San Francisco *Chronicle,* April 1, 1890; Louis A. Coolidge, *An Old-Fashioned Senator: Orville H. Platt of Connecticut* (New York, 1910), pp. 235–37n.

[26] *Cong. Rec.,* 51st Cong., 1st sess. (May 7, 1890), pp. 4246–65, (May 21, 1890), pp. 5112–13; H. Wayne Morgan, *William McKinley and His America* (Syracuse, N.Y., 1963), pp. 128–34; Washington *Post,* May 22, 1890; New York *Journal of Commerce,* April 8, 1890.

[27] Morgan to Manly Curry, March 18, 1889, in Crofts, "The Blair Bill and the Elections Bill," pp. 233–34; Raymond B. Nixon, *Henry W. Grady: Spokesman of the New South* (New York, 1943), pp. 316–30; New York *Tribune,* Dec. 13, 1889.

[28] Henry Cabot Lodge, *Early Memories* (New York, 1913), pp. 125–26; New York *Tribune,* Feb. 12, 1888.

[29] New York *Tribune,* Nov. 7, 1889; *Frank Leslie's Illustrated Newspaper,* Nov. 13, 1889; Lodge, "The Coming Congress," pp. 297–98; John C. Spooner to J. M. Smith, July 20, 1890, John C. Spooner Papers, Manuscript Division, Library of Congress.

[30] *Cong. Rec.,* 51st Cong., 1st sess. (June 26, 1890), pp. 6538–42; J. Morgan Kouser, *The Shaping of Southern Politics: Suffrage Restriction and the Establishment of the One-Party South, 1880–1910* (New Haven, Conn., 1974), pp. 11–44; Thomas B. Reed, "Federal Control of Elections," *North American Review,* 150 (June, 1890), 673–80; New York *Tribune,* March 17, 1890.

[31] Richard E. Welch, Jr., "The Federal Elections Bill of 1890: Postscripts and Prelude," *Journal of American History,* 52 (Dec., 1965), 511–25; *Cong. Rec.,* 51st Cong., 1st sess. (March 15, 1890), p. 2285; New York *World,* March 17, 1890.

[32] Baltimore *Sun,* Feb. 28, 1890; Boston *Journal,* March 18, 1890; New York *Tribune,* March 18, June 18, 1890; Florida *Times-Union,* March 16, 1890, and Mobile *Daily Register,* Oct. 2, 1889, in scrapbooks in Harrison Papers; Charleston *News and Courier,* March 19, April 28, 1890.

[33] New York *Evening Post,* May 22, 1890; New York *Tribune,* July 2, 1890; Washington *Post,* July 2, 1890.

[34] Charleston *News and Courier,* July 3, 1890; Albion W. Tourgee to W. P. Nixon, Aug. 29, 1889, in Crofts, "The Blair Bill and the Elections Bill," p. 235; *Cong. Rec.,* 51st Cong., 1st sess. (July 2, 1890), pp. 6928, 6940–41; Atlanta *Constitution,* July 22, 1890; New York *Herald,* July 23, 1890.

[35] *Cong. Rec.,* 51st Cong., 1st sess. (May 10, 1890), p. 4506, (June 23, 1890), p. 6385; Chicago *Tribune,* March 18, 1890; Dearing, *Veterans in Politics,* pp. 373–400.

[36] Sanford D. Gordon, "Attitudes Towards Trusts Prior to the Sherman Act," *The Southern Economic Journal,* 30 (Oct., 1963), 156–67; William Letwin, *Law and Economic Policy in America: The Evolution of the Sherman Anti-Trust Act* (New York, 1965), pp. 69–70; J. W. Jenks, *The Trust Problem* (New York, 1905), pp. 195–218.

[37] John Sherman, *Recollections of Forty Years,* 2 vols. (Chicago, 1895), 2, 1071–76; *Cong. Rec.,* 51st Cong., 1st sess. (May 1, 1890), p. 4104, (June 18, 1890), p. 6208; New York *Tribune,* June 19, 1890.

[38] Allen Weinstein, *Prelude to Populism: Origins of the Silver Issue, 1867–1878* (New Haven, Conn., 1970), pp. 8–32, 301–53.

[39] Richard P. Bland, "What Shall the Ratio Be?" *North American Review,* 155 (July, 1892), 12; Robert F. Hoxie, "The Silver Debate of 1890," *The Journal of Political Economy,* 1 (Sept., 1893), 535; New York *Tribune,* Nov. 27–29, 1889; Walter T. K. Nugent, *Money and American Society, 1865–1880* (New York, 1968), pp. 263–75.

[40] John Townsend to John Sherman, Dec. 13, 1890, John Sherman Papers, Manuscript Division, Library of Congress; St. Louis *Republic,* June 19, 1890; Brooklyn *Daily Times,* June 18, 1890.

[41] *Cong. Rec.,* 51st Cong., 1st sess. (June 17, 1890), p. 6167; New York *Tribune,* May 2, 1890; Washington *Post,* June 5–8, 1890.

[42] Entry for Jan. 20, 1890, E. W. Halford Diary, Harrison Papers; Sievers, *Harrison: Hoosier President,* pp. 145–48.

[43] Washington *Post,* June 18, 1890; New York *Tribune,* Jan. 20, Feb. 26, June 18, 1890; Chicago *Tribune,* Jan. 21, 1890; William E. Russell, "Political Causes of the Business Depression," *North American Review,* 157 (Dec., 1893), 644–45.

[44] *Cong. Rec.,* 51st Cong., 1st sess. (June 7, 1890), pp. 5814–15; Edward Nelson Dingley, *The Life and Times of Nelson Dingley, Jr.*

(Kalamazoo, Mich., 1902), pp. 326–29; Washington *Post,* June 5–8, 1890; New York *Tribune,* June 19, 1890.

[45] Hoxie, "Silver Debate of 1890," pp. 542–44; W. Rett Lauck, *The Causes of the Panic of 1893* (Boston, 1907), pp. 30–31; Washington *Post,* July 13, 1890; Richard E. Welch, Jr., *George Frisbie Hoar and the Half-Breed Republicans* (Cambridge, Mass., 1971), pp. 149–51.

[46] *Cong. Rec.,* 51st Cong., 1st sess. (July 10, 1890), pp. 7104, 7109, (July 12, 1890), p. 7226; Harrison to Caroline Scott Harrison, July 13, 1890, in Sievers, *Harrison: Hoosier President,* p. 148; New York *Tribune,* July 11–15, 1890; Hartford *Times,* July 14, 1890.

[47] Chicago *Tribune,* March 18, 1890; P. C. Cheney to L. T. Michener, March 23, 1893, Harrison Papers; Lewis L. Gould, "William McKinley, Theodore Roosevelt, and the Expansion of Presidential Power," paper given at the Organization of American Historians annual meeting, April 9, 1976, St. Louis, Mo.

[48] New York *World,* Aug. 3–5, 1890; New York *Times,* Aug. 8, 1890.

[49] Philadelphia *Press,* Aug. 14, 1890; New York *Tribune,* Aug. 14, 1890; Baltimore *American and Commercial Advertiser,* Aug. 17, 1890, in scrapbooks in Harrison Papers.

[50] *Cong. Rec.,* 51st Cong., 1st sess. (Aug. 12, 1890), pp. 8466, 8488–89; New York *Tribune,* Aug. 13–15, 22–25, 1890; Philadelphia *Inquirer,* Aug. 14, 1890; George F. Hoar, "The Fate of the Election Bill," *The Forum,* 11 (March, 1891), 130–32.

[51] Spooner to Henry C. Payne, Aug. 13, 1890, Spooner to W. W. Lockwood, Aug. 18, 1890, Spooner Papers; Dorothy Ganfield Fowler, *John Coit Spooner: Defender of Presidents* (New York, 1961), pp. 133–38.

[52] Welch, *Hoar,* pp. 154–55; Philadelphia *Times,* Aug. 14, 1890; George Frisbie Hoar, *Autobiography of Seventy Years,* 2 vols. (New York, 1903), 2, 155–56.

[53] J. C. Kerr to Dolliver, April 2, 1890, in Ross, *Dolliver,* p. 96; Chicago *Tribune,* April 1–2, June 19–20, 1890; Washington *Post,* June 7, 19, 1890; New York *Tribune,* Sept. 23, 1890; *The Nation,* 51 (Aug. 7, 1890), 101.

[54] Blaine to Harrison, July 21, 1890, Blaine to Harrison, July 22,

1890, Harrison Papers; William E. Curtis, "Friends in South America," *North American Review,* 149 (Sept., 1889), 377–79.

[55] Stoddard, *As I Knew Them,* p. 236; New York *Herald,* June 21, 23, 1890, Aug. 5, 1891; *The Nation,* 50 (June 26, 1890), 502.

[56] Blaine to William P. Frye, July 11, 1890, in Hamilton, *Biography of James G. Blaine,* pp. 686–87; Dingley, *Life and Times of Nelson Dingley,* pp. 330–32; Brooklyn *Times,* June 20, 1890; New York *Evening Post,* June 20, 1890; Philadelphia *Times,* July 15, 1890; *The Nation,* 51 (Aug. 14, 1890), 122–23.

[57] Hamilton, *Biography of James G. Blaine,* pp. 687–88; Cornelius N. Bliss to Charles R. Flint, July 28, 1890, James G. Blaine Papers, Manuscript Division, Library of Congress.

[58] Blaine to Harrison, July 19, 1890, Harrison Papers; Harrison to Blaine, July 23, 1890, in Albert T. Volwiler, ed., *The Correspondence between Benjamin Harrison and James G. Blaine, 1882–1893* (Philadelphia, 1940), p. 112; New York *Tribune,* Sept. 10, 1890.

[59] Washington *Post,* Sept. 27, 1890; New York *Tribune,* Sept. 27, 1890; transcript, Harrison-McKinley conversation, White House special wire, Sept. 1890, in Harrison Papers; Frank W. Taussig, *The Tariff History of the United States* (New York, 1892), pp. 251–83.

[60] *Cong. Rec.,* 51st Cong., 1st sess. (Sept. 27, 1890), pp. 10575–10641, (Sept. 30, 1890), p. 10740; New York *Tribune,* Oct. 1, 1890; Chicago *Tribune,* Sept. 27, Oct. 1–2, 1890.

[61] New York *Tribune,* Oct. 2, 1890; Stoddard, *As I Knew Them,* p. 236.

[62] New York *Press,* Oct. 2, 1890; New York *Tribune,* Oct. 2, 1890; Spooner to Henry C. Payne, Sept. 11, 1890, Spooner Papers; Washington *Post,* Oct. 2, 1890.

[63] Baltimore *American and Commercial Advertiser,* June 2, 1890, in scrapbooks in Harrison Papers; Robinson, *Reed,* pp. 241–49; New York *Tribune,* Sept. 4–5, 1890.

CHAPTER THREE

[1] Cleveland to Lamont, Sept. 13, 1890, Cleveland Papers.

[2] Cleveland to William F. Vilas, Sept. 15, 1889, in Nevins, *Letters of Grover Cleveland,* pp. 210-11; Watterson to Cleveland, April 13, 1890, Cleveland Papers.

[3] Cleveland to Carlisle, April 7, 1890, in Nevins, *Letters of Grover Cleveland,* pp. 221-22; L. T. Michener to E. W. Halford, Oct. 21, 1890, Harrison Papers; W. L. Scott to Cleveland, April 4, 1890, Cleveland Papers.

[4] St. Louis *Republic,* Oct. 16, 1890; New York *Evening Post,* Oct. 20, 1890; Hartford *Times,* Oct. 22, 1890; Norfolk *Virginian,* Oct. 22, 1890: clippings in scrapbooks in Harrison Papers.

[5] Robert Bolt, "A Biography of Donald M. Dickinson" (unpublished Ph.D. dissertation, Michigan State University, 1963), pp. 178-79; James S. Clarkson to Halford, Nov. 20, 1890, Michener to Halford, Oct. 25, 1890, Harrison Papers; Chicago *Tribune,* Nov. 1, 1890.

[6] Thelen, *The New Citizenship,* pp. 1-3, 33-85; New York *Tribune,* Sept. 9, 1890; St. Louis *Globe-Democrat,* Sept. 4, 1890; Morgan, *McKinley,* p. 148.

[7] James S. Clarkson to Halford, Dec. 5, 1891, Harrison Papers; Richard Harmond, "Troubles of Massachusetts Republicans During the 1880s," *Mid-America,* 56 (April, 1974), 85-99; Lois Bannister Merk, "Boston's Historic Public School Crisis," *The New England Quarterly,* 31 (June, 1958), 172-99.

[8] Jensen, *Winning of the Midwest,* pp. 58-68; Kleppner, *The Cross of Culture,* pp. 35-91; Frederick C. Luebke, "German Immigrants and the Churches in Nebraska, 1889-1915," *Mid-America,* 50 (April, 1968), 121-30.

[9] Cyrenus Cole, *Iowa through the Years* (Iowa City, Iowa, 1940), pp. 363-79; New York *Times,* Nov. 7, 1889.

[10] Chicago *Tribune,* Sept. 23, 1890; Louise Phelps Kellogg, "The Bennett Law in Wisconsin," *The Wisconsin Magazine of History,* 2 (Sept., 1918), 3-25; J. J. Mapel, "The Repeal of the Compulsory Education Laws in Wisconsin and Illinois," *Educational Review,* 1 (Jan., 1891), 53-55.

[11] H. C. Payne to Jeremiah Rusk, Dec. 2, 1890, in Richard N. Current, *Pine Logs and Politics: A Life of Philetus Sawyer, 1816-1900* (Madison, Wis., 1950), pp. 253-54; William F. Whyte, "The

Bennett Law Campaign in Wisconsin," *The Wisconsin Magazine of History,* 10 (June, 1927), 377–90.

[12] Ross, *Dolliver,* p. 65; Jean B. Kern, "The Political Career of Horace Boies," *Iowa Journal of History,* 47 (July, 1949), 215–46.

[13] Frank B. Tracy, "The Rise and Doom of the Populist Party," *Forum,* 16 (Oct., 1893), 243; Lawrence Goodwyn, *Democratic Promise: The Populist Moment in America* (New York, 1976), pp. 25–86, 177–212.

[14] P. L. Scritsmier to N. P. Haugen, Oct. 10, 1890, in Jensen, *Winning of the Midwest,* p. 148; Walter T. K. Nugent, *The Tolerant Populists: Kansas Populism and Nativism* (Chicago, 1963), pp. 94–95; Chicago *Tribune,* Nov. 2, 1890.

[15] C. Vann Woodward, *Origins of the New South, 1877–1913* (Baton Rouge, 1951), pp. 175–93; Robert C. McMath, Jr., *Populist Vanguard: A History of the Southern Farmers' Alliance* (Chapel Hill, 1975), pp. 33–89.

[16] Victor Murdock, *"Folks"* (New York, 1921), p. 102; C. Vann Woodward, *Tom Watson: Agrarian Rebel* (New York, 1938), pp. 129–66; Elizabeth N. Barr, "The Populist Uprising," in William E. Connelley, ed., *A Standard History of Kansas and Kansans,* 2 vols. (Chicago, 1918), 2, 1167–68.

[17] Annie L. Diggs, "The Women in the Alliance Movement," *The Arena,* 6 (July, 1892), 166–67.

[18] O. Gene Clanton, *Kansas Populism: Ideas and Men* (Lawrence, Kan., 1969), pp. 37–39, 74–84; Goodwyn, *Democratic Promise,* pp. 157–59.

[19] New York *Tribune,* Aug. 3, 1890; J. L. Lockhart to Arthur C. Mellette, July 13, 1890, in Howard R. Lamar, *Dakota Territory, 1861–1889: A Study of Frontier Politics* (New Haven, 1956), p. 274; Washington *Post,* Oct. 29, 1890.

[20] St. Louis *Republic,* Nov. 5, 1890; Harrison to Howard Cale, Nov. 17, 1890, Harrison Papers; Brooklyn *Standard-Union,* Nov. 5, 1890; New York *Tribune,* Nov. 5, 1890.

[21] Blodgett, *The Gentle Reformers,* pp. 98–99; Gerald W. McFarland, "The Breakdown of Deadlock: The Cleveland Democracy in Connecticut, 1884–1894," *The Historian,* 31 (May, 1969), 394–95;

Roger E. Wyman, "Wisconsin Ethnic Groups and the Election of 1890," *Wisconsin Magazine of History,* 51 (Summer, 1968), 269-93.

[22] Philadelphia *Bulletin,* Nov. 18, 1890; Stuart Noblin, *Leonidas _aFayette Polk: Agrarian Crusader* (Chapel Hill, 1949), p. 227; Frank M. Drew, "The Present Farmers' Movement," *Political Science Quarterly,* 6 (June, 1891), 308-309.

[23] Clanton, *Kansas Populism,* pp. 87-90; Stanley B. Parsons, *The Populist Context: Rural Versus Urban Power on a Great Plains Frontier* (Westport, Conn., 1973), pp. 75-90.

[24] Woodward, *Origins of the New South,* pp. 203-204, 235; Washington *Post,* Nov. 6, 1890.

[25] Noblin, *Polk,* p. 227; Brooklyn *Standard-Union,* Dec. 11, 1890, in scrapbooks in Harrison Papers; New York *Herald,* Dec. 9, 1890; Frank B. Tracy, "Menacing Socialism in the Western States," *The Forum,* 15 (May, 1893), 332-42.

[26] Philadelphia *Inquirer,* Nov. 6, 1890; John B. Elam to Halford, Jan. 8, 1891, Harrison Papers.

[27] Reed to Lodge, Nov. 5, 1890, in Robinson, *Reed,* p. 249; Chicago *Tribune,* Nov. 6, 1890; Harrison to Howard Cale, Nov. 17, 1890, Harrison Papers; St. Louis *Globe-Democrat,* Nov. 16, 1890.

[28] Entry for Dec. 20, 1890, Lodge Diary, in Garraty, *Lodge,* p. 122.

[29] Cleveland to L. Clarke Davis, Nov. 5, 1890, Cleveland to L.Q.C. Lamar, May 1, 1892, in Nevins, *Letters of Grover Cleveland,* pp. 233, 280-81; *The Nation,* 51 (Nov. 13, 1892), 372.

[30] Ray Stannard Baker, *Native American: The Book of My Youth* (New York, 1941), p. 249; New York *Tribune,* Feb. 23, 1892.

[31] New York *Tribune,* Jan. 9, 1891, Jan. 9, 1892; San Francisco *Examiner,* May 13, 1891; Chicago *Tribune,* Nov. 1, 1891.

[32] Barnes, *Carlisle,* pp. 196-98; Kern, "The Political Career of Horace Boies," pp. 228-34.

[33] Bass, *"I Am a Democrat,"* pp. 201-33; Cleveland to William F. Vilas, Oct. 17, 1889, Cleveland to Wilson S. Bissell, Nov. 8, 1890, Cleveland Papers.

[34] Cleveland to E. Ellery Anderson, Feb. 10, 1891, in Nevins, *Letters of Grover Cleveland,* pp. 245-46.

[35] Cleveland to Vilas, Feb. 18, 1891, Cleveland Papers; New Orleans *Daily Picayune,* Feb. 13, 1891; Chicago *Times,* Feb. 13, 1891; Richard Watson Gilder, *Grover Cleveland: A Record of Friendship* (New York, 1910), pp. 31–33.

[36] San Francisco *Examiner,* March 18, 1892; *Cong. Rec.,* 52 Cong., 1st sess. (July 13, 1892), pp. 6128–29; Atlanta *Constitution,* Feb. 13, 1891; *People's Party Paper,* April 14, 1892.

[37] New York *Tribune,* Feb. 23, 1892; Bourke Cockran to Stephen M. White, Feb. 15, 1892, White to Cockran, May 20, 1892, Stephen M. White Papers, Stanford University Libraries, Stanford, Cal.

[38] Nevins, *Cleveland,* p. 491; Washington *Post,* June 23, 1892; *Official Proceedings of the National Democratic Convention* (Chicago, 1892), pp. 76–155.

[39] St. Louis *Republic,* Sept. 18, 1891; Washington *Evening Star,* Nov. 3, 1891: clippings in scrapbooks in Harrison Papers; New York *Times,* Nov. 5, 1891; William C. Endicott to Cleveland, Nov. 7, 1891, Cleveland Papers.

[40] Cleveland to William C. Whitney, July 9, 1892, William C. Whitney Papers, Manuscript Division, Library of Congress; Cleveland to William E. Russell, July 13, 1892, Cleveland Papers.

[41] Parker, *Recollections of Grover Cleveland,* p. 154; Mark D. Hirsch, *William C. Whitney: Modern Warwick* (New York, 1948), pp. 397–412; Nevins, *Cleveland,* p. 498.

[42] Richardson, *Messages and Papers of the Presidents,* 7, 5542–64; *Through the South and West with the President, April 14–May 15, 1891* (New York, 1891); Dorothy Ganfield Fowler, *The Cabinet Politician: The Postmasters General, 1829–1909* (New York, 1943), p. 220.

[43] Chicago *Tribune,* Dec. 1, 1890.

[44] Crofts, "The Blair Bill and the Elections Bill," p. 325; Spooner to Jeremiah Rusk, Jan. 27, 1891, in Fowler, *Spooner,* pp. 156–58.

[45] *Cong. Rec.,* 51st Cong., 2d sess. (March 2, 1891), p. 3825; New York *Tribune,* March 5, 1891; Baltimore *Sun,* March 5, 1891.

[46] New York *Herald,* June 9, 1890; New York *Tribune,* March 5, 1891; Harrison to John A. Sleicher, Aug. 11, 1892, Harrison Papers; Welch, "The Federal Elections Bill," pp. 511–25.

[47] Royal Cortissoz, *The Life of Whitelaw Reid,* 2 vols. (New York, 1921), 2, 176; John W. Foster, *Diplomatic Memoirs,* 2 vols. (Boston, 1909), 2, 253; Solomon Bulkeley Griffin, *People and Politics* (Boston, 1923), p. 304; Foraker, *I Would Live It Again,* p. 133.

[48] Eric L. McKitrick, *Andrew Johnson and Reconstruction* (Chicago, 1960), p. 381; Morgan, *McKinley,* p. 136; Robinson, *Reed,* pp. 160–61; Quay to G. F. Little, Sept. 17, 1890, Stephen B. Elkins to Michener, June 12, 1890, Harrison Papers.

[49] Chicago *Herald,* June 14, 1891; Chicago *Tribune,* June 30, 1891; G. F. Little to Halford, undated (Sept., 1890), W. O. Bradley to Harrison, Jan. 14, 1892, Harrison Papers; C. A. Boutelle to Reed, Aug. 22, 1891, Reed Papers.

[50] Speech in Galveston, Texas, April 18, 1891, in *Through the South and West with the President,* p. 30; Philadelphia *Times,* April 24, 1891.

[51] Walter LaFeber, *The New Empire: An Interpretation of American Expansion, 1860-1898* (Ithaca, N.Y., 1963), pp. 102–49; New York *Mail and Express,* Feb. 5, 1891; Chicago *Tribune,* Feb. 7–9, 1891.

[52] Blaine to Harrison, Feb. 7, 1891, S. Brock to Halford, July 23, 1892, William E. Curtis to Halford, July 26, 1892, Harrison Papers; Tom E. Terrill, *The Tariff, Politics, and American Foreign Policy, 1874-1901* (Westport, Conn., 1973), pp. 175–81; Blaine to John Hopley, Oct. 14, 1891, in Philadelphia *Ledger and Transcript,* Oct. 17, 1891.

[53] Muzzey, *Blaine,* pp. 459–74; Harrison to William B. Allison, May 23, 1891, Harrison Papers.

[54] St. Louis *Globe-Democrat,* June 26, 1891; Louis T. Michener to Halford, Aug. 10, 1891, Harrison Papers; New York *World,* Sept. 10, 1891; Boston *Globe,* Sept. 15, 1891; James M. Swank to Blaine, Feb. 2, 1892, Blaine Papers.

[55] Blaine to Clarkson, Feb. 6, 1892, in Hamilton, *Biography of Blaine,* pp. 699–700; New York *Herald,* Feb. 8, 1892; New York *Times,* Feb. 9, 1892; Resolutions of State Republican Conventions, May, 1892, and Gilbert Pierce to Halford, Nov. 30 (1891), Harrison Papers.

[56] Unidentified clipping, May 4, 1892, in scrapbooks in Harrison

Papers; Blaine to Harrison, May 9, 1892, Russell B. Harrison to Blaine, May 9, 1892, Blaine to Harrison, May 11, 1892, Harrison Papers.

[57] Blaine to Harrison, June 4, 1892, Harrison Papers; E. W. Halford, "Harrison in the White House," *Leslie's Magazine,* 128 (May 3, 1919), 671, 685.

[58] Charles H. T. Collis to Halford, June 4, 1892, Harrison Papers; Cincinnati *Commercial Gazette,* June 5, 1892; New York *Times,* June 4–5, 1892; New York *Mail and Express,* June 5, 1892.

[59] H. V. Boynton to Halford, June 11, 1892, Michener to Halford, June 7, 1892, William Penn Nixon to Halford, June 9, 1892, Harrison Papers; New York *Times,* June 5–11, 1892; James S. Clarkson, "Which Is the True Platt?" undated manuscript, Thomas C. Platt Papers, Yale University, New Haven, Conn.

[60] Hanna to John Sherman, June 14, 1892, Sherman Papers; Harrison to W. O. Bradley, Nov. 16, 1892, Harrison Papers; Robinson, *Reed,* p. 283; Rowland B. Mahany to Blaine, Sept. 20, 1892, Blaine Papers.

[61] New York *Herald,* July 24, 1892; Joseph Frazier Wall, *Andrew Carnegie* (New York, 1970), pp. 537–82; Edward Bemis, "The Homestead Strike," *The Journal of Political Economy,* 2 (June, 1894), 369–96; Henry David, "Upheaval at Homestead," in Daniel Aaron, ed., *America in Crisis* (New York, 1952), pp. 133–70.

[62] *House of Representatives Report No. 2447,* 52nd Cong., 2d sess. (Feb. 7, 1893), p. xxix; Hugh O'Donnell to Whitelaw Reid, July 16, 1892, Memorandum of Frick Visit, July 30, 1892, Whitelaw Reid Papers, Manuscript Division, Library of Congress; Chicago *Herald,* July 8, 1892.

[63] Robert H. Walker, *The Poet and the Gilded Age: Social Themes in Late 19th Century American Verse* (Philadelphia, 1963), pp. 230–31; Baltimore *American,* Aug. 19, 1892, Philadelphia *Evening Bulletin,* Aug. 18, 1892, Cincinnati *Commercial Gazette,* Oct. 5, 1892, in scrapbooks in Harrison Papers.

[64] Nevins, *Cleveland,* p. 508; Chicago *Tribune,* Nov. 10, 1892; New York *Tribune,* Nov. 8–10, 1892.

[65] Joseph H. Manley to Harrison, Nov. 9, 1892, Harrison Papers; Carl N. Degler, "American Political Parties and the Rise of the City: An Interpretation," *Journal of American History,* 51 (June, 1964), 46–47;

John M. Allswang, *A House for All Peoples: Ethnic Politics in Chicago, 1890-1936* (Louisville, Ky., 1971), pp. 23-24.

[66] Jensen, *Winning of the Midwest,* pp. 154-77; Baltimore *Sun,* Nov. 2, 1892; New York *Recorder,* Oct. 20, 1892, in scrapbooks in Harrison Papers. Voter turnout in the northern states was the lowest since 1872, perhaps partly because of the voters' unfamiliarity with the new campaign style.

[67] Noblin, *Polk,* pp. 286-91; *People's Party Paper,* Jan. 7, 1892, July 8, 1892; New York *Tribune,* July 2-6, 1892; Thomas E. Watson, "Why the People's Party Should Elect the Next President," *The Arena,* 6 (July, 1892), 203-204.

[68] Barr, "The Populist Uprising," 2, 1183; James E. Wright, *The Politics of Populism: Dissent in Colorado* (New Haven, Conn., 1974), p. 151; *People's Party Paper,* Sept. 30, 1892.

[69] Wright, *Politics of Populism,* pp. 151-58; Jensen, *Winning of the Midwest,* p. 170; Samuel Gompers, "Organized Labor in the Campaign," *North American Review,* 155 (July, 1892), 93; Theodore Saloutos, "The Professors and the Populists," *Agricultural History,* 40 (Oct., 1966), 238.

[70] Entry for Nov. 10, 1892, Donnelly Diary, in Martin Ridge, *Ignatius Donnelly: The Portrait of a Politician* (Chicago, 1962), p. 309; William Warren Rogers, *The One-Gallused Rebellion: Agrarianism in Alabama, 1865-1896* (Baton Rouge, 1970), pp. 188-235.

[71] *People's Party Paper,* Nov. 25, 1892; Washington *Post,* Nov. 11, 1892.

[72] Harrison to C. N. Bliss, Nov. 16, 1892, Harrison Papers; Richardson, *Messages and Papers of the Presidents,* 8, 5745.

[73] New York *Press,* Nov. 9, 1892, in scrapbooks in Harrison Papers; New York *Times,* Jan. 18, 28, 1893; New York *Herald,* Jan. 28, 1893.

[74] Washington *Post,* Nov. 12, 1892; Orville H. Platt to Wharton Barker, Nov. 15, 1892, Wharton Barker Papers, Manuscript Division, Library of Congress.

[75] Brooklyn *Standard-Union,* Nov. 19, 1892.

CHAPTER FOUR

[1] Richardson, *Messages and Papers of the Presidents,* 8, 5821-25;

New York *Tribune,* March 3-5, 1893; San Francisco *Examiner,* March 5, 1893.

[2] New York *Tribune,* Feb. 2, 1893; New Orleans *Daily Picayune,* March 5, 1893; Atlanta *Constitution,* March 4-5, 1893.

[3] *Review of Reviews,* 7 (April, 1893), 260.

[4] Woodrow Wilson, "Mr. Cleveland's Cabinet," *Review of Reviews,* 7 (April, 1893), 287; Cleveland to Thomas F. Bayard, Feb. 13, 1895, Cleveland Papers; San Francisco *Examiner,* Feb. 11, 1893.

[5] McElroy, *Cleveland,* 2, 6.

[6] Olney description is Theodore Roosevelt's, in Morison, *The Letters of Theodore Roosevelt,* 1, 393; Stephen M. White to A. W. Barrett, Aug. 17, 1893, White Papers; Dewey W. Grantham, Jr., *Hoke Smith and the Politics of the New South* (Baton Rouge, 1958), pp. 43-59.

[7] Entry for June 5, 1896, in Festus P. Summers, ed., *The Cabinet Diary of William L. Wilson, 1896–1897* (Chapel Hill, 1957), p. 97; Josephus Daniels, *Editor in Politics* (Chapel Hill, 1941), pp. 52-53; James A. Barnes, "Myths of the Bryan Campaign," *Mississippi Valley Historical Review,* 34 (Dec., 1947), 399.

[8] Chicago *Tribune,* May 1-2, 1893; New York *Tribune,* May 2, 1893; *The Spectator,* 70 (May 6, 1893), 590, 594-95; Larzer Ziff, *The American 1890s: Life and Times of a Lost Generation* (New York, 1966), pp. 3-23.

[9] Richardson, *Messages and Papers of the Presidents,* 8, 5741-44; R. G. Dun & Co., in Boston *Journal,* Dec. 31, 1892.

[10] Charles Hoffman, *The Depression of the Nineties: An Economic History* (Westport, Conn., 1970), pp. 47-141; New York *Tribune,* Feb. 18-19, 1893.

[11] W. Jett Lauck, *The Causes of the Panic of 1893* (Boston, 1907), pp. 65-94; New York *Tribune,* Feb. 2-10, 14-15, 1893; Brooklyn *Daily Eagle,* Feb. 4, 1893; George R. Gibson, "The Financial Excitement and its Causes," *The Forum,* 15 (June, 1893), 483-93. The Sherman Silver Purchase Act required the Treasury to purchase 4,500,000 ounces of silver each month and to issue in payment Treasury notes redeemable in gold or silver at the Treasury's option.

[12] Henry Lee Higginson to Olney, April 19, 1893, Richard Olney Papers, Manuscript Division, Library of Congress.

[13] New York *Tribune,* May 3-7, 1893; Washington *Post,* May 6, 1893; Jonathan W. Macartney to Reed, May 4, 1893, Reed Papers.

[14] Entry for May 14, 1893, in Charles G. Dawes, *A Journal of the McKinley Years* (Chicago, 1950), p. 28; Albert C. Stevens, "Analysis of the Phenomena of the Panic in the United States in 1893," *The Quarterly Journal of Economics,* 8 (Jan., 1894), 126-44.

[15] Samuel Rezneck, "Unemployment, Unrest, and Relief in the United States During the Depression of 1893-1897," *The Journal of Political Economy,* 61 (Aug., 1953), 325-27; New York *Tribune,* Aug. 2, 1893.

[16] New York *Tribune,* Aug. 16, Oct. 14, Dec. 24, 1893; American Federation of Labor, *Report of Proceedings of the Annual Convention* (New York, 1893), p. 11.

[17] Ray Stannard Baker to J. S. Baker, Dec. 15, 1893, in Robert C. Bannister, Jr., *Ray Stannard Baker: The Mind and Thought of a Progressive* (New Haven, Conn., 1966), p. 43; Carlos C. Closson, Jr., "The Unemployed in American Cities," *The Quarterly Journal of Economics,* 8 (Jan., 1894), 192.

[18] Karel D. Bicha, "The Conservative Populists: A Hypothesis," *Agricultural History,* 47 (April, 1973), 9-24; Henry Markham Page, *Pasadena: Its Early Years* (Los Angeles, 1964), 182-83.

[19] Charles Francis Adams, *Charles Francis Adams, 1835-1915: An Autobiography* (Boston, 1916), p. 200.

[20] Superior *Evening Telegram,* March 21, 1896, in Thelen, *The New Citizenship,* p. 55; Grover Cleveland, *Presidential Problems* (New York, 1904), p. 80.

[21] Cleveland to Carlisle, Jan. 22, 1893, in Nevins, *Letters of Grover Cleveland,* pp. 314-15; Olney Autobiography, in Olney Papers; Washington *Post,* Jan. 22, 1893; Henry Clews, *The Wall Street Point of View* (New York, 1900), pp. 71-73.

[22] Washington *Post,* June 27-July 1, 1893; Atlanta *Constitution,* June 29, July 1, 1893.

[23] Richardson, *Messages and Papers of the Presidents,* 8, 5828; Cleveland to Henry T. Thurber, Aug. 20, 1893, Cleveland Papers.

[24] Nevins, *Cleveland,* p. 532.

[25] *People's Party Paper,* July 14, 1893; New York *Tribune,* July 2–5, 1893; Philadelphia *Press,* Aug. 29, 1893.

[26] Stephen M. White to W. M. Eddy, Aug. 22, 1893, White Papers.

[27] New York *Tribune,* June 28, 1893; William M. Stewart, *The Reminiscences of Senator William M. Stewart of Nevada* (New York, 1906), p. 313; "The Business Outlook," *North American Review,* 157 (Oct., 1893), 385–98.

[28] Leon W. Fuller, "Colorado's Revolt Against Capitalism," *Mississippi Valley Historical Review,* 21 (Dec., 1934), 343. Significantly, the Denver meeting tried to call in debts from southern Democrats in 1891's "force bill" fight. "We saved you then. You can save us now."

[29] New York *Tribune,* July 12–13, Aug. 2–4, 1893; *People's Party Paper,* July 7, 21, 1893.

[30] *Cong. Rec.,* 53d Cong., 1st sess. (Aug. 7, 1893), p. 197; Richardson, *Messages and Papers of the Presidents,* 8, 5833–37; James J. Hill to Cleveland, Aug. 9, 1893, Cleveland Papers; New York *Tribune,* Aug. 6–9, 1893.

[31] *Cong. Rec.,* 53d Cong., lst sess. (Aug. 16, 1893), pp. 410–11, (Aug. 26, 1893), Appendix, p. 552; *Cong. Rec.,* 53d Cong., 2d sess. (March 7, 1894), p. 2673; New Orleans *Daily Picayune,* Aug. 7–9, 1893.

[32] Ross, *Dolliver,* p. 104.

[33] *Cong. Rec.,* 53d Cong., 1st sess. (Aug. 28, 1893), pp. 1004–1008; William E. Curtis to Elizabeth Curtis, Aug. 28, 1893, William E. Curtis Papers, Manuscript Division, Library of Congress.

[34] *Cong. Rec.,* 52d Cong., 2d sess. (Feb. 17, 1893), p. 1734; entry for Aug. 18, 1893, Charles S. Hamlin Diary, Charles S. Hamlin Papers, Manuscript Division, Library of Congress; White to W. M. Eddy, Aug. 22, 1893, White Papers.

[35] New York *Tribune,* Oct. 17–23, 1893; Washington *Post,* Sept. 8, 1893; *Cong. Rec.,* 53d Cong., 1st sess. (Oct. 4, 1893), pp. 2106–19. Seigniorage is the government's profit when it purchases bullion at a

price below the value placed on the metal when coined; it is the difference between intrinsic value and face value.

[36] Josephus Daniels, *Editor in Politics,* p. 54.

[37] Morton to Olney, Oct. 22, 1893, Olney Papers; J. R. McPherson to Cleveland, Oct. 23, 1893, Voorhees to Cleveland, Oct. 24, 1893, Cleveland Papers; Washington *Post,* Oct. 25-27, 1893.

[38] Washington *Post,* Oct. 25, 29, 1893; *Cong. Rec.,* 53d Cong., 1st sess. (Oct. 28, 1893), pp. 2917-26, (Oct. 30, 1893), p. 2958; New York *Tribune,* Nov. 2, 1893.

[39] Raleigh *News and Observer,* Nov. 2, 1893; Andrew Carnegie, "A Word to Wage-Earners," *North American Review,* 157 (Sept., 1893), 365; New York *Tribune,* Nov. 1-3, 1893; F. W. Taussig, "The United States Treasury in 1894-1896," *The Quarterly Journal of Economics,* 13 (Jan., 1899), 204-205.

[40] Louisville *Courier-Journal,* July 10, 1904, in Arthur Krock, ed., *The Editorials of Henry Watterson* (New York, 1923), pp. 98-99.

[41] O. O. Stealey, *Twenty Years in the Press Gallery* (New York, 1906), p. 28; Thomas G. Jones to Cleveland, Nov. 14, 1893, Cleveland Papers; Los Angeles *Times,* Aug. 29, Oct. 31, 1893.

[42] Washington *Post,* Nov. 8-9, 1893; New York *Tribune,* Nov. 8-9, 1893; Morton to John P. Irish, Nov. 8, 1893, J. Sterling Morton Papers, Nebraska Historical Society, Lincoln, Neb.

[43] E. M. Ross to Jackson A. Graves, Nov. 10, 1893, Jackson A. Graves Papers, Henry E. Huntington Library, San Marino, Cal.; Washington *Post,* Nov. 8-9, 1893; Chicago *Tribune,* Dec. 21, 1893, April 3-5, 1894.

[44] *Cong. Rec.,* 53d Cong., 2d sess. (March 1, 1894), pp. 2524-25, (March 7, 1894), pp. 2673-75, (March 15, 1894), p. 2981; Chicago *Times,* March 20-30, 1894; Washington *Post,* March 16, 28-30, 1894. The bill proposed to add about $55,000,000 in silver currency to a money stock of nearly $2 billion.

[45] Washington *Star,* March 17, 1894; George Gray to Cleveland, undated, 1894, Cleveland Papers; Raleigh *News-Observer-Chronicle,* March 31, 1894; Atlanta *Constitution,* March 30-31, 1894; Washington *Post,* March 30, 1894.

[46] San Francisco *Examiner,* March 30, 1894; Cleveland to Everett P. Wheeler, April 16, 1894, in Nevins, *Letters of Grover Cleveland,* p. 351; John Hay to C. S. H., Aug. 5, 1894, in *Letters of John Hay and Extracts from Diary,* 3 vols. (New York, 1969), 2, 318.

[47] Hoffman, *Depression of the Nineties,* pp. xxviii, 63-79, 97-110; Cyrenus Cole, *I Remember, I Remember: A Book of Recollections* (Iowa City, Iowa, 1936), p. 211; Fred A. Shannon, *The Farmers' Last Frontier: Agriculture, 1860-1897* (New York, 1945), pp. 114, 415.

[48] *Bradstreet's,* 22 (April 7, 1894), 209; Adams to Sir Robert Cunliffe, June 21, 1894, in W. C. Ford, ed., *Letters of Henry Adams,* 2 vols. (Boston, 1938), 2, 50.

[49] W. T. Stead, "'Coxeyism': A Character Sketch," *The Review of Reviews,* 10 (July, 1894), 52; New York *Tribune,* March 24-26, 1894.

[50] San Francisco *Examiner,* March 23, 1894; Hill to Cleveland, April 24, 1894, Cleveland Papers; Donald L. McMurry, *Coxey's Army: A Study of the Industrial Army Movement of 1894* (Boston, 1929), pp. 127-292.

[51] A. Cleveland Hall, "An Observer in Coxey's Camp," *The Independent,* 46 (May 17, 1894), 615-16; Thorstein Veblen, "The Army of the Commonweal," *The Journal of Political Economy,* 2 (June, 1894), 456-57; *People's Party Paper,* May 11, 1894; B. O. Flower, "Emergency Measures Which Would Have Maintained Self-Respecting Manhood," *The Arena,* 9 (May, 1894), 822-26.

[52] Stanley Buder, *Pullman: An Experiment in Industrial Order and Community Planning, 1880-1930* (New York, 1967), pp. 147-201; San Francisco *Chronicle,* July 7, 1894; Harrison Gray Otis to Thomas R. Bard, July 18, 1894, Thomas R. Bard Papers, Huntington Library.

[53] Caro Lloyd, *Henry Demarest Lloyd, 1847-1903: A Biography,* 2 vols. (New York, 1912), 2, 147.

[54] Altgeld to Cleveland, July 5, 1894, Cleveland Papers; Grover Cleveland, "The Government in the Chicago Strike of 1894," *McClure's Magazine,* 23 (July, 1904), 227-40.

[55] Washington *Post,* July 5, 1894.

[56] Washington *Post,* July 7, 1894; William E. Curtis to his mother, July 7, 1894, Curtis Papers; Almont Lindsey, *The Pullman Strike: The*

Story of a Unique Experiment and of a Great Labor Upheaval (Chicago, 1942), pp. 147–238.

[57] Morton to John P. Irish, July 21, 1894, Morton Papers; Joseph H. Call to Olney, July 18, 1894, in *Appendix to the Annual Report of the Attorney-General of the United States for the Year 1896* (Washington, D.C., 1896), p. 34; Chicago *Times,* July 21, 1894.

[58] Francis Lynde Stetson to Cleveland, Oct. 7, 1894, Cleveland Papers.

[59] Robinson, *Reed,* pp. 294–304; Roosevelt to Anna Roosevelt, June 24, 1894, in Morison, *Letters of Theodore Roosevelt,* 1, 385; Brady and Althoff, "Party Voting in the U.S. House of Representatives," p. 764.

[60] *Cong. Rec.,* 53d Cong., 2d sess. (Feb. 1, 1894), pp. 1781–97, Appendix, pp. 203–205; Summers, *William L. Wilson and Tariff Reform,* pp. 174–86; F. W. Taussig, "The Tariff Act of 1894," *Political Science Quarterly,* 9 (Dec., 1894), 585–609.

[61] Stephen M. White to Victor Montgomery, June 21, 1894, White Papers.

[62] Washington *Post,* July 2, 1894; Chicago *Tribune,* March 9, 1894; Terrill, *The Tariff, Politics, and American Foreign Policy,* pp. 184–98.

[63] *Cong. Rec.,* 53d Cong., 2d sess. (July 19, 1894), pp. 7710–13, (July 20, 1894), pp. 7730–37, (July 23, 1894), pp. 7801–7809; Washington *Post,* July 20–21, 24, 1894.

[64] New York *Tribune,* Oct. 14, 1894; Cleveland to Wilson, Aug. 13, 1894, Cleveland to Thomas C. Catchings, Aug. 27, 1894, in Nevins, *Letters of Grover Cleveland,* pp. 363–66; Washington *Post,* Aug. 30, 1894.

[65] George R. Peck to Reed, Aug. 29, 1894, Reed Papers.

[66] Roscoe C. Martin, *The People's Party in Texas: A Study in Third Party Politics* (Austin, Tex., 1933), p. 67n; J. Wesley Boynton to Chauncey Depew, March 9, 1894, Chauncey Depew Papers, Yale University, New Haven, Conn.

[67] New York *Tribune,* Oct. 20, 1894; John P. Altgeld, *Live Ques-*

tions (Chicago, 1899), p. 440; Benjamin Harrison, *Views of an Ex-President* (Indianapolis, 1901), p. 401.

[68] Summers, *William L. Wilson and Tariff Reform,* p. 221; Washington *Post,* Nov. 7–8, 1894; New York *Tribune,* Nov. 8, 1894; Chicago *Tribune,* Nov. 7–8, 1894.

[69] Russell A. Alger to Reed, Nov. 8, 1894, Reed Papers; Blodgett, *The Gentle Reformers,* p. 194; Jensen, *Winning of the Midwest,* pp. 224–29; McSeveney, *Politics of Depression,* pp. 87–133.

[70] Chester McArthur Destler, *Henry Demarest Lloyd and the Empire of Reform* (Philadelphia, 1963), p. 272; Willis J. Abbot, "The Chicago Populist Campaign," *The Arena,* 11 (Feb., 1895), 330–37; Alexander Saxton, "San Francisco Labor and the Populist and Progressive Insurgencies," *Pacific Historical Review,* 34 (1965), 425–27.

[71] Kleppner, *The Cross of Culture,* pp. 179–268; Clanton, *Kansas Populism,* pp. 168–69; Wright, *Politics of Populism,* pp. 186–201.

[72] Altgeld to John W. Ela, March 27, 1895, in Altgeld, *Live Questions,* pp. 467–68; John P. Irish to Morton, Nov. 8, 1894, Morton Papers.

[73] Cleveland to Thomas F. Bayard, Feb. 13, 1895, Cleveland Papers; Joseph L. Morrison, *Josephus Daniels: The Small-d Democrat* (Chapel Hill, 1966), p. 24; New York *Tribune,* Dec. 12, 1895.

[74] James S. Clarkson to E. W. Halford, Dec. 5, 1891, Harrison Papers; Donald L. Kinzer, *An Episode in Anti-Catholicism: The American Protective Association* (Seattle, 1964), pp. 140–80; Kleppner, *Cross of Culture,* pp. 251–67.

CHAPTER FIVE

[1] Walter Dean Burnham, *Critical Elections and the Mainsprings of American Politics* (New York, 1970), pp. 1–33, 71–90.

[2] Harrison to Stephen B. Elkins, Feb. 3, 1896, Harrison to Elkins, April 28, 1896, Harrison Papers; Leland L. Sage, *William Boyd Allison: A Study in Practical Politics* (Iowa City, Ia., 1956), pp. 261–64.

[3] Frank A. Flower to Platt, March 6, 1896, Platt Papers. See also the letters from James S. Clarkson to Platt, dated in March and May, 1896, in Platt Papers.

[4] Chicago *Tribune,* Dec. 2–3, 1895; Joseph H. Manley to Reed, Sept. 6, 1894, Manley to Reed, Sept. 14, 1894, Reed Papers; Morris M. Estee to James S. Clarkson, Jan. 11, 1896, Clarkson Papers.

[5] Robinson, *Reed,* p. 327; Benjamin Butterworth to Reed, Oct. 19, 1894, Reed Papers; "Silver and the Tariff at Washington," *Fortnightly Review,* 55 (June, 1894), 837–38.

[6] New York *Tribune,* Nov. 1, 1892.

[7] Foraker, *I Would Live It Again,* p. 238; William Allen White, *Autobiography* (New York, 1946), p. 251.

[8] Canton *Repository,* Feb. 15, 1894, in Stanley L. Jones, *The Presidential Election of 1896* (Madison, Wis., 1964), p. 112.

[9] Foraker, *I Would Live It Again,* p. 99; Roosevelt to Lodge, July 30, 1896, in Morison, *Letters of Theodore Roosevelt,* 1, 552; San Francisco *Examiner,* Aug. 11, 1896.

[10] Margaret Leech, *In the Days of McKinley* (New York, 1959), p. 68; entries for March 14 and March 29, 1896, in Dawes, *A Journal of the McKinley Years,* pp. 72–74; Whitelaw Reid to Hanna, May 4, 1896, Reid Papers.

[11] Frank A. Flower to Platt, March 6, 1896, Platt Papers; William Youngblood to Joseph H. Manley, March 6, 1895, Reed Papers; James A. Waymire to McKinley, April 13, 1896, William McKinley Papers, Manuscript Division, Library of Congress.

[12] New York *Sun,* May 15, 1896, in Robinson, *Reed,* p. 343n; J. Sloat Fassett to Platt, May 30, 1896, Platt Papers; New York *Tribune,* June 17, 1896; Hamilton Disston to Quay, April 1, 1896, Matthew S. Quay Papers, Manuscript Division, Library of Congress; Amos L. Allen to Reed, June 17, 1896, Reed Papers.

[13] *Official Proceedings of the Eleventh Republican National Convention* (n. p., 1896), pp. 81–85; Joseph Benson Foraker, *Notes of a Busy Life,* 2 vols. (Cincinnati, 1916), 1, 463–78.

[14] William Jennings Bryan, *The First Battle: A Story of the Campaign of 1896* (Chicago, 1896), p. 175; Chicago *Tribune,* June 19, 1896; Elmer Ellis, *Henry Moore Teller: Defender of the West* (Caldwell, Idaho, 1941), pp. 257–62.

[15] *People's Party Paper,* June 26, 1896; New York *Tribune,* June 19, 1896; Washington *Post,* June 18–19, 1896.

[16] Foraker, *Notes of a Busy Life,* 1, 487-88.

[17] Cleveland to E. C. Benedict, May 9, 1895, Cleveland Papers; entry for March 2, 1896, in Summers, *Cabinet Diary of Wilson,* p. 38.

[18] J. B. Romans to Dolliver, Feb. 1, 1896, in Ross, *Dolliver,* pp. 120-21.

[19] William H. Harvey, *Coin's Financial School Up to Date* (Chicago, 1895), pp. 43-44; J. Laurence Laughlin, *Facts About Money* (Chicago, 1895); Willard Fisher, "'Coin' and His Critics," *The Quarterly Journal of Economics,* 10 (Jan., 1896), 187-208.

[20] E.g., Ignatius Donnelly, *The American People's Money* (Chicago, 1895); and Mrs. S. E. V. Emery, *Seven Financial Conspiracies Which Have Enslaved the American People* (Lansing, Mich., 1894).

[21] William H. Harvey, *Coin's Financial School* (Chicago, 1894), p. 82.

[22] Jensen, *Winning of the Midwest,* pp. 282-83; Henry Littlefield, "The Wizard of Oz: Parable on Populism," *American Quarterly,* 16 (1964), 47-58.

[23] Altgeld to William J. Stone, June 20, 1895, in Altgeld, *Live Questions,* pp. 486-88.

[24] New York *Tribune,* June 6, 1895; Chicago *Tribune,* June 5-7, 1895; Bryan to T. O. Towles, April 9, 1896, William Jennings Bryan Papers, Manuscript Division, Library of Congress.

[25] Charles M. Rosser, *The Crusading Commoner* (Dallas, 1937), pp. 37-38; Rosser to Bryan, Nov. 23, 1895, Bryan Papers; Louis W. Koenig, *Bryan: A Political Biography of William Jennings Bryan* (New York, 1971), p. 170.

[26] Paolo E. Coletta, *William Jennings Bryan. I. Political Evangelist, 1860-1908* (Lincoln, Neb., 1964), pp. 21-48.

[27] *Cong. Rec.,* 53d Cong., 3d sess., Appendix (Dec. 22, 1894), p. 153.

[28] *Ibid.,* 53d Cong., 1st sess. (Aug. 16, 1893), pp. 410-11.

[29] Washington *Post,* June 2, 1896.

[30] Entry for May 27, 1896, in Summers, *Cabinet Diary of Wilson,* p. 91; San Francisco *Examiner,* June 17, 1896; Chicago *Tribune,* May 17, 1896.

[31] Entries for April 29 and May 26, 1896, in Summers, *Cabinet Diary of Wilson,* p. 73, 90; Washington *Post,* April 30, 1896; Nevins, *Cleveland,* pp. 689–91.

[32] Chicago *Tribune,* June 25, 1896; Washington *Post,* May 31–June 5, 1896.

[33] Morton to John P. Irish, March 14, 1896, Morton Papers; Harvey Wish, "John Peter Altgeld and the Background of the Campaign of 1896," *Mississippi Valley Historical Review,* 24 (March, 1938), 512–13.

[34] New York *Times,* June 18, 28, 1896; William E. Russell to Whitney, June 20, 1896, Whitney Papers; *People's Party Paper,* July 10, 1896; New York *Tribune,* July 1, 1896.

[35] Thomas V. Cator to E. M. Wardell, July 9, 1896, Thomas V. Cator Papers, Stanford University.

[36] Francis B. Simkins, *Pitchfork Ben Tillman, South Carolinian* (Baton Rouge, 1944), p. 315; New York *World,* July 12, 1896; New York *Times,* July 4–5, 1896; Jones, *Presidential Election of 1896,* p. 218.

[37] *Official Proceedings of the Democratic National Convention* (Logansport, Ind., 1896), pp. 250–56; entry for July 9, 1896, Hamlin Diary; New Orleans *Daily Picayune,* July 11, 1896; "Memorandum of a Meeting of Sound Money Men," July 7, 1896, Whitney Papers.

[38] Daniels, *Editor in Politics,* pp. 163–64; Baker, *American Chronicle,* pp. 62–63.

[39] Bryan, *First Battle,* pp. 199–206; New York *Tribune,* July 10, 1896; Willis J. Abbot, *Watching the World Go By* (Boston, 1933), pp. 162–65; Clarence Darrow, *The Story of My Life* (New York, 1932), pp. 91–92.

[40] Chicago *Tribune,* July 11, 1896; New York *Times,* July 11, 1896; Harvey Wish, "John Peter Altgeld and the Election of 1896," *Journal of the Illinois State Historical Society.* 30 (Oct., 1937), 363–65.

[41] Chicago *Times-Herald,* July 10, 1896; Wilson to W. C. P. Breckinridge, July 28, 1896, W. C. P. Breckinridge Papers, Manuscript Division, Library of Congress.

[42] James McGurrin, *Bourke Cockran: A Free Lance in American Politics* (New York, 1948), p. 150; D. S. Alexander, *Four Famous*

New Yorkers (New York, 1923), p. 272; Cleveland to Olney, July 13, 1896, Olney Papers.

[43] Lloyd, *Lloyd,* 1, 259; *People's Party Paper,* Feb. 14, March 20, July 17, 1896; New York *Tribune,* Jan. 21–22, 1896.

[44] New York *World,* Aug. 5, 1896.

[45] B. K. Collier to Cator, July 13, 1896, Cator Papers; Robert F. Durden, "The 'Cow-Bird' Grounded: The Populist Nomination of Bryan and Tom Watson in 1896," *Mississippi Valley Historical Review,* 50 (Dec., 1963), 397–403; *People's Party Paper,* June 26, 1896.

[46] Lloyd, *Lloyd,* 1, 259.

[47] New York *World,* Aug. 3, 1896; Henry D. Lloyd, "The Populists at St. Louis," *The Review of Reviews,* 14 (Sept., 1896), 298–303; Woodward, *Watson,* pp. 318–31.

[48] Roger L. Hart, *Redeemers, Bourbons & Populists: Tennessee, 1870–1896* (Baton Rouge, 1975), p. 220.

[49] Lodge to Moreton Frewen, Sept. 14, 1896, Moreton Frewen Papers, Manuscript Division, Library of Congress.

[50] Morgan, *From Hayes to McKinley,* p. 508; Eugene Hale to William E. Chandler, July 16, 1896, Chandler Papers; T. Bentley Mott, *Myron T. Herrick: Friend of France* (New York, 1929), p. 64.

[51] Bryan, *First Battle,* p. 300; Koenig, *Bryan,* pp. 226–51.

[52] *Speech of William J. Bryan, Democratic Nominee for President, Madison Square Garden, New York, August 12, 1896* (New York, 1896), pp. 3–16; New York *Tribune,* Aug. 13, 1896.

[53] Cleveland to William F. Vilas, Sept. 5, 1896, Cleveland Papers; Chicago *Tribune,* Aug. 7–8, Sept. 3–4, 1896; "Proceedings of the Conference of the National Committee of the Sound Money Democracy," memorandum in the Bynum Papers; Louisville *Courier-Journal,* July 10, 1896; "A Notable Bolt of Newspapers," *The Review of Reviews,* 14 (Aug., 1896), 142.

[54] Coletta, *Bryan,* p. 179; Chicago *Tribune,* Sept. 23, 1896; Daniels, *Editor in Politics,* pp. 190–99.

[55] Coletta, *Bryan,* pp. 174–75; Bryan, *First Battle,* p. 360.

[56] Jensen, *Winning of the Midwest,* p. 275.

[57] Bryan to D. Bride, undated, Bryan Papers; New York *Times,* Nov. 3, 1896; Kenesaw M. Landis to Lamont, Sept. 22, 1896, Lamont Papers; H. H. Markham to Irving C. Stump, Aug. 24, 1896, H. H. Markham Papers, Huntington Library, San Marino, Cal.

[58] Bryan, *First Battle,* pp. 597-604; Barnes, "Myths of the Bryan Campaign," p. 397.

[59] Morgan, *McKinley,* pp. 232-35.

[60] Leech, *McKinley,* p. 88; Reed to Platt, Sept. 20, 1896, Platt Papers.

[61] Leech, *McKinley,* p. 90; Marcus A. Hanna, *Mark Hanna: His Book* (Boston, 1904), pp. 52-53.

[62] Stoddard, *As I Knew Them,* p. 262; Thomas Beer, *Hanna* (New York, 1929), p. 156; McKinley to Hanna, July 7, 1896, Hanna to McKinley, July 8, 1896, McKinley Papers.

[63] Entry for Nov. 22, 1896, in Dawes, *Journal,* p. 106; Stoddard, *As I Knew Them,* pp. 241-42; Dearing, *Veterans in Politics,* p. 460; Frederick W. Holls to Hanna, June 27, 1896, Frederick W. Holls Papers, Columbia University.

[64] Jensen, *Winning of the Midwest,* pp. 287-89; New York *Times,* Oct. 4, 1896.

[65] Untitled speech, 1896, Reed Papers; Ross, *Dolliver,* p. 128; Claudius O. Johnson, "The Story of Silver Politics in Idaho, 1892-1902," *Pacific Northwest Quarterly,* 33 (July, 1942), 286-88.

[66] Entry for Oct. 1, 1896, Dawes, *Journal,* p. 100; Joseph Smith, ed., *McKinley, The People's Choice* (Canton, 1896), p. 38.

[67] Jones, *Presidential Election of 1896,* pp. 291-92; New York *Times,* Nov. 1, 1896; San Francisco *Chronicle,* Nov. 1, 1896; entry for Nov. 2, 1896, in Dawes, *Journal,* p. 104.

[68] Chicago *Tribune,* Nov. 4, 1896.

[69] Jones, *Presidential Election of 1896,* pp. 332-50; James A. Barnes, "The Gold-Standard Democrats and the Party Conflict," *Mississippi Valley Historical Review,* 17 (Dec., 1930), 445-46; Lee Benson, "Research Problems in American Political Historiography," in Mirra Komarovsky, ed., *Common Frontiers of the Social Sciences* (Glencoe, Ill., 1957), pp. 155-71.

[70] New York *Times,* Nov. 6, 1896.

[71] Jensen, *Winning of the Midwest,* p. 57; Blodgett, *The Gentle Reformers,* pp. 220–40; Gilbert C. Fite, "Republican Strategy and the Farm Vote in the Presidential Campaign of 1896," *American Historical Review,* 65 (July, 1960), 787–806.

[72] McSeveney, *The Politics of Depression,* pp. 188–221; Kleppner, *The Cross of Culture,* pp. 316–68.

[73] New York *World,* Nov. 3, 6, 1896; Coletta, *Bryan,* p. 197; Gilbert C. Fite, "William Jennings Bryan and the Campaign of 1896: Some Views and Problems," *Nebraska History,* 47 (Sept., 1966), 247–64; San Francisco *Examiner,* Nov. 11, 1896.

[74] *People's Party Paper,* Nov. 13, 1896; Paul W. Glad, *McKinley, Bryan, and the People* (New York, 1964), p. 197.

[75] Entry for March 4, 1897, in Summers, *Cabinet Diary of Wilson,* pp. 246–50; Chicago *Tribune,* March 3–5, 1897; Raleigh *News and Observer,* March 5, 1897; San Francisco *Examiner,* March 4, 1897.

[76] Glad, *McKinley, Bryan, and the People,* p. 194; Carl N. Degler, "American Political Parties and the Rise of the City: An Interpretation," *Journal of American History,* 51 (June, 1964), 41–49.

CHAPTER SIX

[1] Morgan, *McKinley,* pp. 303–25; William H. Crook, *Memories of the White House* (Boston, 1911), pp. 244–50.

[2] Harrison, "A Day with the President at His Desk," *The Ladies' Home Journal,* 15 (March, 1897).

[3] Leech, *In the Days of McKinley,* pp. 121–33; H. Wayne Morgan, "William McKinley as a Political Leader," *The Review of Politics,* 28 (Oct., 1966), 417–32.

[4] John D. Long, "Some Personal Characteristics of President McKinley," *The Century Magazine,* 63 (Nov., 1901), 144–46; Ira R. T. Smith, *"Dear Mr. President . . .": The Story of Fifty Years in the White House Mailroom* (New York, 1949), pp. 22–45.

[5] Lawrence Shaw Mayo, ed., *America of Yesterday as Reflected in the Journal of John Davis Long* (Boston, 1923), p. 204; W. Hallett

Phillips to Taft, Jan. 13, 1897, William Howard Taft Papers, Manuscript Division, Library of Congress.

[6] McKinley to Gage, Jan. 25, 1897, McKinley to Hanna, Feb. 18, 1897, McKinley Papers; *The Review of Reviews,* 15 (March, 1897), 289-300; Philip C. Jessup, *Elihu Root,* 2 vols. (New York, 1938), 1, 215-34.

[7] Charles S. Olcott, *The Life of William McKinley,* 2 vols. (Boston, 1916), 2, 346; entry for June 17, 1898, Cortelyou Diary, George B. Cortelyou Papers, Manuscript Division, Library of Congress; W. W. Price, "President McKinley's Tours," *The Cosmopolitan,* 34 (Feb., 1903), 383-92.

[8] *Speeches and Addresses of William McKinley* (New York, 1900), pp. 54-55; Richardson, *Messages and Papers of the Presidents,* 8, 6236-44; McKinley to Dingley, Nov. 21, 1896, McKinley Papers; New York *Tribune,* Dec. 6-7, 14, 1896.

[9] Dingley, *Life and Times of Dingley,* p. 431n; *Cong. Rec.,* 55th Cong., 1st sess. (March 31, 1897), 557; F. W. Taussig, *The Tariff History of the United States* (New York, 1931), pp. 327-52; *The Nation,* 64 (April 8, 1897), 256.

[10] New York *Tribune,* July 8-26, 1897; Chicago *Tribune,* July 8, 1897; Lodge to Thomas J. Coolidge, April 7, 1897, Henry Cabot Lodge Papers, Massachusetts Historical Society, Boston.

[11] U.S. Tariff Commission, *Reciprocity and Commercial Treaties* (Washington, 1919), pp. 197-261; William E. Chandler to Kasson, Oct. 19, 1897, Chandler Papers; Kasson to William B. Allison, Oct. 18, 1898, William B. Allison Papers, Iowa State Department of History and Archives, Des Moines.

[12] *The Bulletin of the American Iron and Steel Association* (Nov. 10, 1901); *Speeches and Addresses,* pp. 198-99; Olcott, *McKinley,* 2, 378-84; John W. Foster, "The Reciprocity Treaties and the Senate," *The Independent,* 52 (Dec. 6, 1900), 2897-99.

[13] Washington *Post,* Sept. 19, 1900; Chicago *Tribune,* Nov. 15, 1901; John Dalzell to James H. Wilson, Nov. 21, 1901, James H. Wilson Papers, Manuscript Division, Library of Congress.

[14] James M. Swank to Joseph B. Foraker, Dec. 10, 1910, Joseph B. Foraker Papers, Cincinnati Historical Society.

[15] Hoffman, *Depression of the Nineties,* pp. xxvi–xxviii, 81–89, 177; entry for Aug. 21, 1897, in Dawes, *Journal of the McKinley Years,* p. 126; Ray Stannard Baker, "The New Prosperity," *McClure's Magazine,* 15 (May, 1900), 86–94.

[16] McKinley to George F. Hoar, et al., Dec. 7, 1896, Wolcott to McKinley, Jan. 25, 1897, Wolcott to McKinley, Nov. 22, 1897, McKinley Papers; Washington *Post,* Dec. 20, 1897; New York *Tribune,* June 16–17, 1897.

[17] Walter LaFeber, *The New Empire: An Interpretation of American Expansion, 1860-1898* (Ithaca, N.Y., 1963), pp. 285–300, 333ff; New York *Tribune,* May 15, 1897; *Iowa State Register,* May 22, 1897.

[18] Lodge to W. F. Draper, Dec. 20, 1897, Lodge Papers; Joseph Wisan, *The Cuban Crisis as Reflected in the New York Press, 1895-1898* (New York, 1934); Robert L. Beisner, *From the Old Diplomacy to the New, 1865-1900* (New York, 1975).

[19] Koenig, *Bryan,* pp. 271–73; New York *Tribune,* June 24, 1897.

[20] Richardson, *Messages and Papers of the Presidents,* 8, 6241–42; John A. S. Grenville and George Berkeley Young, *Politics, Strategy, and American Diplomacy: Studies in Foreign Policy, 1873-1917* (New Haven, Conn., 1966), pp. 239–66; A. S. Crowninshield to Long, Feb. 28, 1898, William R. Day Papers, Manuscript Division, Library of Congress.

[21] Richardson, *Messages and Papers of the Presidents,* 8, 6261.

[22] New York *Journal,* Feb. 9, 1898; Washington *Post,* Feb. 9–16, 1898; G. F. W. Holls to Day, Feb. 16, 1898, Day Papers; Lodge to Henry White, Jan. 31, 1898, Lodge Papers.

[23] Washington *Post,* Feb. 16, 1898.

[24] Lodge to McKinley, March 21, 1898, McKinley Papers; *Literary Digest,* 16 (Feb. 26, 1898), 241–44; entry for Feb. 17, 1898, Long Journal, John D. Long Papers, Massachusetts Historical Society, Boston.

[25] Ernest R. May, *Imperial Democracy: The Emergence of America as a Great Power* (New York, 1961), pp. 133–59; Washington *Post,* March 31, 1898; A. W. Dunn, *Gridiron Nights* (New York, 1915), p. 72; entry for March 19, 1898, Straus Diary, Oscar S. Straus Papers, Manuscript Division, Library of Congress.

[26] William Jennings Bryan, *The Second Battle* (Chicago, 1900), p. 83.

[27] Jennie Hobart, *Memories* (Paterson, N.J., 1930), pp. 60–61; New York *Tribune,* March 8, 1898.

[28] Henry Cabot Lodge, *The War with Spain* (New York, 1899), p. 35.

[29] Entries for March 27, 29, April 6–9, 12–13, 1898, Cortelyou Diary; New York *Tribune,* April 11–12, 1898; Cornelius Bliss to Root, April 19, 1898, Elihu Root Papers, Manuscript Division, Library of Congress.

[30] Henry S. Pritchett, "Some Recollections of President McKinley and the Cuban Intervention," *North American Review,* 189 (March, 1909), 397–403; Ida Tarbell, "President McKinley in War Time," *McClure's Magazine,* 11 (July, 1898), 209–24; entries for April 22, June 17, 1898, Cortelyou Diary.

[31] Walter Millis, *The Martial Spirit* (New York, 1939), p. 274; Theodore Roosevelt, *An Autobiography* (New York, 1913), pp. 218–55.

[32] Leech, *In the Days of McKinley,* p. 290; New York *Tribune,* Aug. 13, 1898; Washington *Post,* Aug. 13, 1898; entries for Aug. 8, 12, 1898, Cortelyou Diary.

[33] *Speeches and Addresses,* p. 131.

[34] Finley Peter Dunne, *Mr. Dooley in Peace and in War* (Boston, 1898), p. 9.

[35] Cleveland to Judson B. Harmon, July 17, 1900, Cleveland Papers; New York *Times,* Nov. 17, 1896.

[36] Walter Dean Burnham, "The Changing Shape of the American Political Universe," *American Political Science Review,* 59 (Jan., 1965), 25; *Literary Digest,* 17 (Nov. 19, 1898), 597.

[37] J. Rogers Hollingsworth, *The Whirligig of Politics: The Democracy of Cleveland and Bryan* (Chicago, 1963), pp. 109–20; John J. Broesamle, "The Democrats from Bryan to Wilson," in Lewis L. Gould, ed., *The Progressive Era* (Syracuse, N.Y., 1974), pp. 83–113.

[38] *Literary Digest,* 17 (July 2, 1898), 2–4, (Oct. 8, 1898), 423–24.

[39] Bryan to Mary Baird Bryan, Dec. 10, 1898, Bryan Papers.

⁴⁰Robert L. Beisner, *Twelve Against Empire: The Anti-Imperialists, 1898–1900* (New York, 1968), pp. 18–34, 139–211; Christopher Lasch, "The Anti-Imperialists, the Philippines, and the Inequality of Man," *Journal of Southern History,* 14 (Aug., 1958), 319–31.

⁴¹Richardson, *Messages and Papers of the Presidents,* 8, 6397.

⁴²H. H. Kohlsaat, *From McKinley to Harding: Personal Recollections of Our Presidents* (New York, 1923), p. 68; Long to Joseph L. Bristow, Aug. 8, 1898, Joseph L. Bristow Papers, Kansas State Historical Society, Topeka.

⁴³*Literary Digest,* 17 (Nov. 12, 1898), 566; Thomas J. McCormick, *China Market: America's Quest for Informal Empire, 1893–1901* (Chicago, 1967), pp. 105–25.

⁴⁴*Speeches and Addresses,* pp. 102–5; Julius W. Pratt, *Expansionists of 1898* (Baltimore, 1951), pp. 267–315.

⁴⁵McKinley to Whitelaw Reid, Oct. 31, 1898, Reid Papers; New York *Tribune,* Oct. 8, 20, 1898; Hay to Henry White, Oct. 17, 1898, Henry White Papers, Manuscript Division, Library of Congress; *Public Opinion,* 25 (Nov. 17, 1898), 607–18.

⁴⁶W. G. Edens to Bristow, June 8, 1898, Bristow Papers; "Bryan on Expansion," *Literary Digest,* 17 (Dec. 24, 1898), 740; Edens to Cortelyou, Sept. 29, 1898, Hay to McKinley, Nov. 9, 1898, Cortelyou Papers.

⁴⁷George F. Hoar, *Autobiography of Seventy Years,* 2 vols. (New York, 1903), 2, 315.

⁴⁸*Speeches and Addresses,* pp. 158, 161.

⁴⁹Paolo Coletta, "Bryan, McKinley, and the Treaty of Paris," *Pacific Historical Review,* 26 (May, 1957), 131–46; Bryan to Carnegie, Dec. 24, 1898, Bryan to Carnegie, Dec. 30, 1898, Andrew Carnegie Papers, Manuscript Division, Library of Congress; Carnegie to Bryan, Jan. 10, 1899, Bryan Papers.

⁵⁰Lodge to Theodore Roosevelt, Feb. 9, 1899, Lodge Papers; Washington *Post,* Feb. 6–7, 1899; *Cong. Rec.,* 55th Cong., 3d sess. (Feb. 6, 1899), 1835–48.

⁵¹*Speeches and Addresses,* pp. 185–93; Welch, *Hoar,* pp. 248–49.

⁵²New York *Tribune,* Feb. 15–17, 1899.

[53] *Speeches and Addresses,* p. 168; "The Race Issue in the South," *Literary Digest,* 17 (Nov. 5, 1898), 539; Atlanta *Constitution,* Nov. 4-12, 1898.

[54] "Race Troubles in the Carolinas," *Literary Digest,* 17 (Nov. 26, 1898), 625-26, (Dec. 3, 1898), 652.

[55] *Public Opinion,* 27 (Sept. 28, 1899), 391-92.

[56] *Public Opinion,* 27 (Aug. 31, 1899), 266; Roosevelt to Lodge, Jan. 26, 1899, Theodore Roosevelt Papers, Manuscript Division, Library of Congress; Frederick C. Luebke, *Immigrants and Politics: The Germans of Nebraska, 1880-1900* (Lincoln, Neb., 1969), pp. 166-78; J. H. Gallinger to Root, Nov. 1, 1899, Root Papers.

[57] H. O. Weaver to Allison, Sept. 26, 1899, Allison Papers. Also, Charles M. Pepper to McKinley, Oct. 3, 1899, Charles A. Moore to McKinley, Nov. 9, 1899, Henry C. Payne to McKinley, Oct. 30, 1899, McKinley Papers.

[58] *Public Opinion,* 27 (Nov. 16, 1899), 611-16; D. S. Alexander to Root, Nov. 9, 1899, Root Papers.

[59] James Creelman to Bryan, June 2, 1900, Bryan Papers; Coletta, *Bryan,* pp. 239-45; James K. Jones et al., to Bryan, July 1, 1900, Bryan to Jones, July 2, 1900, Bryan Papers.

[60] Coletta, *Bryan,* p. 256n; New York *Times,* Aug. 6, 1899, April 5, 1900; Washington *Post,* Jan. 20, 1900.

[61] Thomas A. Bailey, "Was the Presidential Election of 1900 a Mandate on Imperialism?" *Mississippi Valley Historical Review,* 24 (June, 1937), 43; New York *World,* July 6-7, 1900; New York *Times,* July 7, 1900; Daniels, *Editor in Politics,* p. 356; Charles M. Rosser, *The Crusading Commoner* (Dallas, 1937), p. 86.

[62] Washington *Post,* Aug. 9, 1900; Chicago *Tribune,* Aug. 9, 1900; Charles F. Manderson to Spooner, May 22, 1900, Spooner Papers.

[63] New York *Tribune,* July 12-13, 1900; *Speeches and Addresses,* p. 302; *The Review of Reviews,* 22 (Sept., 1900), 264-66; Jacob Gould Schurman to McKinley, June 1, 1900, McKinley Papers.

[64] New York *Tribune,* June 22-23, 1900; "The New Reciprocity Treaties," *The Protectionist,* 11 (Jan. 1900), 539-40; Kasson to Hay, Jan. 11, 1900, Papers of John Hay, Manuscript Division, Library of

Congress; *Republican Campaign Textbook, 1900* (Philadelphia, 1900), pp. 438–39.

[65] *Public Opinion,* 29 (Sept. 20, 1900), 361; Perry Heath to Cortelyou, Aug. 20, 1900, Heath to Cortelyou, Sept. 27, 1900, McKinley Papers.

[66] Albert Shaw to Albert J. Beveridge, Aug. 23, 1900, Albert Shaw Papers, New York Public Library; *Public Opinion,* 29 (Nov. 1, 1900), 548; Henry C. Payne, memorandum, July 1, 1900, McKinley Papers; Payne to Spooner, Feb. 7, 1901, Spooner Papers.

[67] James Creelman, "Mr. Cortelyou Explains President McKinley," *Pearson's Magazine,* 19 (June, 1908), 570; entry for March 28, 1899, in Dawes, *Journal,* pp. 185–86; Richardson, *Messages and Papers of the Presidents,* 8, 6360–63.

[68] Bryan to McKinley, Nov. 8, 1900, McKinley Papers; New York *Times,* Nov. 7–9, 1900; Bryan, "The Election of 1900," *North American Review,* 71 (Dec., 1900), 789; Walter LaFeber, "Election of 1900," in Arthur M. Schlesinger, Jr., ed., *History of American Presidential Elections, 1789–1968,* 4 vols. (New York, 1971), 3, 1877–1917.

[69] Morton to Cleveland, Nov. 2, 1900, Cleveland Papers; Claude M. Fuess, *Carl Schurz, Reformer* (New York, 1932), pp. 365–66; Edward M. Shepard, "Support of Mr. Bryan by Sound-Money Democrats," *North American Review,* 171 (Oct., 1900), 446–55.

[70] Michael Paul Rogin and John L. Shover, *Political Change in California: Critical Elections and Social Movements, 1890–1966* (Westport, Conn., 1970), p. 24.

[71] Entry for Nov. 9, 1900, in Dawes, *Journal,* p. 253; Morgan, *McKinley,* p. 508; Long to Helen and Margaret Long, Nov. 14, 1900, Long Papers.

[72] Henry L. West, "The President's Recent Tour," *The Forum,* 31 (Aug., 1901), 661–69; San Francisco *Examiner,* May 18–21, 1900; New York *Tribune,* May 19, 1900.

[73] Lord Herschell to Lord Salisbury, Nov. 25, 1898, Lord Salisbury Papers, Christ Church College, Oxford. I am grateful to Professor Lewis L. Gould, of the University of Texas, Austin, for calling this letter to my attention.

[74] New York *Tribune,* Aug. 3, 6, 25, 1901; *American Economist,* 27 (May 24, 1901), 241, (June 14, 1901), 281; New York *World,* Feb. 5, 1899.

[75] New York *Tribune,* Sept. 6, 1900; New York *Times,* Sept. 6, 1900; Washington *Post,* Sept. 5-7, 1900.

[76] Olcott, *McKinley,* 2, 316; Hay to Henry Adams, Sept. 19, 1901, in William Roscoe Thayer, *The Life and Letters of John Hay,* 2 vols. (Boston, 1929), 2, 267-68; entry for Sept. 10, 1900, in Dawes, *Journal of the McKinley Years,* p. 279.

[77] Entry for Sept. 13, 1901, in Dawes, *Journal of the McKinley Years,* p. 281; Hanna to Henry Corbin, Oct. 12, 1901, Henry Corbin Papers, Manuscript Division, Library of Congress; Allison to Long, Sept. 14, 1901, Long Papers. Czolgosz's trial for the assassination began on Sept. 23, 1901, and lasted only two days. He was executed on Oct. 29.

[78] New York *Tribune,* Sept. 15, 1900.

Index